Uncle John's BATHROOM READER®

PLUNGES INTO THE PRESIDENCY

★ ★ ★ ★ ★

The Bathroom Readers'
Hysterical Society

San Diego, California

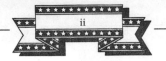

ii

www.bathroomreader.com

The Bathroom Readers' Hysterical Society
Portable Press
5880 Oberlin Drive, San Diego, CA 92121
e-mail: unclejohn@advmkt.com

ISBN: 1-59223-260-4

Library of Congress Catalog-in-Publication Data (applied for)

Printed in the United States of America
First printing: July 2004

04 05 06 07 08   10 9 8 7 6 5 4 3 2 1

THANK YOU
HYSTERICAL SCHOLARS!

The Bathroom Readers' Hysterical Society sincerely thanks the following people who contributed selections to this work.

Julia Bush
Myles Callum
Sharon Cooper
Jenness Crawford
Padraic Duffy
Kathryn Grogman
Kathryn Hamm
Debbie Hardin
Lea Markson
Kathleen McCabe

Graham Meyer
Bethanne Kelly Patrick
Jon Preimesberger
Joyce Slayton
Stephanie Spadaccini
Jameson Spencer
Sue Steiner
Susan Stubbeman
Samuel de Villiers

Project Team:

Amy Briggs, Project Editor

Allen Orso, Publisher

JoAnn Padgett, Director, Editorial and Production

Robin Kilrain, Copy Editor

Vince Archuletta, Cover Design

Lois Stansfield, Interior Design and Composition

Georgine Lidell, Inventory Manager

CONTENTS

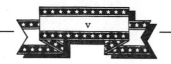

v

EXECUTIVE SUMMARIES

PREFACE

Uncle John's Plunges into the Presidency is about to commence, and you are cordially invited to be part of the experience!

We at the Bathroom Readers' Hysterical Society are thrilled to present our latest, very special creation. This in-depth look at the highest office in the United States of America is filled to the gills with all kinds of goodies for your enjoyment: fascinating facts, wit and wisdom, quips, quotes, and anecdotes all about the men who have led this country through good times and bad—the presidents.

When approaching such a prickly political subject, it can be tough to stay the course. But we've kept in mind the ultimate goal here at Uncle John's: to entertain and educate—not to editorialize. With that in mind, this tome has been written for Madison-Maulers and Gung-Ho-for-Granters alike. There's a little something for everyone. So if your incline is to the right or the left, if you're just firmly seated astride the fence, or even if you march to a different drummer altogether, there's plenty for every political palate. Be sure to read all about:

- All the President's Gaffes

- History's Unluckiest President

- Singing *Assassins* on Broadway

- The True Story of Washington's Teeth, and many more!

Visit our website—www.bathroomreader.com—or drop us an email at unclejohn@advmkt.com. We'd love to hear from you!

As always, go with the flow,
Uncle Al

p.s. Don't forget to vote!

WHO'S GONNA WIN?

There are almost as many ways to predict who's going to be our next president as there are ballots. What's difficult to believe is that some of these ways actually work.

Thousands of people make their livings trying to predict the outcome of presidential elections. Journalists, pollsters, lobbyists, and political scientists all have a stake in the outcome. The months leading up to an election are rife with speculation; everyone—academics and crackpots alike—pulls out their "tea leaves" to try to see how it will all turn out. You don't need to get out your tarot cards, bone up on economic indicators, or count the number of letters in your candidate's name. We've got the answers right here.

IT'S THE HEIGHT, RIGHT?
The most common belief is that the taller candidate is the guy to beat. In his 1965 book *Language on Vacation*, Dmitri Borgmann found that in the nineteen U.S. presidential elections between 1888 and 1960, the taller candidate won the popular vote all but once, when 6 feet 2 inch tall Franklin Roosevelt beat the taller Wendell Willkie (6 feet 2½ inches) in 1940. Psychologist John Gillis published *Too Tall, Too Small* in 1982 in which he claimed that the taller candidate won 80 percent of the twenty-one presidential elections from 1904 to 1984. Keep in mind that finding accurate data on the heights of the candidates, especially the losers, can be difficult; it may be best to back up your arsenal of predictive measures with a few more methods, even if in eight of the last ten elections, the taller candidate has won.

IT'S ALL IN A NAME?
So how does name length measure up? Borgmann also has a hypothesis about names. Between 1876 and 1960, the candidate with the most letters in his last name won the popular vote twenty out of twenty-two times. (Maybe that's why the 2000 election was so close!) Of course don't forget that the winner of

---

Thomas Jefferson once ate a tomato in public to prove it wasn't poisonous.

the popular vote is sometimes trumped by the winner of the electoral college, for instance in the Tilden–Hayes contest of 1876 and the Cleveland–Harrison battle in 1888. In recent years, the longer-named candidate has won only three out of eleven contests, so this theory might need to be put to bed.

First names play into elections too. Some observers point out that from FDR until Bill Clinton, a president with an unusual first name always followed a president with a common first name, and vice versa: Franklin, Harry, Dwight, John, Lyndon, Richard, Gerald, Jimmy, Ronald, George. But there again, the theory falls off in recent years.

IT'S THE ECONOMY, STUPID

More serious scholars like to crunch the numbers to make their predictions. Political scientist James Campbell demonstrates that a good way to predict our next president has been the growth rate (the percent change in the size of the economy) during April, May, and June of the election year. If the growth rate of the Gross Domestic Product (GDP, the combined value of all the spending in the country in a given year, plus the value of all exports minus the value of all imports) during this time is 2.6 percent or higher, the incumbent president or someone from his party will likely win. If the number is 1.5 percent or lower, then the incumbent party will lose. But what if the growth rate falls between these numbers? Then the future is predictably murky. Since 1952 this method has predicted the outcome in every presidential contest but one in 1968, when Vice President Hubert Humphrey lost to Richard Nixon, most likely because of the Vietnam War.

"GALLUP"ING TO THE WHITE HOUSE

The Gallup Poll has been determining what they call the President's Approval Rating for more than sixty years, by asking the public whether they approve or disapprove of the way the president is handling his job. Emory University political scientist Alan Abramowitz has found that if the president's approval rating in mid-June of the election year is 51 percent or higher, he or his party will probably win. If his approval rating is 45 percent or lower, he or his party will probably lose. And once again anything

between these numbers leaves us (surprise!) with an uncertain future. Since the mid-1950s, the Gallup approval rating has been perhaps the single greatest predictor of presidential election results, particularly in reelection years. Since 1952, the leader in the Gallup Poll taken between September 21 and 24 and between October 12 and October 16 has won every election. In the weeks between these crucial points and the November election, talking heads continue to analyze every blip in the percentage points. However, it is invariably the Gallup Poll taken on these dates that would tell them everything they need to know.

DIFFERENT SCHOOLS OF THOUGHT

Maybe all the pros should just pay attention to the amateurs when it comes to predicting election winners. According to the children's book publisher Scholastic, students from grades one through twelve have nailed the election outcomes for every presidential race for the past fifty years (except the close Kennedy–Nixon contest in 1960).

BuyCostumes.com, a company specializing in—you guessed it—costume sales, has a unique way to soothsay. Using the sales of Halloween masks depicting the two major candidates since 1980, the company has shown that mask sales correlate with the results of each election. In 2000, sales of the George W. Bush mask outpaced Al Gore's mask by 14 percent. In 1996 Bill Clinton's sales led Bob Dole's by 16 percent. So keep your eye on the men in the masks in October.

Lastly, who knew that what happens on a football field can predict who sleeps in the White House? Our last predictive measure has been the performance of Washington, DC's own Redskins in their last home game just prior to Election Day. For the past fifteen elections, a Redskins win at home means a win for the incumbent party and a hometown loss means a loss for the incumbent party. So if the Republicans or Democrats are betting people, they better have a serious sitdown with Redskins owner Dan Snyder and coach Joe Gibbs. It just might mean the election.

• • • Its presidential alums are the two Adamses, two Roosevelts, and Kennedy.

THE RULES OF THE PRESIDENTIAL GAME

If you wanna be prez, then you have to know the rules.

WHO CAN BECOME PRESIDENT?
Anybody can become president as long as that person is a native-born citizen of the United States, at least thirty-five years old, and has lived in the United States for at least fourteen years.

VICE PRESIDENT?
Because the vice president can become president at any time, the requirements for that position are the same as for becoming president: a native-born U.S. citizen, at least thirty-five years old, and fourteen years as a resident. Additionally, the Constitution requires that the vice president be from a different state than the president. This stipulation was added to keep one state from becoming too politically powerful.

WHO MAKES UP THE PRESIDENT'S CABINET?
The modern presidential cabinet consists of the president, vice president, and heads of the fifteen executive departments: state, treasury, justice, defense, interior, agriculture, commerce, labor, health and human services, housing and urban development, transportation, energy, education, veteran affairs, and homeland security.

    The size of the cabinet has grown over the years. George Washington, who began the practice of meeting with the top members of his administration, had a cabinet that included only the secretary of state, secretary of the treasury, the secretary of war, and the attorney general!

THIRD TIME'S THE CHARM?
Before 1951, there wasn't anything on paper to limit a president's number of terms. Most presidents limited themselves to two terms in deference to a tradition started by George Washington. When

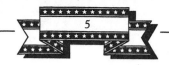

Thomas Jefferson defended the self-imposed limit at the end of his second term, the tradition was set.

Along the way, however a few presidents have sought to break with tradition. Ulysses S. Grant, in his retirement, hoped to be drafted for a third term in 1880, but his party looked elsewhere. Woodrow Wilson also would have accepted a third nomination had it come his way in 1920, but it did not.

The only president to have served more than two terms was Franklin D. Roosevelt, who was elected to four terms. Although opponents cried "No Third Term" when Roosevelt ran in 1940, the Democratic Party and the rest of the nation thought it best to stick with him as world war swept through Europe. Elected again, Roosevelt died soon after the start of his fourth term. After his death the Republican Party, when it returned to power in Congress, sought to prevent another president from having more than two elected terms, successive or not. It pushed the Twenty-second Amendment to ratification in 1951. Surprisingly, the president remains the only member of the federal government to have a term limit.

NEXT IN LINE
Not to be morbid, but the following is the order of succession if the president were to die:

1. Vice President
2. Speaker of the House of Representatives
3. President Pro Tempore of the Senate (longest serving senator of the majority party)
4. Secretary of State
5. Secretary of the Treasury
6. Secretary of Defense
7. Attorney General
8. Secretary of the Interior
9. Secretary of Agriculture
10. Secretary of Commerce
11. Secretary of Labor
12. Secretary of Health and Human Services
13. Secretary of Housing and Urban Development
14. Secretary of Transportation
15. Secretary of Energy
16. Secretary of Education
17. Secretary of Veteran Affairs
18. Secretary of Homeland Security*

*The secretary of homeland security may be moving on up. Legislation pending in 2004 would move the office up to eighth place, just ahead of the secretary of the interior.

There are more threats against the First Lady than the vice president, says the Secret Service.

NUMBER ONE: GEORGE WASHINGTON

Served from 1789 to 1797

Vital Stats: Born on February 22, 1732, in Pope's Creek, Virginia. Died on December 14, 1799, in Mount Vernon, Virginia
Age at Inauguration: 57
Vice President: John Adams
Political Affiliation: None (first term), Federalist (second term)
Wife: Martha Dandridge Custis (married 1759)
Kids: None to speak of. Washington was just the father of his country.
Education: Private Tutor
What he did before he was president: Ferry Operator; Surveyor; Tobacco Planter; Commander in Chief of the Continental Army; Delegate to the First and Second Continental Congresses; President of the Constitutional Convention
Postpresidential Occupations: Planter; Distiller

MEMORABLE QUOTES

"The General is sorry to be informed that the foolish and wicked practice of profane cursing and swearing, a vice heretofore little known in an American army, is growing into fashion. He hopes the officers will, by example as well as influence, endeavor to check it . . . a vice so mean and low, without any temptation, that every man of sense and character detests and despises it."
—General George Washington's order from August 3, 1776

"Observe good faith and justice towards all nations. Cultivate peace and harmony with all . . . And can it be that good policy does not equally enjoin it? It will be worthy of a free, enlightened, and at no distant period a great nation to give to mankind the magnanimous and too novel example of a people always guided by an exalted justice and benevolence."
—Washington's advice from his "Farewell Address," September 17, 1796

Of all the presidents Warren G. Harding had the biggest feet. He wore size 14 shoes.

AN ASSASSINATION OF CHARACTER

Although Andrew Jackson suffered the nation's first assassination attempt, it was an earlier assault on his honor that actually drew blood.

The Secret Service does a fantastic job protecting the president from harm, but can they protect the chief executive from nose tweakers? A grave threat to a man's honor in the nineteenth century, nose tweaking was a danger faced squarely by President Andrew Jackson, the first president allegedly to receive a very serious twist of the beak. Denying it until the day he died, Andrew Jackson railed against the possibility that any man had dared to touch his nose. But some say it really did happen.

GOT YER NOSE!

In 1833 the president was accosted by a disgruntled man named Robert Randolph. In one account, Randolph boarded a docked steamboat on which President Jackson was traveling. He made his way to Jackson's cabin and found the president sitting behind a desk. Extending his own hand, Jackson saw Randolph begin to remove his glove. But rather than shaking the president's hand, Randolph reached across the desk to grab Jackson's nose, twisting it so hard that it began to bleed uncontrollably.

Randolph didn't have some strange nose-grabbing fetish. He did have a bone to pick with the president though, and a twisting of Jackson's nose was sufficient vindication. Why? Well, in those days a man's nose, being the most prominent feature of his face and always exposed to the scrutiny of others, was considered to be a solid indication of his character. Allowing any other man to touch, tweak, twist, or tickle one's nose was a serious affront to a gent's ego and a serious blow to his honor. Although Jackson's nose was bloodied, the more serious injury was to his reputation. Randolph had as much as publicly called him a dirty liar with that one tweak.

So what was Randolph so angry about? A former Naval purser, Randolph had lost his job because of Andrew Jackson, who had

---

The White House requires 570 gallons of paint to cover its outside surface.

revoked Randolph's commission after he had been charged with submitting false financial reports. But the roots of Randolph's problems go further back into another Washington scandal.

WOMAN TROUBLES

Long before Andrew Jackson ran for president, he and his wife had caused one of the nation's earliest sex scandals. As a young man Jackson married Rachel Robards, a divorcée and the daughter of a tavern keeper in Nashville, Tennessee. Unfortunately Jackson married Rachel before her divorce was finalized. When the paperwork finally went through, the two were married again and life went on, but charges of Rachel's bigamy plagued the Jacksons many times in their lives. The most notable incident occurred during Jackson's 1828 run for the presidency when his opponents publicly scrutinized Rachel's "scandalous" behavior—despite the fact that the incident had occurred almost thirty-five years before. Their efforts proved unsuccessful as Jackson won the election in a landslide. Sadly Rachel died before Jackson took office, and he blamed her death on those who slandered her name. "May God Almighty forgive her murderers, as I know she forgave them. I never can," he said.

After Jackson took office another scandal quickly arose. Secretary of War John Eaton had married the former Margaret "Peggy" Timberlake, a widow and daughter of a DC tavern owner. Eaton was not only Jackson's secretary of war, but his close friend and adviser as well; Jackson had been fond of Peggy since meeting her some years before while boarding at her father's tavern. In fact the president had encouraged their marriage. But the grandes dames of Washington society and wives of Jackson's cabinet members did not approve of Peggy and socially shunned her. Jackson was outraged. He believed the cabinet wives' behavior was a thinly veiled attack on his presidency, instigated by his political rivals. Perhaps of more consequence was the fact that Jackson could not help but see the matter as a replay of the assault on his own beloved wife's honor. As a result Jackson spent his first years in office going to great lengths to defend Peggy Eaton.

NOTORIOUS

The Washington, DC, doyennes slighted outspoken and attractive

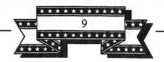

Peggy for a number of reasons. Her status as a tavern owner's daughter lowered her stock in their eyes. Of greater importance were the whispers that Peggy was an adulteress. Shortly before her marriage to Eaton, Peggy had been married to John Timberlake, a purser in the navy aboard the U.S.S. *Constitution*. Timberlake had been good friends with Eaton and had entrusted him with looking after Peggy while he was away at sea. Unfortunately Eaton looked after Peggy a little too closely and the two were soon rumored to be "involved." In 1828 Timberlake died at sea, allegedly committing suicide after hearing about the affair. Eaton and Peggy married less than a year later, which did little to quiet the scandalous talk about town.

When almost a year later an investigation of the *Constitution*'s accounts, which had been kept by Timberlake in his position as ship's purser, turned up missing funds, Jackson again viewed the matter as an attempt to discredit not only Peggy's reputation but his presidency as well. Jackson's name became embroiled in the matter when an accusation surfaced that Timberlake had stolen the money to give his friend Eaton to save Peggy's father's tavern from financial ruin. Jackson was apparently able to defuse the looming scandal, as neither Timberlake nor Eaton was ever charged with any crime. But the funds were still missing. Who would take the blame? It would be Timberlake's naval successor, none other than the future nose-tweaker Robert Randolph.

THE FALL GUY

Although the investigation ultimately determined that no intentional wrongdoing was involved, Randolph was nevertheless dismissed from the navy—on Jackson's orders. Disgraced and unemployed, Randolph's opportunity to exact justice came a little over a month later when Jackson's steamboat docked in Randolph's home town.

But what actually happened to Jackson's nose is still up for debate. Until the day he died, Jackson insisted that no man had ever touched his nose. Maybe, maybe not. But Peggy Eaton said she enjoyed teasing Jackson about the incident, just to see his vehemently overblown denial that it had ever happened.

MR. PRESIDENT AT THE BAT

"May the sun never set on American baseball."—Harry S. Truman

You don't need to watch the Ken Burns documentary *Baseball* to know just how important the sport is to the United States. So it should come as no surprise that the commanders-in-chief have had a special relationship with the game too, even though the hometown team, the Washington Senators, wasn't known for its winning records.

THE FIRSTS

The first president ever to attend a baseball game was Andrew Johnson, who watched the New York Mutuals defeat the Washington Nationals in 1866. The Mutuals and the Nationals were amateur clubs, as were all baseball players until the Cincinnati Red Stockings became the first professional club in 1869. Johnson was also the first president to host a team at the White House, when the Brooklyn Atlantics were his guests. Hosting teams quickly became a tradition at the White House, with both Chester A. Arthur and Grover Cleveland inviting clubs. During the ballplayers' visit, President Arthur made the now-dubious statement, "Good ball-players make good citizens."

The first president to attend a professional baseball game was Benjamin Harrison, in 1892. On a June afternoon, President Harrison saw the Washington Senators do what they did best for many years in the nation's capital—lose, this time to the Cincinnati Reds by a score of 7 to 4.

The predictably poor performance of the hometown team didn't dissuade future presidents from attending games, though. The last president who failed to attend a baseball game while in office was Teddy Roosevelt. He thought it was a game for "molly-coddles" and not physical or manly enough for his tastes. Ironically, Teddy was also the first president to receive a lifetime pass to attend all professional games.

One of Andrew Jackson's most famous duels began over a horse race.

TR's successor, William Howard Taft, began a tradition in 1910 that is still kept today. At the Senators' opening day game at National Park, Taft was invited to throw out the first ball. Taft was a more appropriate liaison between the office of the president and baseball than Roosevelt was. He was a great lover of the game, and he had been a catcher on a sandlot team in his younger and lighter days. After the game, the Senators star pitcher, Walter Johnson, who had caught the ball that Taft threw, sent the ball to the White House to get Taft's autograph on it.

THE FIGUREHEADS

An acting president's position in baseball has been as a sort of figurehead. He has no power over the functioning of the game, but by being the leader of the nation he seems to be, by extension, the leader of the national game. The ritual of the president's throwing out the first pitch on opening day has now acquired a sense of giving approval, of authorizing the season to begin. Indeed, Franklin Roosevelt once actually did authorize the season to start when he wrote the famous "green light" letter during World War II.

In January 1942, a month after the attack on Pearl Harbor and three months before the scheduled opening day, baseball commissioner Kenesaw Mountain Landis wrote to Roosevelt to ask whether baseball should be suspended during the war effort. Roosevelt replied that for reasons of employment and recreation the game should continue during the war. However he did state his opinion that draftable players should go into the service. They did, leaving baseball with many very young or very old (for baseball) players, disabled players (an outfielder for the St. Louis Browns during this time, Pete Gray, had only one arm), and players who were 4-F (ineligible for military service) for other reasons, like color blindness.

President Roosevelt also gave the green light to light at ballgames. He threw a switch at the White House on May 24, 1935, that lit a bulb at Crosley Field in Cincinnati to kick off the first night game ever.

With the exception of the "green light" letter, the position of the president as the phantom head of baseball hasn't translated into much efficacy. During the players' strike of 1994–1995, when the World Series was canceled, President Bill Clinton ordered the

---

Thomas Jefferson took a cold footbath every morning for 60 years.

players and the owners to end the strike by February 6, 1995. They didn't, and the 1995 season started late. After he left office, former president Jimmy Carter wrote an article in *USA Today* urging the public and the National Baseball Hall of Fame to forgive Pete Rose for gambling and allow him to be reinstated. As of this writing, it still hasn't happened.

THE FIELD

A few presidents were pretty good players in their day. Dwight Eisenhower played semipro ball just before going to West Point for one season. Strangely, though, he played under a pseudonym and only revealed it after his presidency was over. He never explained why and then instructed his staff not to answer any questions about it. He only claimed that he wouldn't go into it because it was "too complicated."

When George H. W. Bush was in college at Yale University, he was the first baseman and captain of the school's extremely successful baseball team. Bush threw left-handed and batted right-handed, an unusual combination. Some experts said that Bush might have been a candidate for the majors (and for a slightly higher batting average) if he had batted lefty. Five of Bush's teammates, though, were drafted by major league teams. The Yalies' highest level of success was when they went to the College World Series in 1948, losing to the University of Southern California. Bush also met Babe Ruth when playing ball for Yale. In a public ceremony Ruth presented him with the manuscript of his autobiography.

And, of course, President George W. Bush was the managing general partner of the Texas Rangers from 1989 to 1994. After working on his father's 1988 presidential campaign, Bush the Younger participated in the purchase of the franchise from a family friend and fellow oilman. During the years of Bush's tenure as the managing general partner, the team arranged to build a new stadium and laid the groundwork for their first ever play-off appearance in 1996. After a brief flirtation with becoming the commissioner of baseball, Bush resigned from his position with the Rangers when he was elected the governor of Texas.

Email was introduced into the White House in 1992.

THE NICKNAME GAME

*Sure, to their faces it was Mr. President,
but behind their backs it was a whole different story*

John Adams. As vice president, Adams was obsessed with figuring out the most honorable title for his boss, President Washington. He so pestered his fellow politicians with suggestions—"Your Excellency" and "Mr. President" to name just a few—that they finally came up with one of their own. Except that it wasn't for Washington, but for the plump Adams himself: His Rotundity.

James Monroe. Monroe was proud of his Revolutionary past, and his closet reflected it: powdered wigs and old-fashioned britches were a must. People were so disturbed by his insistence on wearing outdated clothes that they named him the Last Cocked Hat.

Martin Van Buren. More at ease crafting backroom deals than giving speeches in front of crowds, Van Buren rose to prominence by retooling the Democratic Party he loved into a well-oiled political machine. With a trick always up his sleeve, he quickly became known as the Little Magician. However, when a series of financial panics sent the nation into a tailspin, a disillusioned public came up with a less flattering name for their commander in chief: Martin Van Ruin.

But before you discard Van Buren into the dustbin of presidential history, be aware that you probably use one of his nicknames all the time: He was affectionately dubbed Old Kinderhook, a reference to his hometown in New York, and during his run for office, booster organizations sprang up around the country called OK Clubs. At his rallies supporters shouted OK to voice their approval, and what had been up to then an obscure phrase from New England quickly became an ingrained part of American culture.

James Buchanan. This anal-retentive president had to have everything just right: Buchanan promptly returned a $15,000 payment one day after noticing it was ten cents short. To be fair, he

---

Zachary Taylor chewed tobacco and was famous for never missing a spittoon when he spat.

also sent three cents to a proprietor whom he had accidentally underpaid for a meal. Yet his penny-pinching was infinitely more interesting than his honesty, and Ten-Cent Jimmy was born.

Benjamin Harrison. An eloquent man on the campaign trail, Harrison wasn't exactly the warmest guy in person. Chances are, you were in for a frosty reception running into the White House Iceberg, who was so cold, he even wrote his own children out of his will.

Ronald Reagan. Reagan was often called the Gipper for his work in the movie *Knute Rockne, All American*, in which Notre Dame's football team is inspired to win one for his terminally ill character. But people are just as likely to call him Dutch, for a slightly less inspiring reason: his alcoholic father, while observing his baby Ronald crying up a storm one day, commented, "For such a little bit of a fat Dutchman, he sure makes a hell of a lot of noise."

Ulysses S. Grant. President Grant's father wasn't exactly Ward Cleaver. Convinced his son would never amount to anything, he decided to call the boy Useless.

William Henry Harrison. During his campaign, he was known as Tippecanoe, named after the creek where he celebrated a victory over Tecumseh's Native American forces. Yet his presidency would be better described by another nickname of his: after giving the longest inauguration speech in history, he quickly fell ill from the cold and died one month into his presidency—this short tenure being another dubious record for Old Granny.

Lucy Hayes. First Ladies aren't immune to the name game. When the teetotalling wife of Rutherford B. Hayes, our nineteenth president, banned all alcohol from the White House—even going to the extreme of allowing only water at state dinners—an anti-temperance organization dubbed her Lemonade Lucy.

Martin Van Buren's autobiography does not mention his wife even once.

WASHINGTON, DC: THE PRESIDENT'S HOMETOWN

"Somebody once said that Washington was a city of Northern charm and Southern efficiency."—John F. Kennedy

No matter where a president hails from, Washington, DC, quickly becomes the chief exec's hometown. Designed by a Frenchman with quadrants and confusing diagonal streets, the District is a fascinating and baffling place. Here's a quick little guide to the lovely U.S. city that is the nation's capital along the Potomac River.

WASHINGTON'S PLAN

- French-born Pierre Charles L'Enfant, a onetime volunteer for the Americans during the War for Independence, was appointed by President George Washington as the architect of a grand scheme for the new capital city of the United States. It was one of the first planned communities of the New World.

- L'Enfant's plan specified the placement of the major federal buildings and monuments (there were already plans to memorialize the Founders, even before they died!), as well as sweeping parkland to enhance the majesty of the structures.

- Washington, DC, was originally 10 miles square, crossing the Potomac River into Virginia. Both Virginia and Maryland donated land for the capital city. The Virginia portion, however, was later given back to Virginia in 1846 at the request of the commonwealth.

- Unfortunately for L'Enfant, he never got to finish his project. In February 1792 President Washington fired him because con-

---

Eisenhower was a skilled chef, famous for his vegetable soup, steaks, and cornmeal pancakes.

struction was behind schedule, thanks in part to labor shortages in the capital city. One after another, architects replaced him, each leaving his own thumbprint on L'Enfant's grand scheme. They were less than faithful to his original intent.

OUT ON THE STREETS

- L'Enfant divided the city into quadrants (northwest, northeast, southeast, southwest), with the Capitol at the center. So when addressing a letter to Washington, DC, make sure you include the quadrant designation.

- The National Mall extends from the Capitol all the way down to the Lincoln Memorial. Running east to west, Constitution Avenue borders the mall on the north side and Independence Avenue on the south.

- As you walk north or south of the mall, you'll see that the east-west streets have names of letters that go all the way up to W. After W Street, east–west streets take on two-syllable names, then three-syllable, and then the names of trees and flowers. These names are in alphabetical order—but sometimes they skip a letter or repeat. It looks a lot more disorganized the farther you get from downtown DC.

- If someone tells you they live on J Street in Washington, they're pulling your leg. There is no J Street in the District. Why? Legend has it that architect L'Enfant despised John Jay, the first Chief Justice of the Supreme Court (no one seems to know why) and that he refused to name a street after him.

- However much L'Enfant might have hated Jay, it is implausible that he would have gotten away with such a petty gesture: his plans were subject to the scrutiny of a board of commissioners. It's more likely that there is no J Street because the letters I and J in eighteenth-century English, especially when handwritten, were often indistinguishable and largely interchangeable. Thus to have both an I and a J Street would have been confusing to local letter carriers.

A 1940 book published a proof of the Pythagorean Theorem derived by James Garfield.

- Numbered streets start at 1st and then run north to south to 52nd Street NW and 63 Street NE. But numbered and lettered streets alike sometimes skip a block or two, and then suddenly reappear.

- Confused yet? Avenues named after the states radiate out from the Capitol and White House and intersect downtown. Downtown avenues meet at traffic circles, which are disorienting tests of patience for every driver who must pass through them.

THE WHITE HOUSE

- L'Enfant's plan called for the White House to be nearly ten times its current size, to balance the scale of the building in relationship to the Capitol building. Later architects scaled back this plan, and now the White House is relatively modest in relationship to the buildings that surround it.

- The Ellipse, a circular park on the south side of the White House, contains the Zero Milestone, the point from which all distances are measured from Washington. L'Enfant included the milestone in his original plan of the city to emphasize Washington's importance in the world.

- James Hoban won a government-sponsored competition for his Georgian design of the president's house. Hoban went on to supervise the building's construction and was paid the grand sum of $500 for his efforts (not surprisingly, when given a choice he picked the cash settlement in lieu of an honorary medal). Thomas Jefferson entered the same contest anonymously as A.Z. and lost.

- When White House residents or guests stand in the second-floor Oval Room, they have a clear view of the bronze statue contained within the Jefferson Memorial (dedicated in 1943), which honors the author of the Declaration of Independence—surely an inspirational view and a nice way to console TJ for not winning the architecture prize.

The White House Family Theater can accommodate 30 people.

WASHINGTON'S WEDDING CAKE

- Standing tall on 17th Avenue, NW, the Eisenhower Executive Office Building, or EEOB, is tough to miss. Until 1999 called the Old Executive Office Building, the decadent building has housed the State, War, and Navy departments. Its French Empire-style stands in stark contrast to the Georgian-style White House next door.

- Now housing the White House staff overflow from the West Wing, the structure has seven floors, more than 900 columns, and two dozen chimneys topped with oversized chimney pots.

- Mark Twain called the EEOB "the ugliest building in America" and Herbert Hoover said it was the "greatest monstrosity in America," but architectural critics have generally disagreed with their assessments.

- In the early twentieth century there were plans drawn to sheathe the EEOB in a Greek Revival-style facade to make the building fit in with the look of its august neighbors. But the Depression in the 1930s forced decision makers to shelve this idea. Today it is a much-beloved building in the city, often referred to as the Wedding Cake.

WASHINGTON'S SUPER DOME

- In 1901 Congress decreed that the Capitol dome (set atop a hill—thus the term Capitol Hill) must remain the highest point in Washington; it is 287 feet, 5.5 inches high. Thus high-rise office buildings in the city are no taller than about 13 floors.

- The Capitol has no back door. Actually, it has no back! The building was designed with an East Front and a West Front, the latter of which faces the National Mall. Both sets of "front" steps have been the site of presidential inaugurations.

- The architecture and configuration of the ceilings in Statuary Hall in the Capitol are such that whispers can be heard from

one side of the room to the other. So speaking softly wouldn't protect anyone when speaking out of turn—even before the advent of microphones.

- Congress has its own underground railroad, an 18-passenger electric subway that travels about 20 mph and runs between the three Senate office buildings and the Capitol. The late Strom Thurmond (for years the nation's oldest legislator) is said to have taunted his younger colleagues who were relaxing on the train as he himself walked briskly alongside it.

- Want to check up on your representatives and make sure they're doing their jobs? Well, you can tell when Congress is in session by looking for the flags that fly over the House and Senate. At night, when it's tougher to see the flags, a light shines from the *Goddess of Freedom*, the statue that sits on top of the Capitol dome. This practice is thought to have originated in the middle of the nineteenth century, when many representatives lived near the Capitol building. These signals told legislators to get back to work.

LICENSE PLATE POWER!

- District residents are the only U.S. citizens without representation in Congress. DC has long fought for statehood—with no luck to this point. The District does have two "shadow" senators and a representative, however, who lobby the Congress on behalf of citizens of the District—but they are the only nonvoting members of the legislature.

- In 2000 to protest their situation, DC citizens changed the logo on their new license plates from "Nation's Capital" to "Taxation Without Representation." Before he left office, President Bill Clinton had these confrontational tags put on the presidential limo, but George W. Bush replaced them with just plain District plates.

A 40-quart Peerless Ice Cream Freezer was added to the White House kitchen in 1912.

THE STATE OF THE STATE OF THE UNION

Just how does the president check in with the people?

Touching base is important, so it's a great thing that the authors of the Constitution made that part of the president's job. Constitutional requirement: Article II, Section 3 requires that the president "shall from time to time give to the Congress Information of the State of the Union, and recommend to their Consideration such Measures as he shall judge necessary and expedient." Here's a quick punch list of facts about the State of the Union address.

FIRST ADDRESS
In January 1780, just eight months into his first term, President George Washington delivered his address to a joint session of Congress at Federal Hall, New York City.

SHORTEST ADDRESS
Washington's 1790 speech was also the shortest, coming in at only 833 words and clocking in at about five to seven minutes.

LONGEST ADDRESS
President Harry S. Truman's 1946 address was the longest at more than 25,000 words. Truman, however, took pity on Congress by sending it over as a written message rather than delivering it in person.

FIRST ADDRESS IN WRITING
In December 1801, Thomas Jefferson was the first president to send his address only as a written message to Congress. Subsequent presidents followed his example by mailing the speech for the next 112 years.

NEVER GAVE THEIR ADDRESSES
Sadly William Henry Harrison and James A. Garfield each died during his first year in office before he could give the speech.

FIRST MODERN ADDRESS DELIVERED IN PERSON
President Woodrow Wilson in 1913 revived the practice of delivering the address in person before a joint session of Congress.

ONLY MODERN PRESIDENT
NEVER TO GIVE THE SPEECH IN PERSON
Never delivering the message before Congress, Herbert Hoover only sent in written messages from 1930 to 1933.

FIRST TO CALL THE SPEECH
THE STATE OF THE UNION ADDRESS
President Franklin D. Roosevelt in 1935.

FIRST RESPONSE BY THE OPPOSITION PARTY
In 1966 television networks gave the Republican Party thirty minutes to respond to President Lyndon Johnson. Ironically one of the two selected speakers was Michigan representative and future president Gerald R. Ford.

FIRST PRESIDENT TO RECOGNIZE
MEMBERS OF THE AUDIENCE
President Ronald Reagan in 1982 began the practice of presidents giving recognition to honored guests seated in the congressional gallery.

FIRST ADDRESS TO BE POSTPONED
In 1986, when the space shuttle *Challenger* disaster occurred on the day that President Reagan was to deliver his address, the speech was rescheduled for the following week.

MOST GROUNDBREAKING FOREIGN POLICY
In his December 1823 message to Congress, President James Monroe spelled out his Monroe Doctrine—telling the European powers not to mess with the United States in the Western

---

Warren G. Harding once gambled away an entire set of White House china.

Hemisphere. "The American continents . . . are henceforth not to be considered as subjects for future colonization by any European powers."

MOST MEMORABLE DOMESTIC POLICY
Lyndon B. Johnson spelled out the details of his Great Society programs in the first evening State of the Union address in 1965. "The Great Society asks not how much, but how good; not only how to create wealth but how to use it; not only how fast we are going, but where we are headed."

MOST ELOQUENT
President Abraham Lincoln's 1862 address given on December 1 during the Civil War was quite simple and very powerful.

> Fellow-citizens, we cannot escape history. We of this Congress and this Administration will be remembered in spite of ourselves . . . The fiery trial through which we pass will light us down in honor or dishonor to the latest generation . . . We, even we here, hold the power and bear the responsibility. In giving freedom to the slave we assure freedom to the free—honorable alike in what we give and what we preserve. We shall nobly save or meanly lose the last best hope of earth. Other means may succeed; this could not fail. The way is plain, peaceful, generous, just—a way which if followed, the world will forever applaud and God must forever bless.

MOST AWKWARD
President Bill Clinton's 1999 address, given during his impeachment trial. The Senate acquitted him three weeks later.

MOST WEIRD
During President Bill Clinton's 1997 address, the TV networks put Clinton on a split screen with the announcement of the verdict in the O. J. Simpson civil trial.

To help curb his appetite, John Adams had boiled cornmeal pudding served before his meal.

FIRST TO BE BROADCAST ON THE RADIO
President Calvin Coolidge's address in 1923.

FIRST TO BE BROADCAST ON TELEVISION
President Harry S. Truman's speech in 1947.

FIRST TO BE BROADCAST LIVE ON THE INTERNET
President George W. Bush's speech in 2002.

FIRST TO BE BROADCAST VIA HIGH-DEFINITION TELEVISION
President George W. Bush's speech in 2004.

★　★　★　★　★

THE JELLYBEAN PRESIDENT

During Reagan's years at the White House, a jar of jellybeans could always be found in the Oval Office, on *Air Force One*, and in the Cabinet meeting rooms. The president began this love affair with the chewy candy when he stopped smoking in the late 1960s. Jellybeans helped ease his nicotine cravings, and licorice was Reagan's favorite flavor. At about the same time, the Rowland family, both California candy makers and devout Republicans, began sending the then-governor of California a 20-pound shipment of jellybeans every month to help him kick the tobacco habit.

In 1976, the Rowlands went on to introduce the Jelly Belly brand to the world. Jelly Belly jellybeans looked like ordinary jellybeans, but their gourmet flavors were out of this world. To honor him when he became president, Jelly Belly sent Reagan 7,000 pounds of red, white, and blue jellybeans for his 1981 inauguration. The blueberry jellybean was invented just for the occasion. (They needed a bean in just the right shade of blue.) Reagan loved the patriotic beans, but licorice still remained his favorite.

Bulletproof glass was installed in the three south windows of the Oval Office in 1941.

NUMBER TWO: JOHN ADAMS

Served from 1797 to 1801

Vital Stats: Born on October 30, 1735, in Braintree, Massachusetts. Died on July 4, 1826, in Quincy, Massachusetts.
Age at Inauguration: 61
Vice President: Thomas Jefferson
Political Affiliation: Federalist
Wife: Abigail Smith (married 1764)
Kids: Abigail Amelia (1765–1813); John Quincy (1767–1848); Susanna (1768–1770); Charles (1770–1800); Thomas Boylston (1772–1832)
Education: Harvard University
What he did before he was president: Lawyer; Teacher; Political Agitator; Delegate to the First and Second Continental Congresses; Delegate to the Massachusetts Constitutional Convention; Commissioner to France; Minister to the Netherlands and England; U.S. Vice President
Postpresidential Occupations: Writer

MEMORABLE QUOTES

"I pray Heaven to bestow the best of blessing on this house, and on all that shall hereafter inhabit it. May none but honest and wise men ever rule under this roof!"
—John Adams's first letter after moving into the White House, November 2, 1800

"I have one head, four limbs and five senses, like any other man, and nothing peculiar in any of them . . . I have no miniature, and have been too much abused by painters ever to sit for any one again."
—John Adams's answer to a biographical information request, March 11, 1809

James Buchanan liked to give parties featuring sauerkraut and mashed potatoes.

OLD IKE PLUGS SOME TOBACCO

The story of Old Ike, Woodrow Wilson's tobacco chewing ram.

World War I was underway, Woodrow Wilson was president, and Americans were making contributions to the war effort. What could the president offer his people in addition to his public service?

President Wilson and his wife hit upon a great idea—get a flock of sheep! Wait, it's a better idea than you might think: with a shortage of manpower because of the war, the president could cut down on the amount of gardeners he needed, since the sheep would trim the lawn. After sheering time, Mrs. Wilson could auction off the wool, with the proceeds going to the Red Cross. Everybody would win!

So, thirteen ewes were shipped in to the White House. They immediately ate everything in sight, ironically making more work for the gardeners. However Mrs. Wilson's part of the plan worked much better: The first shearing yielded ninety-eight pounds of wool, which ended up raising more than fifty thousand dollars at auction. Yet this wasn't the most memorable part of the Wilsons' experiment with animal husbandry: That would lie with Old Ike, the tobacco-chewing ram.

BUTTING FOR BUTTS

Ike, sent along with the ewes to keep them company, was addicted to chew. Unfamiliar with the human custom of spitting, Ike was content to let tobacco juice would run down his chin and stain his fur. And when he was done with the chew, he'd swallow the whole thing. Nicotine-addicted barn animals were not as rare as one might think: in the South farm hands would sometimes give animals tobacco as a joke. However, as any nicotine-addicted person knows, this type of joke can turn into a serious habit. Poor Ike. He would do anything to get his fix, often butting people holding cigars or foraging for discarded cigarettes.

Were our first 2 presidents Democrats or Republicans? Neither—they were Federalists.

In 1920, with the war over, the great sheep experiment came to a close. President Wilson gave the entire flock—still headed by Ike—to L. C. Probert, an official with the Associated Press. Ike spent his remaining days doing what you would expect a virile ram to do with nothing but ewes around; the flock quickly grew to more than seventy animals. Mr. Probert eventually used their wool to make blankets, a couple of which he gave as gifts to President Calvin Coolidge. An old, frail Ike was finally put down in 1927—but not until Mr. Probert gave him one last piece of chew. He died peacefully, with the tobacco still in his mouth.

★　★　★　★　★

DEAD ON THE FOURTH OF JULY

The lives of the Founding Fathers were intertwined in many ways, none more so that those of John Adams and Thomas Jefferson. But what had began as a spirited friendship was almost destroyed by vicious political rivalries. After a bitter defeat in the 1800 presidential election, Adams skipped Jefferson's inauguration. The two did not speak for more than ten years after that.

In 1812, the two decided to let bygones be bygones and struck up one of the most memorable correspondences in U.S. history. The letters they sent back and forth from Adams's farm in Quincy, Massachusetts to Jefferson's Virginia home, Monticello, have been a valuable resource for historians, political scientists, and biographers alike.

As their lives were intertwined, so were their deaths. Both the second and third presidents died on the same day—July 4, 1826, the 50th anniversary of the signing of the Declaration of Independence. Ninety-two at the time of his death, Adams had vowed to live until the Jubilee of the nation's birth. His last words were, "Thomas Jefferson survives." Little did he know, that Jefferson himself had died earlier that day at Monticello.

That's not all. Five years later, another president also died on the nation's birthday. The fifth president, James Monroe, died on July 4, 1831. On a happier note, one president was born on the 4th of July. Calvin Coolidge, the 30th president, was born on July 4, 1872.

A George W. Bush "Collectible Talking Action Figure" speaks 25 phrases.

CLOSE CALLS I

Some presidents escaped an ignominious end by a hairbreadth.
You'd be surprised how many got so lucky.

S ure, we all get ticked off at the president sometimes. And
sometimes we'd like to take a potshot at him, but we never
would. In the history of the United States, thirteen men and
women actually have. Lucky for the country and the men in
office, nine of them failed. Some of our presidents served out their
terms by the merest accident of fate—a shaky chair, a misfiring
gun. History would have looked a lot different if we hadn't had so
many close calls.

RICHARD LAWRENCE: ANDREW JACKSON

The morning of January 30, 1835, Richard Lawrence sat on a
chest in his shop in Washington, DC, clutching a book and laughing to himself. Suddenly he stood up, dropped the book and said,
"I'll be damned if I don't do it!"

He left the shop and headed to the Capitol. There he waited
in a portico for Andrew Jackson to emerge from the funeral of
Congressman Warren Davis. The elderly president Jackson hob-
bled into view, leaning on the arm of the U.S. treasury secretary.
Lawrence leapt from the crowd, leveled a pistol at the president's
chest, and pulled the trigger. The gun misfired: the cap exploded
noisily, but didn't ignite the powder. Not to be deterred, Lawrence
pulled out a second pistol, again fired at point-blank range, and
again, nothing happened. The bullet and powder had fallen out
of both pistols in his pocket. An enraged Jackson struggled away
from his companions and attacked Lawrence with his cane,
shouting, "Let me alone! Let me alone! I know where this came
from." Jackson assumed—incorrectly—that political opponents
sent the assassin.

Richard Lawrence was born in England around 1800. He
immigrated to the United States when he was twelve and lived
quietly for many years as a house painter. In November 1832 he
suddenly decided to return to England. He got as far as Philadel-

---

phia and turned back. He told his shocked brother-in-law that he found the papers in Philadelphia were full of vicious attacks on his character—and they call it the City of Brotherly Love. This was, in modern parlance, Lawrence's first psychotic episode. At the time, everyone just agreed he was a lunatic.

King Richard
In the months that followed, Lawrence developed an extravagant sense of fashion. Decked out in exorbitantly expensive finery, Lawrence would stand completely still in his doorway for hours, allowing passersby to bask in his presence. He believed he was King Richard III of England and, as such, owned two English estates. He stopped working, assuring his friends he would be wealthy as soon as the American government gave him the money from these estates. President Jackson, because he opposed the national bank, was preventing this transfer of funds. Lawrence came to a "natural" conclusion: remove Jackson, remove the opposition, and get the money. It made perfect sense, at least to Lawrence anyway.

At his trial Lawrence angrily stood and announced, "It is for me, gentlemen, to pass upon you, and not you upon me." The jury and prosecuting attorney, Francis Scott Key (better known for composing "The Star Spangled Banner" than his legal career) quickly agreed Lawrence was insane. Lawrence lived out the rest of his days in the Government Hospital for the Insane in Washington, DC, the first man to attempt to assassinate the president.

JOHN SCHRANK: TEDDY ROOSEVELT
The day after President McKinley died from Leon Czolgosz's attack, John Schrank awoke from a dream. In it he saw McKinley sit up in his coffin, point an accusing finger at Theodore Roosevelt, who succeeded him, and intone, "This is my murderer, avenge my death."

Eleven years later William Howard Taft was president and campaigning for reelection; but Roosevelt wasn't out of the picture and ran as a third-party candidate. Schrank became obsessed with preventing Roosevelt's reelection. According to what he called the Four Pillars of Our Republic, Schrank's personal theory of govern-

---

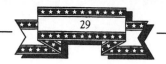

ment, a three-term president would lead to the erosion of our civil rights and a descent into dictatorship. On September 14, 1912, the anniversary of his first vision, Schrank was again visited by the ghost of William McKinley. This fearful specter told Schrank, "Let not a murderer take the presidential chair. Avenge my death." Schrank agreed.

Schrank bought a gun for $14.00 and started stalking Roosevelt, the candidate for the Bull Moose Party. From Charleston, to Augusta, to Atlanta, to Birmingham, and on to Chattanooga, Nashville, Louisville, Evansville, and Chicago, Schrank followed but never got his chance. Finally, on October 14 in Milwaukee, Schrank had his moment.

Waiting for Roosevelt to leave the Hotel Gilpatrick for his evening speech, Schrank stepped into a local bar. There he requested the band play John Philip Sousa's "Stars and Stripes Forever," and danced happily to the music. Thanking them, he paid for his drink, and joined the crowd outside the hotel.

As Roosevelt walked from the hotel to his waiting car, Schrank pushed his way forward, calmly drew a gun from his pocket, and fired on Roosevelt at point-blank range. Before he could fire again, a former football player in the crowd tackled him and pinned him to the ground. Teddy quickly assured the crowd he was fine, saying, "Oh, no! Missed me that time, I'm not hurt a bit."

Roosevelt got into his car and continued to his evening engagement. On the way one of his companions noticed a hole in his overcoat. Opening it Roosevelt found his shirt soaked with blood but refused to seek medical treatment. When his friends insisted, he replied, "I will deliver this speech or die, one or the other."

At the hall the waiting crowd had heard nothing of the attack. Roosevelt stepped up to the podium to their cheering and opened his jacket, showing the bloody shirt. He cried, "It takes more than one bullet to kill a Bull Moose!" With blood dripping down his pants and onto the floor, he gave his planned speech, continuing for almost an hour. As time passed, though, he seemed to be losing steam, leaning more and more unsteadily on the podium.

The Word is Mightier than the Gun
It may seem ridiculous to risk his life over a speech, but it's actu-

---

Andrew Jackson sometimes coughed up blood because of a bullet lodged near his heart from a duel.

ally the speech that saved Teddy's life. When Roosevelt finally submitted to examination, the doctor found a hole in the manuscript. The bullet had gone through the folded fifty-page speech and his spectacles case, losing all its force by the time it hit Roosevelt. On hearing this story Senator Dixon said, "That must have been a great speech . . . if it could stop a bullet." Teddy's hot air saved his life, but it failed to win him the election. He lost to Woodrow Wilson.

As for Roosevelt's assailant, Schrank was found insane at his trial. Schrank demanded that the gun and bullet be displayed at the New York Historical Society. When told the bullet was still in Teddy's chest, he exclaimed, "That is my bullet! . . . And I want it to go to the New York Historical Society." Schrank lived the rest of his life in an asylum, where he came to be known as "Uncle John." (It's no relation. We promise.) He was well mannered and even-tempered, a favorite among the guards. When a guard once asked him if he hunted, he replied, "Only Bull Moose."

★　　★　　★　　★　　★

FOR THE BIRDS

- Zachary Taylor's canary, Johnny Ty, died when they brought him a mate. They thought they found him a lovebird, but it turned out that both birds were both males.

- Among the presidents who kept parrots, Teddy Roosevelt had a macaw named Eli Yale. Dolley Madison used to like to stroll around with her green parrot perched on her shoulder.

- President Kennedy and his family had two parakeets named Bluebelle and Marybelle.

- The Coolidges had a virtual aviary on their hands: three canaries, a thrush, a mockingbird, and a goose named Enoch.

- James Buchanan kept a pair of bald eagles.

WARTIME WUNDERKINDER

"Experience is the teacher of all things."
—Julius Caesar

There is a strong tradition of military service running through the Oval Office. In fact, thirty-one commanders in chief could put military experience on their resumes prior to becoming president. Some served in state militias during times of peace; others commanded entire armies during the War for Independence, the War of 1812, and the Civil War. Their ranks have run the gamut from private to general to supreme allied commander. But strangely enough some of the presidents with little or no military experience held down the position of commander in chief and oversaw some of the greatest military victories in U.S. history.

A 1,920-HOUR TOUR, A 1,920-HOUR TOUR
Some might say that the best wartime president was Abraham Lincoln, who preserved the Union during the trials faced in the Civil War (1861–1865). Prior to taking office Lincoln wasn't exactly a soldier himself. He did serve an eighty-day stint during the Black Hawk War when the Fox and Sauk tribes took up arms against the United States. Having seen no action in his first thirty days, he re-upped for another twenty days and then a second twenty-day stint. During his last month, Lincoln served in the Independent Spy Corps, charged with (although unsuccessful at) tracking down Chief Black Hawk. In all his time Lincoln never saw any battle action, but he did save a Native American from being lynched.

IN HIS NATION'S SERVICE
Woodrow Wilson had no military experience whatsoever. With a background in academics (he's the only president to hold a PhD), Wilson served as the president of Princeton University and governor of New Jersey before ascending to the presidency. He was

... The others are Jackson, Van Buren, Taylor, Fillmore, A. Johnson, and Cleveland.

known by the rather unintimidating nickname of the School-master in Politics, but he must have been a quick military study to become an effective commander during World War I. Fewer than eighteen months after the United States entered the Great War, Germany declared an armistice. The greatest accomplishment of Wilson's wartime administration, however, may have been the use of volunteers to staff governmental wartime agencies that made it possible to dissolve the agencies at the end of the war, bringing federal spending back down to levels close to those seen before it began. Smart guy, that Wilson.

FRANKLIN GETS RESULTS

Franklin Roosevelt presided over two of the worst American crises of the twentieth century: the Great Depression and World War II. As a public policy visionary, Roosevelt would have seemed better suited to dealing with the former, but who knew that the latter would highlight his leadership ability? The closest FDR ever came to military service was an appointment to the position of assistant secretary of the navy under Woodrow Wilson (incidentally, the same position his cousin Teddy had held in the first McKinley administration).

Despite Roosevelt's lack of direct military experience, he took a major role in determining the strategy that would march the country toward victory during World War II. On the domestic front, FDR's leadership revved up the military and industrial war machine; his words inspired Americans to make personal sacrifices for the war effort. FDR's strong diplomacy with the leaders of Great Britain and the Soviet Union ensured success over the Axis powers. Germany was within a month of surrendering when he died, and the tide was beginning to turn in the Pacific. FDR's leadership during the war and the programs he enacted also helped pull the country out of the Depression.

NUMBER THREE: <u>THOMAS JEFFERSON</u>

Served from 1801 to 1809

Vital Stats: Born on April 13, 1743, in Goochland County, Virginia. Died on July 4, 1826, in Charlottesville, Virginia.
Age at Inauguration: 57
Vice President: Aaron Burr (first term); George Clinton (second term)
Political Affiliation: Democratic–Republican
Wife: Martha Wayles Skelton (married 1772).
Kids: Martha "Patsy" (1772–1836); Jane (1774–1775); Unnamed son (b. and d. 1777); Maria "Polly" (1778–1804); Lucy Elizabeth (1780–1781); Lucy Elizabeth (1782–1785)
Education: The College of William and Mary
What he did before he was president: Farmer; Lawyer; Inventor; Architect; Delegate to the Second Continental Congress; Governor of Virginia; Minister to France; Secretary of State; U.S. Vice President
Postpresidential Occupations: Planter; Writer; Educator

MEMORABLE QUOTES

"I have sworn upon the altar of God eternal hostility against every form of tyranny over the mind of man."
—Thomas Jefferson's letter to Dr. Benjamin Rush, September 23, 1800

"If you are obliged to neglect any thing, let it be your chemistry. It is the least useful and the least amusing to a country gentleman of all the ordinary branches of science."
—Thomas Jefferson's advice to his grandson, January 3, 1809

All U.S. presidents have worn glasses, though some didn't like wearing them in public.

LEADING LADIES

Okay, you've heard of Hilary Rodham Clinton, Mary Todd Lincoln, and Lady Bird Johnson. But what were the first two names of First Ladies Arthur, Cleveland, and Coolidge? If you don't know— well, not many do—but you'll just have to puzzle it out.

ACROSS

1. Get one's mitts on
5. Falls off
9. Pile up
14. Dishy Barrett
15. Russia's ___ Mountains
16. Watch name
17. "Now ___ me down ..."
18. Prefix with legal
19. Threaded fasteners
20. First Lady ___ ___ Arthur
23. Haitian religious practice
24. Beer brand of western New York
28. H.S. class
29. "Iliad" city
32. Chilean poet Pablo
33. Party
35. One-named model-actress
36. First Lady ___ ___ Cleveland
40. Cafe au ___
41. "Woo woo!"
42. ___ Shriver, sister of JFK
45. D.I., perhaps
46. What savings accts. pay
49. Tense and constricted
51. Actor Ving ___
53. First Lady ___ ___ Coolidge
56. Boarded
59. Say it's so
60. Satiric Sahl
61. Dazzled
62. Cafe handout
63. Rocker Tori
64. Travelers company since 1996
65. Kind of school
66. Hawaiian goose

DOWN

1. Mourn
2. Deodorant on a ball
3. Not digital
4. Howled like a hound on the scent
5. Happy to the max
6. Dundee hillside
7. Mystery writer Nevada
8. "Da bomb," e.g.
9. Show starter
10. Affectation
11. Sun Devils' campus, briefly
12. Mind the kids
13. Brillo alternative
21. "___ your life!"
22. Remote room?
25. Kyoto contest
26. Dutch cheese
27. Euclid or Caesar follower
30. State south of Wash.
31. Molly Bloom words
33. Ball wear, perhaps

George Washington's pets included 36 hounds and Polly the parrot.

34. Young newts
36. Goat-legged deity
37. Skater's domain
38. "Act your age!"
39. Graph starter
40. Scented necklace
43. It covers the lens and iris
44. Greek "H"
46. Phrase following "Hi honey"
47. Brain cell
48. Bad fly
50. Rascal
52. Mad Ave guy
54. Anon's partner
55. "___ fishin'"
56. Actress Scala
57. It precedes "Blast-off!"
58. Make a doily

Turn to page 315 for the solution.

Franklin D. Roosevelt passed the bar exam in 1907, then he dropped out of law school.

WHICH BUSH IS IT?

*Can you tell the difference between the sayings of the
latest father and son to sit in the Oval Office?*

George H. W. Bush and George W. Bush have a lot in
common. They both play golf, they both have lived in
Texas, and, oh yeah, they both have been president. The
other thing they share is a certain way with words. Don't misunderestimate your ability to tell who said what. Just take our little
guessing game.

"POPPY" GEORGE OR GEORGE "DUBYA?"

1. "I'm conservative, but I'm not a nut about it."

2. "Security is the essential roadblock to achieving the road map
to peace."

3. "America's freedom is the example to which the world expires."

4. "It's no exaggeration to say the undecideds could go one way or
another."

5. "I don't feel the compulsion to be the glamour, one-shot, smart-
comment kind of guy. I think experience, steadiness, knowing how
to interact with people is the way to get things done better."

6. "I am mindful not only of preserving executive powers for
myself, but for predecessors as well."

7. "I'm not the most articulate emotionalist."

8. "The United States is the best and fairest and most decent
nation on the face of the earth."

9. "Our nation must come together to unite."

Most common presidential religious affiliation: Episcopalian, followed by Presbyterian.

10. "Where there is suffering, there is duty. Americans in need are not strangers, they are citizens, not problems, but priorities. And all of us are diminished when any are hopeless."

11. "The surest way to win the war against poverty is to win the battle against ignorance. Even though we spend more on education than any other nation on Earth, we just don't measure up."

12. "We must live up to the calling we share. Civility is not a tactic or a sentiment. It is the determined choice of trust over cynicism, of community over chaos. And this commitment, if we keep it, is a way to shared accomplishment."

13. "I want a kinder, gentler nation."

14. "If it weren't for this deficit looming over everything, I'd feel like a spring colt."

15. "This foreign policy stuff is a little frustrating."

16. "I've coined new words, like, misunderstanding and Hispanically."

★　★　★　★　★

THE TWO MRS. BUSHES

"Who knows? Somewhere out in this audience may even be someone who will one day follow in my footsteps, and preside over the White House as the president's spouse. I wish him well!"
—Barbara Bush speaking at Wellesley College's commencement

"She was pretty intimidating . . . She still can be. She's terrific, though. She's a wonderful mother-in-law. And she loves her children—and, of course, I love one of them, too."
—Laura Bush on her mother-in-law, Barbara

ANSWERS: 1. Poppy, 2. Dubya, 3. Poppy, 4. Poppy, 5. Poppy, 6. Dubya, 7. Poppy, 8. Poppy, 9. Dubya, 10. Dubya, 11. Poppy, 12. Dubya, 13. Poppy, 14. Poppy, 15. Dubya, 16. Dubya

So far, 22 presidents served no more than one term.

A FINE MESS:
THE ELECTION OF 1800

*Did you spend five weeks in November and December 2000,
with eyes glued to the TV awaiting the final results of the
presidential election? Well, you should have been around in the
winter of 1800. Things were even worse then.*

The American people know a lot about close presidential
races; the 2000 election sure was tight. The official difference was three electoral votes out of 538—a razor thin
margin. But that was nothing compared to some other elections
from past years. Uncle John's delved deep into the past to find the
closest of the too close to call.

The first and closest ever race was the election of 1800,
which wasn't just nearly a tie, it *was* a tie. To complicate matters,
the two men who tied for first were running mates, presidential
candidate Thomas Jefferson and his vice presidential candidate
Aaron Burr. It was a constitutional crisis just waiting to happen.

LACK OF VISION
So how on earth did they get into such a mess? Well, the writers
of the 1787 Constitution came up with some clever schemes for
their newly created nation, but the first crack at choosing president and vice president was not their finest hour. Basically the
original scheme was that the presidency went to the guy with the
most electoral votes while the runner-up made due with the office
of vice president.

One thing the Founding Fathers hadn't planned on was the
existence of political parties. So they didn't anticipate that a president and vice president could be from different ones and completely
at odds with each other for four years. Just imagine a scenario where
George W. Bush got teamed up with Al Gore. The way Article II of
the Constitution was first drafted, that's exactly what could have
happened. In fact in 1796 it did. Federalist John Adams got saddled
with the Democratic-Republican Thomas Jefferson, a kick off to a
bitter political rivalry between the two men.

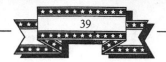
But the most important possibility they overlooked was that a vice presidential candidate could walk away with the whole she-bang and leave his running mate in the dust (or at least in the vice president's seat)—a feat Aaron Burr almost accomplished in 1800.

AND THE WINNER IS . . .

By 1800, presidential tickets had developed and the Federalists and Democratic-Republicans were on them. Each man who ran for president chose a colleague to be his veep; Federalist John Adams had picked fellow-Fed Charles Pinckney while Jefferson chose Burr, a gifted New York politician. Before the election took place the Federalists had shrewdly arranged for one elector to throw one vote to Governor John Jay, so that Adams would be ensured of a one-vote advantage over Pinckney if the Federalists won. But Jefferson and Burr's electors made no such arrangements. The result? Both men garnered seventy-three votes each, deadlock. (In case you're wondering, Adams got sixty-five votes; Pinckney, sixty-four; and Jay even garnered one.)

The Constitution says that any election that results in a tie must be decided in the House of Representatives, where each state has one vote determined by its congressional delegation. There were sixteen states in 1800, so nine of them formed a majority. The problem was that the Federalists controlled enough of those state delegations that they could prevent Jefferson's election by throwing their support to Burr, even though he was the declared *vice* presidential candidate. Now why would they do that?

THE CHOICE WAS THEIRS

The simple answer is fear of Jefferson, whom many saw as the American embodiment of the godless French revolution, a man who was, in fact, a fervent supporter of the battle cries of French freedom and the king's overthrow. But many feared Jefferson also stood for the mob and mob rule. "A violent democrat, a vulgar demagogue, a bold atheist, and a profligate man" was how one newspaper described him. President of Yale, Timothy Dwight, as he surveyed the early election returns, lamented sarcastically, "We have now reached the consummation of democratic blessedness. We have a country governed by blockheads and knaves."

In contrast, Burr was admired—or tolerated—by many. Even

. . . They include Dutch, English, Irish, Scottish, Welsh, Swiss, and German.

Abigail Adams admitted "the bold, daring and decisive Burr would serve the country better." A dashing ladies' man and gifted lawyer, Burr was also perceived by others as not being the most trustworthy sort. This belief caused many Federalists to think they could more easily sway and influence Burr as president to see their point of view, whereas Jefferson would be much harder for the Federalists to control.

Two major obstacles stood in Burr's way. One was the plain fact that Jefferson was the presidential candidate. Burr had made assurances, both public and private, that the Virginian would have his unqualified support and loyalty. To overtly violate those promises would ruin Burr politically. So when the tie was announced Burr kept silent, neither saying he would decline to accept the office nor that he wished to win it either. And the second obstacle for Burr? Why, the man he would eventually strike down in a duel four years later, Alexander Hamilton.

ENTER THE THIRD MAN

Hamilton, the former secretary of the treasury and a power in the Federalist Party, turned out to be the lynchpin for the election. As an influential man, he had a tough decision to make. On the surface he had cordial relationships with both Jefferson and Burr, but underneath it all he harbored deep mutual suspicions of both men. Who should he throw his weight behind?

Political rivals Jefferson and Hamilton tangled when they were both members of Washington's cabinet. They both harbored very strong ideas about what the new republic should become. Hamilton believed in an economy based on industry and a strong central government, Jefferson preferred agriculture and a weak central government. Each thought the other's vision was ludicrous and potentially dangerous.

Hamilton and Burr, however, were rivals of a different sort. Both men were New Yorkers and Revolutionary War heroes, but they were often at odds with each other. One of the first instances occurred in 1791 when Burr defeated Hamilton's father-in-law to win a seat in the U.S. Senate, denying Hamilton a valuable congressional ally. Their rivalry continued into April 1800 when New York's legislative delegation, a group that would decide the presidential election later that year, came up for election them-

George Washington was the only president elected unanimously.

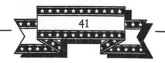

selves. Tirelessly scouring the city and state, Burr put together a pro-Democratic–Republican slate that won and undercut much of Hamilton's power in New York. The Empire State's twelve electors went to Jefferson in December.

But Hamilton's visceral hatred of Aaron Burr seemed to go beyond political rivalry. He often warned friends that "Mr. Burr is unprincipled, both as a public and a private man. In fact, I take it he is for or against nothing but as it suits his interest and ambition." Or how about this one: "Mr. Burr is bold, enterprising, and intriguing . . . and I feel it is a religious duty to oppose his career." Some say Hamilton's feelings were nothing more than jealousy, while other experts say Hamilton feared that Burr's self-serving ambition threatened the welfare of the country. Either way, Hamilton's choice in 1800 was Jefferson.

A MAN WITHOUT A PARTY

In 1800, Hamilton's endorsement actually put him at odds with his own party. He often complained about becoming "an isolated man," as he lamented in a letter to James Bayard, Delaware's sole congressional representative. After the tie Hamilton wrote reams of letters arguing against Burr. To Senator DeWitt Clinton: "Jefferson or Burr?—the former without all doubt . . . The latter has no principles . . . and will listen to no monitor but his own ambition." To another: "There is no doubt but that upon every virtuous and prudent calculation Jefferson is to be preferred. He is by far not so dangerous a man and he has pretensions to character."

ALL'S WELL THAT ENDS WELL

It appears Hamilton's letters did the trick. After 33 rounds of voting that stretched over six days, in February 17, 1801, Jefferson finally won; he took nine votes and Burr garnered five. (On that same day, James Bayard, perhaps at last yielding to Hamilton's pleas, abstained, reducing Burr's tally from six to five.) Luckily for the infant America, the debacle turned out just fine. The country got the presidential candidate it wanted. Most important of all, the Twelfth Amendment to the Constitution was passed in 1804. It requires electors to cast separate votes for president and vice president, making sure that this mess would never happen again.

George *Washington* is the only president who didn't live in *Washington*, DC, during his presidency.

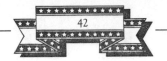

DOES CHARLES ATLAS KNOW ABOUT THIS?

*Legendary for his tremendous energy and physical activity as president,
Teddy Roosevelt might have been the original 90-pound weakling who
spent his youth merely fighting to breathe.*

Teddy Roosevelt may have never had sand kicked in his face
at the beach, but his weakling status seemed a sure bet during his childhood. Few would have guessed that this future
president would be remembered as the solid, robust guy who led
the Rough Riders, trekked through the Wild West, and never met
a physical challenge he didn't want to embrace. His reputation for
bravery would have been impossible to predict because "Teedie"
started out as a small and sickly boy. How small and sickly was he?
Well, he was so small and sickly that no one thought he would
live past his fourth birthday, much less go on to become president.

A RUNT OF A CHILD

As a young child, Teedie struggled with asthma, endless coughs,
colds, nausea, fevers, and nervous diarrhea, which he described at
the age of three as a "toothache in my stomach." All these illnesses led to insomnia and malnutrition. He was so weak and ill
that for much of his childhood, he couldn't even attend school.
Young Teedie had to learn at home with a steady stream of tutors
to satisfy his active and intensely curious mind that was bound by
his puny frame.

At times he rarely felt well for more than ten days straight
and was forced to spend many subsequent days in bed. On the
Roosevelt family's lengthy trip to Europe in 1869, he was plagued
by breathing problems and extended headaches. He wrote in his
diary about attacks of gastroenteritis, toothache, and asthma. Yet
in between it all, he displayed amazing energy, running from one
sightseeing spot to another, hiking, biking, and soaking up the
world until his poor health would flare up again.

TEDDY GETS PHYSICAL

A doctor who examined him around age twelve recommended fresh air and exercise. He made it clear to the Roosevelts that if Teddy didn't act on this advice the development of his strained and battered lungs was in serious danger. His influential and constantly busy father also worried that his son was too pale and thin. Coupled with the advice of the doctor, Theodore Senior at that point told Teddy, "You have the mind but you have not the body and without the help of the body the mind cannot go as far as it should. You must *make* your body." And with that, Teddy embarked on a personal training regimen that would forever transform him—both in mind and body.

Taking advantage of the family's considerable wealth, his father transformed their family home's second floor into a posh home gym, outfitting it with state-of-the art exercise equipment of all kinds. It was there that Teddy began to spend his free time to develop the physique and personal discipline that would later make him famous. In that gym Roosevelt benched-pressed and pushed and lifted and stretched and followed routines that would make any current body builder proud. He was dedicated and consistent. And as any good personal trainer would tell us today, he saw results. His muscles grew, his chest expanded, and he got healthier.

BOXING DAYS

But even that wasn't enough. After two solid years of body building, asthma attacks could still lay him low. So Roosevelt decided to take up boxing. He knew that he wanted to go to Harvard University and needed to be able to compete both academically and physically with America's finest young men. So he continued working out and boxed regularly with his brother and others.

Finally, by the age of seventeen, Roosevelt beat the weakling within. In 1875, he competed against his brothers and cousins in fifteen athletic contests, including running, jumping, vaulting, wrestling, and boxing. Teddy won all but one of them! He had completely transformed himself; he went from wimpy to wonderful. His thin frame was no longer weak; it was strong, wiry, and muscular. In the process, he had developed an iron self-discipline for which he was always known as an adult.

ENERGETIC EXPLORER

TR's energy and passion for physical activity became legendary. He spent several years in the Wild West, honing his skills as a cowboy. He would ride for hours at a time, sometimes all through the night. He gained celebrity status for physical bravery by charging up Kettle Hill in Cuba during the Spanish-American War amid gunfire and horrendous heat. As governor of New York he wrestled with a middleweight wrestling champion every week.

As president, Roosevelt was difficult to keep up with as he rode horses through Rock Creek Park while discussing policies with cabinet members, visitors and advisers. In summers he chopped down trees to relax and rode at top speeds around Long Island on his horses in between conducting official national business.

One of Roosevelt's most lasting legacies comes directly from his devotion to fitness and all this running around. His programs supporting natural resource conservation stemmed largely from his personal love of the great outdoors. He loved to ride, hunt, and explore through the national parks, and he established the first national wildlife refuge. Roosevelt spent many weeks recharging his batteries in these wild and wonderful American places—stretching his mind and his muscles, testing his endurance, and simply breathing deeply of the clean, fresh air he had so much difficulty inhaling as a child.

★　　★　　★　　★　　★

HIT THE BOOKS, JUNIOR!

"I believe in rough, manly sports. But I do not believe in them if they degenerate into the sole end of any one's existence. I don't want you to sacrifice standing well in your studies to any over-athleticism; and I need not tell you that character counts for a great deal more than either intellect or body in winning success in life. Athletic proficiency is a mighty good servant, and like so many other good servants, a mighty bad master . . . A man must develop his physical prowess up to a certain point; but after he has reached that point there are other things that count more."

—Teddy Roosevelt's words on athletics to his son, Ted, Junior

The Bushes are related to Benedict Arnold, Marilyn Monroe, Winston Churchill *and . . .*

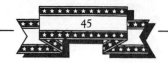

IN LOCO PRESIDENTIS

*You probably wouldn't let the unconscious, anesthetized,
or generally incapacitated mind the store,
but would you let them mind the country?*

It seems like a pretty necessary and not terribly difficult thing to do—make sure someone is always running the country. But it took America's lawmakers almost 200 years to get most of the kinks out of the presidential succession process. Not until the Twenty-fifth Amendment to the Constitution was passed in 1967 was the procedure for replacing an incapacitated president clarified. So what happened before that? Well, the government sort of made things up as it went along.

THAT DEPENDS ON WHAT
THE MEANING OF "PRESIDENT" IS

The first real test of the succession process came when William Henry Harrison died after only a month in office. Harrison had delivered his inauguration speech in cold, windy weather without an overcoat. Harrison caught a cold that quickly turned into pneumonia. Within a month he was dead.

The Constitution said that given the president's death, his *powers and duties* should go to the vice president, who at that time was John Tyler. But not everyone was sure that Tyler actually became *president*. While he might have the president's powers and duties, was it really the same thing as being president? Wasn't he only *acting,* so to speak? Tyler didn't think so. He quickly had himself sworn in as president and even gave an inauguration speech at the ceremony.

Congress decided not to argue the point, which was almost as good as giving Tyler a nod of approval. Of course not everyone was pleased with the "decision" and some dubbed Tyler His Accidency throughout his term of office. Tyler selected no one to be his vice president, so if he happened to kick the bucket or get kicked out of office, Congress would have to elect his successor to serve until the next presidential election. But every vice president

since Tyler who has come to power via a death in office has been perfunctorily sworn into the office of president.

LEADERSHIP LIMBO

The next important question of succession was what to do if a president became unable to carry out his duties. James Garfield spent seventy-nine days hovering between life and death after he was mortally wounded by an assassin's bullet, but presidential powers never transferred during that time. Woodrow Wilson had a severe stroke with over a year left in his second term. His condition stayed a mystery as he remained in virtual seclusion afterward, with his wife taking over the duty of communicating his wishes to the outside world. But this may have been for the best. Wilson's vice president, Thomas Marshall, not a well-known statesman, was best known for a remark he made during the speech of a long-winded senator talking about the needs of the country. Marshall commented loudly enough to be heard by everyone: "What this country *needs* is a good five-cent cigar."

One of the biggest reasons that Garfield and Wilson remained in power during these times was that there was nothing that compelled the vice president to surrender the powers of office if the president ever recovered. It took a long time to fix this problem, but in 1965 Congress passed the Twenty-fifth Amendment, which was ratified by the states two years later. Now there was finally a mechanism for the president to declare himself unable to serve and to later resume his powers by declaring himself capable again. If the president were to fall into a coma and unable to transfer power, then the vice president and a majority of the executive department heads can do it for him; when the Chief recovers, then he gets his powers back.

"I AM IN CONTROL HERE"

Finally, there would be somebody to mind the store. This should have made us all rest a little easier when Ronald Reagan was shot in 1981. Except the Twenty-fifth Amendment wasn't invoked in this case. In surgery, under anesthesia, and in critical condition, President Reagan was clearly unable to exercise his powers and duties. Vice President George H. W. Bush was away in Texas,

---

Ronald Reagan was the first president to have been divorced.

which left the White House was in a state of confusion as it waited for Bush's flight to arrive in DC.

Reagan's top presidential advisers scrambled to hold a chaotic meeting in the White House Situation Room immediately after the incident. There was the question of who was in charge prior to Bush's arrival. Secretary of State Alexander Haig seized the reins in the Situation Room meeting, saying, "The helm is right here. And that means right in this chair for now, constitutionally, until the vice president gets here." Former national security advisor Richard Allen later wrote that despite knowing that there were constitutionally two other people (the Speaker of the House and the president pro tempore of the Senate) ahead of the secretary of state in the line of succession, no one argued with Haig.

Perhaps Haig wishes someone had reminded him of the correct order of succession, especially before he talked to the press. After the Situation Room meeting, Haig spoke at a hurriedly convened White House press conference where he assured the press that he was in charge: "I am in control here." Those five little words guaranteed Haig a lifetime of infamy as the secretary of state who hadn't remembered his civics lessons.

THEN, WHO IS IN CONTROL HERE?

So if Haig wasn't actually in control, then who was? Basically, for a short period of time, no one was in charge of the country. Power never officially transferred to anybody. Pundits have speculated that Reagan's aides were afraid that an official transfer of power to the vice president would only feed a sense of panic about the president's chances of survival. That's right. What they believed was that citizens would feel safer with no one officially at the helm instead of a temporary transfer of presidential powers to Vice President Bush. Interesting logic, wouldn't you say?

Oddly enough in 1985, Bush did become the first acting president during a much less turbulent time. Ronald Reagan needed surgery to remove a cancerous polyp in his intestine. He signed over the presidential powers to Vice President Bush for about eight hours on July 13, 1985. When he came to, Reagan reclaimed his duties and George H. W. Bush would just have to wait until 1988 to get them back.

NUMBER FOUR: JAMES MADISON

Served from 1809 to 1817

Vital Stats: Born on March 15, 1751, in Port Conway, Virginia. Died on June 28, 1836, in Montpelier, Virginia.
Age at Inauguration: 57
Vice President: George Clinton (first term); Elbridge Gerry (second term)
Political Affiliation: Democratic–Republican
Wife: Dolley Payne Todd (married 1794)
Kids: None
Education: The College of New Jersey (later known as Princeton University)
What he did before he was president: Politician; Delegate to the Continental Congress; Delegate to the Constitutional Convention; U.S. Congressman; Secretary of State
Postpresidential Occupations: Planter; Writer; University Rector; State Legislator; Presidential Adviser

MEMORABLE QUOTES

"Since the general civilization of mankind, I believe there are more instances of the abridgment of the freedom of the people, by gradual and silent encroachments of those in power, than by violent and sudden usurpations."
—James Madison in his speech in the Virginia Convention, June 6, 1788

"The capacity of the female mind for studies of the highest order cannot be doubted, having been sufficiently illustrated by its works of genius, of erudition, and of science."
—James Madison in a letter to Albert Picket, September 1821

Four of the first five presidents hailed from Virginia.

DON'T CALL THEM DUMMIES!

Old presidents never die—they just perform at Walt Disney World.

S ome may think of Walt Disney World's Hall of Presidents as an air-conditioned port in a storm of the hot Orlando, Florida, sun. But once visitors step right in, they'll find (in addition to a cool place to sit down) a unique and stirring tribute to some of the greatest political minds and heroes of America, the forty-three presidents. When Walt Disney began dreaming about his theme parks, he wanted a patriotic exhibit to honor American presidents. He envisioned an attraction where all the presidents— dead and alive—would be onstage together and where his childhood hero, Abraham Lincoln, would address the audience with a rousing speech. Walt did get his wish, which came true because of a bird brain.

BIRD BRAIN?
While traveling through New Orleans, Walt Disney found a way to achieve his dream when he bought an antique mechanical bird. It was an automaton or machine that imitates the actions of a living creature. Walt Disney found and bought an antique automaton that recreated the actions of a bird in a cage. After studying the "brains" and inner workings of the bird, Walt set his technicians, still known today as Imagineers, to inventing mechanical creatures for his theme park, Disneyland, in Anaheim, California. He called the technology that propelled the lifelike machines Audio-Animatronics.

WINKIN', BLINKIN' LINCOLN
Once Walt and his team had successfully analyzed the antique automaton, they moved on to creating an Animatronic "human" replica of President Abraham Lincoln. The first part of the figure built in the Disney studios was Lincoln's head, which could wink,

---

Kennedy was the only president to win a Pulitzer Prize, for his biography, *Profiles in Courage.*

blink, move its mouth to speak, and perform twenty-two movements overall. Dimensions for the head were taken from an actual death mask of Abe Lincoln, making the features so realistic that the sight of it sitting on a black box terrified a janitor. He took off down the hallway and refused to clean the room it was in.

When the entire figure of Lincoln was completed, the robot performed at the 1964 World's Fair. This first Audio-Animatronic president could make fifty-seven movements. Audiences saw a Lincoln who could put his hands behind his back, shrug his shoulders, stand up from a seated position, and deliver a powerhouse speech.

In July 1965, an exhibit titled "Great Moments with Mr. Lincoln" opened in the Opera House on Disneyland's Main Street. The lifelike Lincoln rose from his chair and gave a stirring performance using the voice of actor Royal Dano and a script that combined quotes from the Great Emancipator's actual speeches. In the early days however, Animatronic technology sometimes failed, and Lincoln fell over in a heap, leaving some viewers wondering if they'd watched a reenactment of his assassination. Luckily, the Imagineers have worked out a lot of the bugs since then, so audiences can still enjoy "Great Moments with Mr. Lincoln" at Disneyland today.

PRESIDENTS: DEAD AND ALIVE

By 1971 when Walt Disney World opened in Orlando, Florida, Imagineering technology had progressed far enough to create Walt's original dream of a stage full of presidents. Animators could use computers and sophisticated electronics to synchronize sounds and animation that allowed figures to move in a fluid, realistic manner—and not fall over in heaps.

In the original Hall of the Presidents, thirty-six Audio-Animatronic U.S. presidents were introduced to the public. Everyone from George Washington to Richard Nixon was present and accounted for. In the following years Gerald Ford, Jimmy Carter, Ronald Reagan, George H.W. Bush, Bill Clinton, and George W. Bush all made it to the stage. Disney's presidents' hall is the only place where you can see all the men who have held the office at once. Today the show begins with a film presentation narrated by Maya Angelou about the origins of the U.S.

Constitution, the relationship between it and the presidents who have sworn to protect and uphold it. But the film is only the warm-up act for the real stars.

The curtains part dramatically to reveal the main attraction, the robotic representations of the commanders in chief, who are introduced one by one. Each president acknowledges his introduction with a nod or gesture. Meanwhile the other presidents chat among themselves, nod their heads or shift in their seats just like restless, live actors. After the visitors meet all the former U.S. presidents, the current animatronic president delivers a patriotic opening address. (As of this writing, only Presidents Bill Clinton and George W. Bush have personally recorded their own remarks.) And in an animated finale, President Abraham Lincoln rises and delivers a speech fashioned from his own words.

THE DISNEY'S IN THE DETAILS

From its placement in the park to the fabric of the costumes of its "performers," every detail of Disney's Hall of Presidents was carefully worked out. Just approaching the hall is a patriotic experience for visitors. The president's hall was placed in Liberty Square, a recreation of colonial America. Just outside the hall, cast in the same mold as the original is a replica of the Liberty Bell that rang upon the ratification of the Constitution in 1789.

To keep the mechanical performers realistic, Disney's craftspeople researched everything. This is one of the few places where fashion buffs can see just what the most powerful men in the country were wearing when they lived. They meticulously studied film footage to capture presidential speech patterns and movement as well as detailed studies of their class rings and shoes. Each president since Lyndon Johnson's administration has done his best to help Imagineers create the most accurate depiction of himself. The figure of President Clinton wears a watch that actually belonged to the former president, and even former First Lady Hillary Rodham Clinton gave the Imagineers the skinny on how her husband combed his hair. Not one to overlook fashion, George W. Bush made sure his ensemble was tailormade according to his preferences: dark blue suit, white shirt, and red tie.

PRESIDENTIAL HALL CONTROVERSY

Of course America's presidents are never strangers to controversy—even if they're robots. During the post-Watergate years, the Nixon figure was so unpopular that it was greeted by snickers or boos from the audience, but that reaction has faded over time. During the Clinton impeachment scandal, the hall held firm and continued to feature the sitting president's robotic persona despite the ongoing controversy. The popularity of the Hall of Presidents itself has also had ups and downs when faced with newer, more exciting thrill rides and attractions. But come what may, whenever visitors to the Magic Kingdom need a shot of patriotism—or a jolt of air-conditioning—the Hall of Presidents will be there to serve the people.

★　★　★　★　★

YARDSTICK, YARDSTICK ON THE WALL
WHO'S THE TALLEST ONE OF ALL?

Line 'em all up and see who is head and shoulders above the rest. The top five heights of all the presidents and the men who grew to them!

1. **6 foot 4 inches:** Abraham Lincoln

2. **6 foot 3 inches:** Lyndon B. Johnson

3. **6 foot 2 1/2 inches:** Thomas Jefferson

4. **6 foot 2 inches:** George Washington, Chester A. Arthur, William H. Taft, Franklin D. Roosevelt, George H. W. Bush, Bill Clinton

5. **6 foot 1 inch:** Andrew Jackson, Ronald Reagan

Franklin Delano Roosevelt was related by blood or marriage to 11 former presidents.

THE PRESIDENT SEZ I

Some of the most memorable words from our commanders in chief.

"Government is not reason, it is not eloquence, it is force; like fire, a troublesome servant and a fearful master. Never for a moment should it be left to irresponsible action."
—George Washington

"Associate with men of good quality if you esteem your own reputation; for it is better to be alone than in bad company."
—George Washington

"In politics the middle way is none at all."
—John Adams

"We hold these truths to be self-evident that all men are created equal, that they are endowed by their Creator with certain inalienable rights, among these are life, liberty, and the pursuit of happiness, that to secure these rights governments are instituted among men. And for the support of this declaration, with a firm reliance on the protection of divine providence, we mutually pledge our lives, our fortunes, and our sacred honor."
—Thomas Jefferson

"Those who labor in the earth are the chosen people of God, if he ever had a chosen people, whose breasts he has made his peculiar deposit for substantial and genuine virtue."
—Thomas Jefferson

"Enlighten the people generally, and tyranny and oppressions of body and mind will vanish like evil spirits at the dawn of day."
—Thomas Jefferson

"The essence of Government is power; and power, lodged as it must be in human hands, will ever be liable to abuse."
—James Madison

"The best form of government is that which is most likely to prevent the greatest sum of evil."
—James Monroe

"I consider, then, the power to annul a law of the United States, assumed by one State, incompatible with the existence of the Union, contradicted expressly by the letter of the Constitution, unauthorized by its spirit, inconsistent with every principle on which it is founded, and destructive of the great object for which it was formed."
—Andrew Jackson

"Whenever I hear anyone arguing for slavery, I feel a strong impulse to see it tried on him personally."
—Abraham Lincoln

"Fourscore and seven years ago our fathers brought forth on this continent a new nation, conceived in liberty and dedicated to the proposition that all men are created equal. Now we are engaged in a great civil war, testing whether that nation or any nation so conceived and so dedicated can long endure. We are met on a great battlefield of that war. We have come to dedicate a portion of it as a final resting place for those who died here that the nation might live. This we may, in all propriety do. But in a larger sense, we cannot dedicate, we cannot consecrate, we cannot hallow this ground. The brave men, living and dead who struggled here have hallowed it far above our poor power to add or detract. The world will little note nor long remember what we say here, but it can never forget what they did here."
—Abraham Lincoln

Woodrow Wilson is the only president to have earned a PhD degree.

THE UNLUCKIEST PRESIDENT

Some say you have to be lucky to become president.
President Pierce would beg to differ.

President Franklin Pierce had rotten luck in life. What's more, he seems to have rotten luck in death, too, having both become one of the most obscure U.S. presidents and, when actually thought about, considered one of the greatest failures in the office due to his inability to prevent the country from slipping into civil war. Here are a few examples of his misfortunes:

PERSONAL PROBLEMS

- A strange, inscrutable omen? In his youth, Pierce fell into a river on Election Day.

- At the start of his third year at Bowdoin College, when the class rankings of all the undergraduates were first posted, Pierce was dead last.

- While leading troops in a charge during the Mexican War, Pierce's horse reared up suddenly at the sound of artillery fire. First Pierce's groin was thrown against the pommel of his saddle, incurring what one biographer called "an excruciating and sense-taking though hardly permanent injury." The horse then fell over and broke its leg; Pierce himself fainted and twisted his knee badly in the tumble. Then rumors flew that the reason he was no longer leading his troops was that Pierce had chickened out. Whispers of cowardice dogged him for the rest of his life.

- Pierce suffered from depression his entire life. It cast a melancholy pall over all his achievements. When elected U.S. Representative from New Hampshire at the astonishingly young age of 28, he wrote, "I find that the remark that 'Tis distance lends enchantment to the view' is no less true of the political than

the natural world." Sounds excited to be heading to Washington, doesn't he?

- Pierce was afflicted with the unlucky combination of being an alcoholic but unable to hold his liquor.

MARITAL DISCORD

- Pierce's wife, Jane, suffered from ill health all her life and hated politics. She also suffered from depression. Jane was, in fact, so depressed when the Pierces lived in the White House that Franklin would find any way to stay away, including riding his horse aimlessly through the streets of the District.

- Jane became an ardent abolitionist while in Washington; Franklin was a lifelong proponent of slavery.

- Jane also suffered from chronic pulmonary disease, which was presumed to be tuberculosis by doctors of the time. Washington's climate worsened her condition. It's said that there were fewer social functions in the White House during the Pierce presidency than during any other—and it sounds as if it was with good reason.

FAMILY TRAGEDIES

- Franklin Junior, the Pierce's first child, died three days after birth. Pierce never even met the boy, as Jane hadn't accompanied him to Washington that year on account of her health. He found out about the birth, and death, only by mail.

- Franklin and Jane's second son, Frank, died of typhus at age four.

- Between the 1852 election and the inauguration in 1853, the Pierces were traveling between Boston, Massachusetts, and Concord, New Hampshire, when the train car they were riding in derailed and rolled down a hill. Their third son, Benjamin, was killed in the accident—the only fatality at the scene. Jane decided that by this tragedy God was removing all distractions from Franklin's life so that he could better tend to his presiden-

---

Taft inaugurated the custom of the president throwing out the ball to start the baseball season.

tial duties. Franklin, needless to say, found this idea immensely unsettling.

POLITICAL PROBLEMS

- When he was a relatively unknown representative, Pierce was publicly accused of lying by powerful politician John C. Calhoun. At the time Pierce had the bad luck of having laryngitis and could not defend himself.

- Pierce's inauguration took place in a snowstorm.

- Pierce struggled against malaria throughout his presidency.

- Pierce's vice president, William R. King, died before even making it to Washington to serve his term. He was sick in Cuba at the time of the inauguration, and died in Alabama, shortly after traveling back to the United States.

- In the midterm elections during Pierce's presidency, his party was routed, losing their House majority.

- Pierce is the first president in history to run for reelection but fail to be nominated by his party.

HE STILL HAD HIS LOOKS

- Despite all his hard luck, Pierce generally scores high marks in the looks department.

- Pierce boasted an unblemished forehead, piercing dark gray eyes, and tousled dark locks.

- Standing 5 feet 10 inches tall, he had the strong posture and broad chest of a soldier.

The Tafts owned the first White House automobile.

IN THE DOGHOUSE WITH LBJ

President Harry S. Truman said: "If you want a friend in Washington, get a dog." LBJ had many dogs, but they kept getting him into trouble with the public.

L ike many presidents before him, President Lyndon Johnson kept dogs as pets during his administration. Often pups have been used as props to help politicians seem likable and human, but LBJ was a certified dog fanatic. The only catch was that his close canine relationships kept landing the president in hot water with the American public.

A REAL PAIN IN THE EAR

President Johnson's beagles Him and Her were true celebrities. Not only did they have their pictures in *LIFE* magazine, but Johnson would often walk them while he talked to the press. A small scandal erupted when it was discovered that Him wore a tag saying "#1" and Her wore one saying "#2" The reason? The burgeoning feminist movement did not appreciate that Him was ranked top dog over Her.

The most famous and scandalous Him-and-Her incident occurred in May 1964. Johnson was trying to get the beagles to perform a trick in front of a bank of photographers and an investment task force that had gathered in the Rose Garden. Him wouldn't hold still, so Johnson leaned down and lifted the dog up onto his haunches by his long floppy ears. Him yelped loudly, but LBJ tried to brush it off nonchalantly. "If you ever follow dogs, you like to hear them yelp," he said, "It does them good to let them bark." By the end of the day, photographs of the president suspending a yelping dog in the air by its ears had made virtually every news outlet across the globe and turned into a public relations disaster.

Dog lovers flooded the White House with angry phone calls, letters, and telegrams, and experts spoke out in the press against Johnson's harmful behavior. At the time, beaglers defended their

---

Theodore Roosevelt craved attention. It was said he wanted to be "the bride at every wedding . . ."

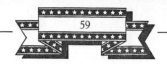

president by pointing out that hunters commonly tug dogs' ears in order to make sure they're in "good voice." Breeders often reached into wriggling litters of beagle pups to lift them by their ears—as long as the pups were still small. However, the consensus was that lifting full-grown dogs by their ears was generally hurtful. A spokesman for the American Society for the Prevention of Cruelty to Animals put it best when he said, "If somebody picked you up by the ears, you'd yelp too." There was even a float in the Rose Bowl Parade that year of a giant beagle whose ears would raise up while a speaker in his mouth cried "Ouch!"

SINGING WITH YUKI

When Luci Johnson Nugent found a stray dog at a Texas gas station, she took it home and named it Yuki. On a visit to her father at the White House, she brought the little mixed-breed with her. LBJ and Yuki hit it off right away, and seeing how her father loved the little guy, Luci gave the dog to her dad. LBJ was so taken with his new companion that he bought little boots for Yuki to wear in the rain. He even tried to sneak Yuki into Lynda Baines Johnson's official wedding portraits until Lady Bird put her foot down and ordered an aide to "get that dog out of here right now. He will not be photographed."

Yuki did manage to work his way into other venues though. He hung out in the Oval Office and under the table during cabinet meetings. He also became known for "singing" with the president. It may not have been the smartest move when Johnson invited television cameras into the Oval Office to see Yuki sit on his lap and sing with him. First the two "dueted" on a folk song and then an aria. The critics were not amused. Outraged music lovers felt that the president and his pooch had mocked classical music. But Johnson loved the uproar and noted, "Not all the comments are bad. This one says that I sing almost as good as the dog. " Johnson even treated foreign dignitaries to the spectacle of him howling with Yuki. Some say they found the display less than dignified.

". . . and the corpse at every funeral."

WILL CLUB SODA GET THAT OUT?

Him, Her, and Yuki weren't the only dogs to have the run of the White House during the Johnson administration. A little girl from Illinois made a gift to LBJ of a white collie named Blanco, who was a little on the nervous side. FBI director J. Edgar Hoover also gave the Johnsons another beagle; this one was named "J. Edgar" but soon became known as just plain Edgar.

With all these pooches around, White House dog caretaker Traphes Bryant begged Johnson to keep the animals confined when inside the house for fear they'd ruin the carpets. But accidents happen. When Lady Bird Johnson showed Pat Nixon around the house before it changed hands, she had to apologize for all the stains on the white carpet of the family quarters.

★ ★ ★ ★ ★

PRIMETIME PRESIDENTS
Turn on the TV and what do you see? Lot's of presidents

1963: After losing races for the presidency and the governorship of California, Richard Nixon appeared on *The Jack Paar Program*. He played the piano and a song of his own composition.

1976: A good sport, Gerald R. Ford appeared on *Saturday Night Live* alongside his imitator, Chevy Chase. President Ford teased Chase by saying, "I'm Gerald Ford, and you're not."

1994: On another episode of *Saturday Night Live*, George H. W. Bush critiqued Dana Carvey's well known impression of him. "It's totally exaggerated! It's not me. Those crazy hand gestures. The pointing thing. I don't do 'em!"

1994: Bill Clinton is asked on MTV if he prefers boxers or briefs. He answers, "Usually briefs." (Too much information, we think.)

Chester A. Arthur enjoyed walking at night and seldom went to bed before 2 a.m.

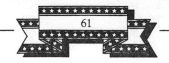

NUMBER FIVE:
JAMES MONROE

Served from 1817 to 1825

Vital Stats: Born on April 28, 1758, in Westmoreland County, Virginia. Died on July 4, 1831, in New York City, New York.
Age at Inauguration: 58
Vice President: Daniel D. Tompkins
Political Affiliation: Democratic–Republican
Wife: Elizabeth Kortright (married 1786)
Kids: Eliza (1786–1840); Maria Hester (1804–1850)
Education: The College of William and Mary
What he did before he was president: Lawyer; Office in the 3rd Virginia Regiment and Continental Army; Delegate to the Continental Congress; Member of the Virginia Assembly; U.S. Senator; minister to France and England; Secretary of State; Secretary of War
Postpresidential Occupations: Writer

MEMORABLE QUOTES

"From the commencement of our Revolution to the present day almost forty years have elapsed, and from the establishment of this Constitution twenty-eight . . . what has been the effect? To whatever object we turn our attention . . . we find abundant cause to felicitate ourselves in the excellence of our institutions. During a period fraught with difficulties and marked by very extraordinary events the United States have flourished beyond example."
—James Monroe' s first inaugural address, March 4, 1817

"Louisiana . . . and the Floridas . . . have been ceded to us . . . We now, fellow-citizens, comprise within our limits the dimensions and faculties of a great power under a Government possessing all the energies of any government ever known to the Old World, with an utter incapacity to oppress."
—James Monroe's second inaugural address, March 5, 1821

While president, Ulysses S. Grant was arrested for driving his horse too fast and was fined $20.

DON'T ASK AMY

*What was it really like to be a third grader living
in the White House? Amy's keeping mum.*

When President Jimmy Carter went to the White House in 1977, he and First Lady Rosalynn took their four children with them. Carter's three sons—Jack, Chip, and Jeff—were all grown up, a state that rendered them totally uninteresting to the media. News people turned their attention to the president's nine-year-old daughter, Amy Lynn, with her long blond hair, roller skates, and her Siamese cat, Misty Malarky Ying Yang. Soon young Amy had captured the national spotlight.

THINGS WERE PEACHIER IN GEORGIA

Raised in the small town of Plains, Georgia, shy, bookish Amy found the pressure of her newfound fame a tough challenge to handle. At an age where just going to school can be an ordeal, Amy had to face the nation's appetite for news about her life. Her parents, who wanted Amy to remain as much like an ordinary third grader as possible, enrolled her in public school in Washington, DC; but the Carters forgot that ordinary third graders aren't driven to class by a chauffeur in a presidential limo. And they don't bring along Secret Service agents either. Classmates gaped at Amy when she first arrived, and the media showed up to make school days into circus daze. Citing safety reasons Amy's teachers kept her inside during recess every day. Understandably, Amy was miserable. Eventually the Carters transferred their daughter to a private school, but that didn't end her fishbowl life.

Amy's behavior at dinner—state dinners that is—also attracted national attention. Some folks dream of attending a White House gala to break bread with the president of the United States, but such events were a huge yawn to a nine-year-old Amy who just saw him as Dad. As a solution, the Carters let her read at the table to ward off boredom and to keep her out of trouble. They'd already used this "novel" tactic during their inaugural ball, so they were likely surprised when a hue and cry developed over

---

Franklin Pierce gave his inaugural address from memory, without the aid of notes.

Amy's burying her nose in a book at state dinners. Media pundits criticized the family for bad manners and warned of possible offense to foreign leaders. Fortunately no miffed head of state ever broke off relations with the U.S. government because Amy turned pages through the soup course.

LEAVING MARKS ON THE WHITE HOUSE

Of course life at the White House also had its perks. The wood floors of the grand East Room were the perfect texture for roller-skating. Rumor has it that they still bear the marks of Amy's roller skates. A tree house was also built for the first daughter on the South lawn—a hidden place where she could play with friends or simply read in peace. Just in case she got tired of the cat, one of her teachers gave Amy a dog called Grits, a name taken from Carter's campaign slogan, *Grits and Fritz*. (Walter "Fritz" Mondale was Carter's vice president.)

And it turns out that the Clintons were not the first to host sleepovers in the Lincoln bedroom. Amy Carter had them beat on that count when she and her friends had a Halloween slumber party in the legendary bedroom where Lincoln's apparition is said to appear. The girls never did get to see the famous ghost, but there was plenty of screaming when the first lady and one of the maids—both covered with sheets—burst in to the room.

ASK AMY

The grade-schooler also did her bit for public service, promoting education and putting in appearances without complaint. But Amy continued to find the spotlight difficult; in one interview when asked if she had anything to say to America's children, Amy famously answered, "No."

ADVICE FROM AMY

Things didn't get much better when President Carter made his reelection bid in 1980. In a televised debate with opponent, Governor Ronald Reagan, President Carter announced that he'd asked Amy what the most important issue was and that she had answered "nuclear weapons." Though Carter was pointing out the importance of disarmament to future generations, many viewers

President John Tyler was a granduncle of Harry S. Truman.

didn't like the idea of their president bringing up the advice of a thirteen-year-old in a presidential debate. Critics latched on to the term "Ask Amy" as one tactic to help defeat the sitting president.

Even after leaving the White House, Amy made news and continued to be criticized by the media. While attending Brown University she became a political activist and protested against CIA recruitment on college campuses and against apartheid. Arrested three times, Amy went on trial for her part in a campus demonstration, and the media analyzed her every move. Eventually she was found innocent. Once Amy left the university for academic reasons, she finally found her way out of the public spotlight.

WHATEVER HAPPENED TO AMY?
Books continued to play a big part in Amy's life. Having obtained a master's degree in fine art, Amy illustrated two of her father's books. She also met her husband, Jim Wentzel, while working at a bookstore. Today the couple has a young son named Hugo, and Ms. Amy Carter (she kept her maiden name) protects her family's privacy by refusing all interviews. So if reporters want to know the pros and cons of being the child of a president, they can't ask Amy anymore.

★　★　★　★　★

YOU SHOULDN'T HAVE
Several presidents and their families were given living gifts.
Is there a diplomatic way to refuse?

The Marquis de Lafayette presented Thomas Jefferson two Briards, herding dogs bred in France. He also gave John Quincy Adams an alligator.

The King of Siam presented this President Buchanan with a herd of elephants, even though he was a democrat!

Martin Van Buren received a pair of tiger cubs from the sultan of Oman, but Congress made him send them to the zoo.

DO IT YOURSELF <u>PRESIDENCY</u>

Don't like how the President is running the country?
Then maybe you can found your own. American history is full of
people who decided to start their own way of running things.

E ver envy the president's powers? Think you could do a better
job? Well, you're not alone. Several Americans thought they
ought to be the ones in charge, so they declared themselves
independent and tried to go it alone. Here's a short collection of
their serious and not-so-serious attempts at founding new nations.

THE SERIOUS . . .
The Cherokee Nation. In 1802 the state of Georgia and the federal government had reached a deal: if Georgia dropped its claims
to vast tracts of land to its west, then the Feds would "urge" the
predominantly Cherokee Native Americans to relocate from the
state. The Cherokee were understandably not happy about the
arrangement, so few moved from Georgia. By 1827 the Cherokee
Nation had ratified a constitution of its own asserting sovereignty
as an independent nation. Deciding that the Cherokee hadn't
quite gotten the hint, Congress then passed the Indian Removal
Act of 1830. Still defiant, the Cherokee Nation brought its case
all the way to the Supreme Court, where it won. Yet President
Andrew Jackson wasn't to be intimidated by the Supreme Court.
Despite having sworn allegiance years ago to a Cherokee Chief
who had saved his life, Jackson defied the Court decision and
marched the Cherokee west along the Trail of Tears.

Mecklenburg County. It was 1819 and former President John
Adams, still a die-hard Federalist, was itching to discredit his old,
bitter rival Thomas Jefferson. An amazing opportunity fell into his
lap with the discovery of the Mecklenburg Declaration of Independence, in which Mecklenburg, North Carolina, purportedly
declared independence from England a full year before Jefferson

. . . A list of their dates and topics is at www.fdrlibrary.marist.edu

penned the Declaration of Independence for the colonies in 1776. Adams argued this made Jefferson's document (and Jefferson himself) irrelevant; Jefferson countered and claimed that the Mecklenburg document was a phony. Historians now also doubt its authenticity, but what is not in doubt is the bitterness that resulted from the declaration of this Declaration.

The Republic of Indian Stream. With Canada and New Hampshire squabbling over their border, a frustrated group of citizens caught in the middle said to heck with both of them. In 1832 they declared themselves the United Inhabitants of Indian Stream Territory, forming their own constitution and legislative assembly. Canada and New Hampshire became rival suitors each trying to woo the community to their side. The situation soon deteriorated with mob violence and kidnappings. Things came to a head, literally, when a Canadian justice was hit in the head with a sword. His assistant was shot in the groin. New Hampshire threatened to send the militia into the Republic to end the madness; finally Canada gave up and washed its hands of Indian Stream. The short-lived republic rejoined New Hampshire—and Congress compensated the Canadian assistant's wife for her husband's groin wound.

Empire of the United States. San Francisco had a sensation on its hands in 1859 with the self-proclaimed emperor of the United States, Joshua Norton. His fan base grew and grew as the press reported more and more on his bizarre antics: he dissolved Congress, sold bonds backed by the Imperial Treasury, and ordered Abraham Lincoln and Jefferson Davis to report to his house to patch things up during the Civil War. The police charged him with lunacy, but they wouldn't keep him in jail for fear of a public backlash. When he died in 1880, his funeral was attended by 10,000 people.

North Dakota. William "Fighting Bill" Langer, hugely popular following his 1933 election as governor of North Dakota, quickly ran afoul of the law and was convicted of fraud. Yet instead of stepping down, Langer got together some friends, fortified the governor's mansion, and declared North Dakota an independent

Theodore Roosevelt officially gave the White House its current name in 1901. Before that . . .

nation. Members of the supreme court of North Dakota had to come in person to the mansion to talk him into giving up. He was eventually found innocent of fraud after a retrial (during which he bribed the judge's son). Surprisingly he was reelected governor.

New Atlantis. Ernest Hemingway's brother Leicester founded this republic in 1964, which at its inception comprised six people living on an 8-by-30-foot raft in the Caribbean Sea. Although Leicester spent most of the money he had made from his book *My Brother, Ernest Hemingway* on construction, the raft still was far from impressive. Basically made of bamboo and pipes, it was anchored to the sea floor by a rusted Ford engine block. He dreamed of it serving as the headquarters of his International Marine Research Society, but his dream was short-lived: within a few years, a storm destroyed much of the raft, forcing the inhabitants to abandon it. Local fisherman then cannibalized the rest of the platform for its lumber. Leicester survived the death of his New Atlantis but tragically couldn't escape the fate of so many members of his famous family: he committed suicide in 1982.

The Republic of Minerva. In 1972 Morris "Bud" Davis, an engineer from California, declared two coral reefs in the South Pacific Ocean his sovereign domain. While a sea resort of 60,000 residents that could double as a tax shelter was his ultimate goal, he began modestly by building a stone tower topped by a flashing light and the Minervan flag. One country quickly responded to his desire for statehood: the Tongan King Taufa'ahau Tupou IV, eager to assert his own sovereignty, showed up with a hundred-man militia and tore down the flag.

AND THE NOT-SO-SERIOUS
The Independent Kingdom of Talossa. In 1981 at age thirteen, Robert Ben Madison decided that his bedroom was actually the Independent Kingdom of Talossa, that he was its king, and that he had jurisdiction over half of his hometown of Milwaukee, Wisconsin. King Madison now has over 60 Talossan "residents" that keep in contact over the internet, write Talossan books about burial mounds and the Talossan language, and run elections.

The Conch Republic. In the spring of 1982 Key West, Florida and it businesses faced growing problems with falling levels of tourism: the U.S. Border patrol set up roadblocks on Highway 1, which connects the Florida Keys to the mainland, to impede drug traffickers. In protest, an irate city council quickly issued an edict proclaiming their independence as The Conch Republic. They declared war on the United States, then immediately surrendered, asking for a monetary aid package so they could celebrate their defeat in style. The highway was soon reopened, and ironically, celebration of this event has become a boon to tourism.

North Dumpling. Dean Kamen wanted to construct a wind turbine on his privately owned island off the coast of New York in 1992. When the state denied his request, he promptly seceded, creating his own navy, flag, and currency based on the value of Pi (the never-ending number that expresses the ratio of every circle's circumference to its diameter). He boasts a nonaggression pact with President George H. W. Bush, and even appointed Ben and Jerry his joint chiefs of ice cream.

★　★　★　★　★

PRESIDENTIAL ROADSIDE GUIDE

Check out these presidential stops along the way.

Presidential Pet Museum. *Lothian, Maryland.* Located 19 miles from the White House, this stop features the largest collection of presidential pet memorabilia anywhere. Founder and dog breeder Claire McClean purloined a few snippets of hair from Ronald Reagan's pooch, Lucky, to start her collection.

The Lincoln Monument. *Laramie, Wyoming.* If you're driving west along Route I-80, it's tough to miss this 12 1/2 foot tall sculpture of Lincoln's head. Looming over the highway, the statue sits atop a 30 foot pedestal so all may see it.

John Quincy Adams named one of his sons George Washington.

A GRAVE MISTAKE

Somebody call Oliver Stone!
President Zachary Taylor's death could have been a conspiracy!

The scene is this: a sultry July 4 in Washington, DC. President Zachary Taylor is out in the cruel sun attending an Independence Day ceremony at the Washington Monument (where construction was progressing lethargically after the laying of the cornerstone two years earlier). The swampy, humid climate of the capital city oppressed the crowd. Taylor, still dapper at age sixty-five in a heavy black suit, sweated copiously.

As soon as the ceremony had ended, Taylor indulged in large amounts of iced buttermilk and iced cherries to try to cool himself off. Soon he started to feel ill. His doctors tried a number of different remedies but his condition rapidly deteriorated. Taylor died five days later, July 9, 1850.

DEATH IS JUST A BOWL
OF CHERRIES (AND ARSENIC?)

Sounds suspicious, don't you think? Well, even if you don't think so, historian Clara Rising did—strongly enough that she offered to pay $1200 out of her own pocket in 1991 for Taylor to be exhumed. Her theory was that Taylor, who opposed the spread of slavery into the territory acquired in the Mexican War, was done in by proslavery forces, possibly in cahoots with Senator Henry "The Great Compromiser" Clay and/or vice president Millard "Inconsequential" Fillmore. She first became suspicious about Taylor's death after she confirmed with a medical examiner that the symptoms of the so-called intestinal disorder that he died of were also consistent with the symptoms of arsenic poisoning. The five-day descent from illness to death also struck her as fishy, given that Old Rough and Ready, even at age sixty-five, was in great physical shape. Her near-religious devotion to all things Zachary (as she always referred to him) got her agitating for an exhumation so Taylor's remains could be tested for traces of arsenic. Not so coincidentally, she was also preparing a book on

---

At 16 George Washington was an enthusiastic spelunker; he loved exploring caves.

Taylor at the time, which she never neglected to mention in interviews.

DIGGING DEEPER

When Taylor's grave was opened on June 18, 1991, the examiners found that the casket was too rotten to be moved. Fortunately, though, the body had been placed inside a lead liner, which was still intact, before being placed in the casket. The workers solemnly wrapped the liner and remains of the casket in an American flag. The bundle was reverentially presented to the amassed crowd and then brought to the morgue for testing.

An electric saw buzzed through the lead liner encasing Taylor's body. Rising saw her hero for the first time. She said, "It was a sacred moment," which inspired in her "a very warm sort of feeling." Taylor's remains were well preserved, owing to a small hole in the liner that had allowed air in to dry out the body. His socks, gloves, and burial shroud were still intact, although discolored. His hair, including the distinctive bushes of his eyebrows, was still in place, despite the near-complete absence of skin for it to cling to. The examiners collected samples of Taylor's hair, fingernails, and bones, then closed up the liner. They returned the former president to his tomb a few hours later.

The testing took another eight days, during which newspapers and magazines worked themselves up about the consequences of a positive finding. Lincoln would no longer be the first president to be assassinated. The issues that led to the Civil War would have turned deadly eleven years before Fort Sumter. And quiet Millard Fillmore would have to be reconsidered as the evil mastermind of his time.

THE RESULTS ARE IN

On June 26 the laboratory report was made public. It showed that Taylor's teeth had little natural decay although he may have ground them and that he had an abscess. However, it did not show any evidence of arsenic poisoning. There was arsenic in the hair and nail samples, but the amounts were small enough to be explained by natural occurrences in the environment and the nonlethal amounts in medicines of the time. The level of arsenic

in the samples would have been hundreds or thousands of times higher had Taylor been poisoned. "It's not borderline. He was not poisoned," said George R. Nichols II, the chief medical examiner of Kentucky.

Rising seemed to collapse the stages of grief by exhibiting simultaneously denial, anger, and acceptance in her statements following the release of the unambiguous results. "We found the truth. The truth also contains the fact that his political enemies benefited from his removal, whether they removed him or not. You can still point the finger and say they got away with it even if nature did him in."

The results also suggested that nineteenth-century quackery might have precipitated Taylor's death. Some of the remedies his doctors gave him may have contained mercury and quinine. They also used one of the most common medical techniques of the day, bleeding. Modern doctors believe that these treatments may have done more harm than good. The most likely explanation for Taylor's death now is an intestinal illness aggravated by acute sunstroke from the July 4 ceremony, along with a little help from his doctors.

The real murder in this case may have been Clara Rising's career and aspirations of fame and fortune, both for herself and for the president she championed. Thirteen years after the exhumation, Taylor remains as obscure as ever, the first in a line of four largely ineffectual presidents who failed to avert civil war. And Clara Rising's book remains unpublished.

★   ★   ★   ★   ★

TWENTY-ONE GUNS FOR 1776

A twenty-one-gun salute is a very special honor, reserved for presidents and former presidents (as well as for foreign dignitaries and heads of state). Some say that the salute actually commemorates the year 1776, which is why the guns are fired thus: one-seven-seven-six.

NUMBER SIX:
JOHN QUINCY ADAMS

Served from 1825 to 1829

Vital Stats: Born on July 11, 1767, in Quincy, Massachusetts. Died on February 23, 1848, in Washington, DC.
Age at Inauguration: 57
Vice President: John C. Calhoun
Political Affiliation: Democratic-Republican
Wife: Louisa Catherine Johnson (married 1797)
Kids: George Washington (1801–1829); John (1803–1834); Charles Francis (1807–1886); Louisa Catherine (1811–1812)
Education: Harvard University
What he did before he was president: Lawyer; Professor; Minister to the Netherlands, Prussia, Russia, and Great Britain; U.S. Senator; Secretary of State
Postpresidential Occupations: U.S. Congressman

MEMORABLE QUOTES

"Having now a good opportunity I cannot let it slip without writing a few lines to you as it is not often that I have that pleasure . . . in writing to so kind and tender a Mamma as you have been to me for which I believe I shall never be able to repay you."
—John Quincy Adams in a letter to his mother, Abigail Adams, April 12, 1778

"While dwelling with pleasing satisfaction upon the superior excellence of our political institutions, let us not be unmindful that liberty is power; that the nation blessed with the largest portion of liberty must . . . be the most powerful nation upon earth."
—John Quincy Adams in his first annual message to Congress, December 6, 1825

DYSFUNCTIONAL ERECTION

Who knew it would take fifty years to honor
"The Father of His Country"?

What weighs 40,000 tons, towers 555 feet 5 1/8 inches high over the nation's capital, has 897 steps to the top, is made of 36,491 stones, and can boast with certainty that George Washington *never* slept there? The Washington Monument!

Today surrounded by 50 flags at the base, symbolizing each of the 50 states, the white marble obelisk is the jewel in the crown of the National Mall—but it took a surprisingly long time for the nation to get around to building it.

DESIGN DEBATES

Immediately after the War for Independence, the Continental Congress made plans to honor General George Washington. As far back as 1783, there was a plan for an equestrian statue of Washington to be placed near the Capitol building—once they figured out where the capital *city* was going to be. But the new nation was busy, and the capital moved several times, making it difficult to find a good spot for a tribute.

After Washington died in 1799, Congress again made noises about erecting a monument in his honor, and they settled on creating a tomb in the Capitol building. But they forgot to ask his family's opinion. Washington's heirs did not want to move his remains, which stayed firmly planted in his tomb on the grounds of his home, Mount Vernon, in Alexandria, Virginia.

As the 100th anniversary of Washington's birth approached, there was again a push to memorialize the first president. Congress coughed up $5,000 in 1832 for a marble statue intended for the Capitol Rotunda. However artist Horatio Greenhough's creation—a 20-ton seated seminude figure—was not exactly what most folks had in mind. This statue ended up at the Smithsonian Institution in 1908.

... Franklin D. Roosevelt would watch only short films with happy endings.

In 1833 George Watterson (a former Librarian of Congress) formed the Washington National Monument Society, whose purpose was to finally erect a fitting memorial. The society held a design competition that architect Robert Mills won. His original plan was a much more elaborate design than the current simple obelisk seen today. Mills wanted an even bigger obelisk surrounded by a colonnade, which was to be interspersed with statues of other Revolutionary War heroes and capped by a classically inspired statue of a toga-clad Washington driving a chariot. There were even plans to entomb the remains of these heroes in underground catacombs. But money—and enthusiasm—were short-lived. In 1848, the Society decided to just build the obelisk and worry about the colonnade later. Excavation was begun later that year, and the cornerstone was laid on the Fourth of July.

BUILDING BLOCKS AND STUMBLING BLOCKS

The society encouraged all states and territories to donate memorial stones to be used in the interior walls of the monument. Donations poured in from other sources as well, including blocks from Native American tribes, businesses, and even foreign countries. Perhaps the most well known memorial stone came in the early 1850s from Pope Pius IX: a marble stone that had been part of the Temple of Concord in Rome. In March 1854, however, members of the Know-Nothings (an aptly named anti-Catholic, anti-immigrant political party) stole the stone and allegedly threw it into the Potomac River.

Donations to the society began to dry up in 1854, and Congress was reluctant to step in and help. The nation was embroiled in controversy over the spread and existence of slavery; a monument to honor the Father of the United States seemed a folly to build when that very nation was in danger of being torn apart. Social turmoil and economic uncertainty stalled the plans. The monument would stand unfinished for more than twenty years as the country went to war with itself and then struggled to put itself together again.

MONUMENTAL MAKEOVERS

After the Civil War ended Congress appropriated $200,000 to resume construction of the Washington Monument. Plans for the colonnade were finally scrapped, and the size of the obelisk was changed to make it conform more to classical Egyptian proportions. Construction finally began again in 1879. The new architect, Thomas L. Casey of the U.S. Army Corps of Engineers, incorporated the original donated memorial stones in the interior walls. The first memorial stone to be placed was the Alabama stone. The last two stones to be placed were installed in 1982: the Alaska stone, which is made of solid jade; and another stone donated by the Vatican to replace the original that was pilfered. The monument was opened to the public on October 9, 1888, and it typically has more than 800,000 visitors each year.

Beginning in 1997 the Washington Monument closed down to undergo a huge restoration effort. Scaffolding enfolded the exterior so the outside could be cleaned and repaired. On the inside, the masonry and historic donated stones were restored. On the practical side, the elevators, heating, and cooling systems were upgraded too! The new elevator cab features glass panels so riders can view the commemorative stones on the 180-, 170-, 140-, and 130-foot levels. The elevator takes viewers to the top in only 70 seconds, but the ride down takes 138 seconds so people can really see the stones.

As of this writing, the monument grounds are still undergoing security upgrades in the wake of the September 11, 2001, terrorist attacks. But the monument itself remains open to visitors, who can still ride the elevator to the top and enjoy sweeping views of the Lincoln Memorial, the White House, the Jefferson Memorial, the Capitol, and the city beyond.

DID'JA EVER NOTICE?

Because the monument was left unfinished (at about 150 feet tall) for so long, it is actually two colors. Even though the same type of stone was used after construction resumed, it had to be mined from a different quarry, and the white shade could not be matched exactly. If you look closely you can see the change in color about a third of the way up.

A VIDAL LINK WITH THE PRESIDENCY

Blue-blooded novelist Gore Vidal has presidential connections that are thicker than water but thinned with acid from his sharp pen.

Best-selling author Gore Vidal certainly has a way with words and a familiarity with American history. With historic novels like *Burr*, *Lincoln*, and *1876* to his name, Vidal buries himself in the political doings—and dones—of the United States. His personal connections (he claims to be related to Al Gore and is, however, a fifth cousin to Jimmy Carter), political affinities (he may be the last of the "small-r" republicans), and prose preoccupations have caused him to write about many presidents, to declaim many more, and to consider all of them at one time or another.

Herewith, a Gore-y set of musings on a the presidents.

GEORGE WASHINGTON
"Washington is our first millionaire, with no great love of the people . . . Of course, he acquired his fortune in the most honest way, by marrying it."

JOHN ADAMS
"On September 5, 1774, forty-five of the weightiest colonial men formed the First Continental Congress at Philadelphia. The weightiest of the lot was the Boston lawyer [and future president] John Adams, known as the best-read man in Boston. Short, fat, given to bouts of vanity that alternated with its first cousin self-pity, he was thirty-nine years old when he joined the Massachusetts delegation to the Congress."

THOMAS JEFFERSON
"There is a problem with Thomas Jefferson. There always has been a problem. On the one hand, he is the voice of the best aspect of the United States, which was the notion that every person had

life, liberty, and the inalienable rights, including the pursuit of happiness, which turned out to be the joker in the deck."

ABRAHAM LINCOLN

"Lincoln, like Bismarck at the same time in Germany, took a loosely federated nation with nothing much in common but a language and made a centralized (eventually militarized) federal state."

THEODORE ROOSEVELT

"As president, Theodore Roosevelt spoke loudly and carried a fair-sized stick. When Colombia wouldn't give him the land that he needed for a canal, he helped invent Panama out of a piece of Colombia; and got his canal."

FRANKLIN DELANO ROOSEVELT

"The best president of the 20th century was the FDR of 1933–37. He saved corporate capitalism. I can't say, in retrospect, this was such a good thing, but I was a kid when the Bonus Army marched on my hometown of Washington during Hoover and revolution was in the air. The next year FDR was in office."

HARRY S. TRUMAN

"Truman replaced the republic that Lincoln had thoughtfully left in place with a national security state, a militarized economy with bases on every continent. And he allowed our civil liberties to fade away. The first warning was when he required all government workers—several million people from Post Office workers up to Cabinet members—to swear loyalty oaths to the republic that was no more. Pure Stalin."

JOHN F. KENNEDY

"He didn't have it. He had no plan. He was playing a game. He enjoyed the game of politics, like most of them do. There was no real substance to him. He was quite intelligent, very shrewd about people, but he liked the glamour of it all. He loved war, he had a very gung-ho attitude. I began to part company with him about

the Bay of Pigs. Then we all forgave him, and he started the invasion and started to beef up the troops in Vietnam."

BILL CLINTON
"Clinton, people took seriously, because he was a wonderful speaker, he was a great explainer, he understood the economy, everybody knew that. The other presidents just went blank on the subject of economics. Clinton could lecture your ear off."

GEORGE W. BUSH
"George W. Bush, yes, he is very dumb . . . When I was at Exeter, Poppy [George H. W.] was at Andover, and Poppy's son George W. also went to Andover, where he was a cheerleader. A very distinguished cheerleader."

★　　★　　★　　★　　★

PRESIDENTIAL CENTS

Take a look in your pocket. Chances are,
you've got a handful of presidents.

- Abraham Lincoln was the first president depicted on a U.S. coin. To commemorate the centennial of his birth in 1909, a bronze one-cent piece was adopted which evolved into the copper penny.

- Would Washington have minded being the second president profiled on coin? He made his debut on the twenty-five-cent piece in 1932 to honor the bicentennial of his birth.

- The third president, Thomas Jefferson, is also the third president on a coin. In 1938, they slapped his likeness on the nickel.

- All three of these presidents are special: they're the only ones to appear on both paper money and metal coins.

THE BUCK STOPS HERE

Guess who's the highest paid president. You might be surprised.

Congress has given the president a raise only five times in history, but some presidents have made a lot more than others—thanks to inflation. We've done the math to find out what their yearly salaries would be worth, on average, in twenty-first century dollars. Here's the list of the well paid and the not-so-well-paid presidents.

THE TEN HIGHEST PAID

President	Salary in His Day	What's It Worth Now? *
1. William Taft	$75,000	$1,445,454
2. William McKinley	$50,000	$1,106,719
3. Richard Nixon	$200,000 $50,000 expense account	$1,084,831
4. Woodrow Wilson	$75,000	$1,048,379
5. Theodore Roosevelt	$50,000	$1,015,151
6. Grover Cleveland	$50,000	$1,001,093
7. Benjamin Harrison	$50,000	$984,313
8. Dwight Eisenhower	$100,000 $50,000 expense account	$963,253
9. Franklin Roosevelt	$75,000	$915,013
10. Herbert Hoover	$75,000	$903,458

THE TEN LOWEST PAID

President	Salary in His Day	What's It Worth Now? *
1. Bill Clinton	$200,000 $50,000 expense account.	$282,648
2. Andrew Johnson	$25,000	$300,446
3. James Madison	$25,000	$321,110
4. George H. W. Bush	$200,000 $50,000 expense account.	$334,554
5. John Adams	$25,000	$357,543
6. Abraham Lincoln	$25,000	$374,518
7. Thomas Jefferson	$25,000	$378,526
8. James Monroe	$25,000	$395,184
9. Ronald Reagan	$200,000 $50,000 expense account.	$424,609
10. George Washington	$25,000	$427,314

COMPENSATION COMPENDIUM

- President Grant received the first raise from Congress at the start of his second term, his salary increasing from $25,000 to $50,000. The next four presidential raises are as follows: Taft had his salary raised to $75,000; Truman, in his second term, to $100,000 plus a $50,000 expense account; Nixon to $200,000 with a $50,000 expense account; and George W. Bush to $400,000 with a $50,000 expense account.

- Sometimes Congress gives the president a raise, not because he is underpaid but because they are: traditionally, no government employee can make more than the president. Yet unlike the president, many of them have built cost-of-living increases into their salaries. When their pay starts butting up against that of the president's, they tend to become more generous.

Andrew Jackson bought 20 spittoons for the East Room for $12.50 each.

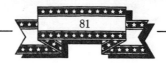

- George Washington, Herbert Hoover, and John F. Kennedy refused their salaries.

- While many presidential expenses are picked up by other departments and agencies, not all of them are: Thomas Jefferson left office owing $10,000 just for wine.

- Crime doesn't pay: the two impeached presidents, Bill Clinton and Andrew Johnson, are dead last on the lowest paid list. But maybe you just have to know when to get out: President Nixon, who resigned before he could be impeached, is the third highest paid president.

- This list does not take into account presidential pensions, which Congress began doling out in 1958. It started at $25,000 per year and included both an office and staff. The payment is now based on the annual pay of a cabinet secretary: in 2001 this came out to $161,200.

- The vice president doesn't work for free either: in 2004, the salary for the second in command is $202,900.

* Each President's salary was adjusted for inflation for every calendar year in which he held office. These adjusted salaries were then averaged. Presidents since Truman have had a $50,000 expense account that was included in this list as part of the presidential salary.

John Tyler was on his knees playing marbles when informed that he had become president.

ASSASSINS ON BROADWAY?

John Wilkes Booth sings a patriotic anthem to the South. Garfield assassin Charles Guiteau points a revolver at the audience, singing, "What a Wonder is a Gun." Would a musical about presidential assassins be as bad an idea as "Springtime for Hitler"?

H ere's an idea for a musical. Picture this. Let's get all the presidential assassins together on a stage and let them tell their side of the story in song! Sounds like a surefire Broadway hit, doesn't it? Well, it sure did to Stephen Sondheim and his collaborator John Weidman.

IF AT FIRST YOU DON'T SUCCEED . . .
Sondheim is no stranger to bizarre subject matter. One of his most critically acclaimed plays, *Sweeney Todd*, winner of eight Tony Awards, including best musical for 1979, features a nineteenth-century barber who slices up his clients and serves them à la carte as meat pies. Try taking your sweet grandmother from out of town to see that one. Sondheim started his career as the lyricist for *West Side Story*, and has since written plays about escaped lunatics (*Anyone Can Whistle*), pointillist paintings come to life (*Sunday in the Park with George*), and fairy tales gone dreadfully awry (*Into the Woods*)—all of them of not great commercial successes. Even so, ask any starlet on the Great White Way and they will tell you he's the hottest thing in musical theater today.

PLOT? WHAT PLOT?
Premiering at the end of 1990, the musical *Assassins* showed audiences an hour and a half of surreal insight into the lives and motives of the men and women who've taken a shot at the president. But this is a chorus lineup like none you've ever seen. Each assassin, from John Wilkes Booth to John Hinckley, carries a gun—and is not afraid to use it. Staged like a vaudeville revue, the scenes have no plot to tie them together. Assassins from differ-

---

James K. Polk's family name had originally been Pollock, a common Irish name.

ent centuries talk to one another, and they each get their chance in the spotlight. Each character's motivation is different; some desire love, fame, or money while others long for freedom from tyranny or freedom from stomach pain—but each one expresses a unique frustration with the "American dream" and how killing a president may lead to redemption. Not exactly light stuff.

NOTHING NEW UNDER THE SUN
Amazingly Sondheim was not the first person to think of writing a theater production about the ins and outs of presidential assassination. That honor goes to Charles Gilbert, Jr., whose play, also titled *Assassins*, was produced in 1979 at an alternative theater in Pittsburgh, Pennsylvania. Gilbert was inspired by a book he stumbled on in the library that collected together bits of poetry and memoirs of the lives of American assassins. Initial reviews of his play were tepid, noting that it "could turn into a remarkable piece, with work." Gilbert shelved the idea, and he was shocked to receive a letter from Sondheim in 1988 asking for permission to use the work as the basis for a new musical.

Sondheim and Weidman used pieces of Gilbert's play, including the carnival opening, but substantially changed it, most notably by removing the plot and adding music. Like Gilbert they used historical accounts of the assassins' lives to build the play; most of the details depicted on stage are true. Years later Gilbert had the chance to direct the Sondheim–Weidman version of his play. He says it was like being reunited with a child given up for adoption: the family resemblance is there, but it's clearly a product of someone else's parenting.

WORK IN PROGRESS
Assassins was originally produced at Playwrights Horizons, a tiny 150-seat theater founded to stage experimental works. It has no orchestra pit, so the singers could only be accompanied by piano, drums, and synthesizer. Sondheim intended for the show to have full orchestrations, which do appear on the cast album, and for it to have one more musical number called, "Something Just Broke." The song, which was used in the London production, is the only piece depicting the citizens' point of view as they react and grieve.

Sondheim felt it was needed as a touchstone for the audience, but he never had a chance to add it to the original New York production.

"SHOOT THE PREZ, WIN A PRIZE"
The play opens with a carnival scene. In front of a booth festooned in stars and stripes and marked "Shoot the Prez, Win a Prize," a hawker calls each of the assassins to step right up and shoot the president. (In case you were wondering, subtlety is not the strong point of this show.) We later see Giuseppe Zangara, who shot at FDR, sing while strapped down to an electric chair, and Charles Guiteau cakewalk up the gallows to his own death. Lynette "Squeaky" Fromme, who shot at Gerald Ford, joins Hinckley in a demented love ballad that she sings to Charles Manson, and he to Jodie Foster. The play has its comic moments, but audiences were usually too confused or appalled to laugh.

NO GRASSY KNOLL HERE
In the climactic scene of *Assassins*, John Wilkes Booth walks into the Texas Book Depository on November 22, 1963. There he talks Lee Harvey Oswald out of shooting himself and into shooting JFK, a conspiracy theory you won't see covered on *20/20*. This eleven-minute, nonmusical scene is so powerful that it was recorded on the original cast album. But some audience members found it much too close to home. One woman said that when she saw Oswald, she thought, "I don't want to go through that again."

BLINK AND YOU MISS IT
Assassins previewed off-Broadway on December 18, 1990, opening officially on January 27, 1991. Unfortunately, the timing could not have been worse for a black comedy about shooting presidents as the Gulf War broke out during previews. According to members of the cast, after the war was announced, the audience stopped laughing. In light of what some viewed as the play's antipatriotism, it's no surprise that *Assassins* didn't make the transfer from off-Broadway to Broadway. André Bishop, the original artistic director, thinks it wasn't just the war—audiences didn't want to see a play about assassins. It closed February 16, after just seventy-three performances.

NEGATIVE FEEDBACK
Critical reaction to the play was mixed. The *New York Times* review called it daring and gutsy, but added that the play's "potential is unfulfilled." One reviewer called it a "chilling vision of evil reaching out to evil"—definitely not what your average theatergoer expects in an evening's entertainment of song and dance.

Audiences themselves were often less forgiving. Cast members recall being booed and hissed at curtain calls, and some say they lost friends over the play. One audience member summed up the general reaction. Turning to his companion at the end, he said, "I liked it, but who are you supposed to feel for?"

OLD MUSICALS NEVER DIE, THEY JUST WIN TONYS
Despite its disastrous first run, *Assassins* has lived on in numerous amateur productions. You can hardly spend four years on an American college campus without seeing a production. The show even found its way back to the Great White Way. A Broadway revival was scheduled for November 2001, but after the September 11 attacks, the theater pulled it from the lineup, saying it was not "the appropriate time."

It's a good thing they waited for an appropriate time and received a much warmer reception the second time around. In 2004, an *Assassins* revival was staged on Broadway in the space that used to house Studio 54, which has been converted into a theater. Opening on March 26, 2004, this new production was a resounding success. The *Wall Street Journal* called the cast, "The Best Ensemble on Broadway!" and the *New York Times* raved that Sondheim's score was "Astonishing." To cap it all off, the production garnered a 2004 Tony Award for Best Featured Actor in a Musical, Best Director of a Musical, and (the real prize) Best Revival of a Musical. What a difference a few years can make!

BUT WHAT'S THE POINT?
Sondheim says that this is his only musical in which he would not change a thing, and it looks as though time has proven him correct. But what's the overall point of the show? Is it a glorification of the assassins? A warning about the dark side of the American dream? When asked, Sondheim only cryptically replied, "The piece should speak for itself."

NUMBER SEVEN: ANDREW JACKSON

Served from 1829 to 1837

Vital Stats: Born on March 15, 1767, in The Waxhaws, South Carolina. Died on June 8, 1845, in Nashville, Tennessee.
Age at Inauguration: 61
Vice President: John C. Calhoun (first term); Martin Van Buren (second term)
Political Affiliation: Democratic
Wife: Rachel Donelson Robards (married 1791, second marriage 1794)
Kids: Andrew Jackson, Jr. (adopted) (1808–1865)
Education: Studied law in Salisbury, North Carolina
What he did before he was president: Lawyer; U.S. Congressman; U.S. Senator; Tennesee Supreme Court Judge; Major General of the U.S. Army; Governor of the Florida Territory
Postpresidential Occupations: Retired

MEMORABLE QUOTES

"I feel in the depths of my soul that it is the highest, most sacred, and most irreversible part of my obligation to preserve the union of these states, although it may cost me my life."
—Andrew Jackson's second inaugural address, March 4, 1833

"You must, to get through life well, practice industry with economy, never create a debt for anything that is not absolutely necessary, and if you make a promise to pay money at a day certain, be sure to comply with it. If you do not, you lay yourself liable to have your feelings injured and your reputation destroyed with the just imputation of violating your word."
—Andrew Jackson in a letter to his son, April 14, 1835

Calvin Coolidge loved having his head rubbed while he ate breakfast in bed.

GHOSTS IN THE
WHITE HOUSE

*Things that go bump in the night, spectral laundry-hanging, and
prodigious profanity—the White House can sure be a spooky place.*

For more than 200 years America's top dog has roomed in
the White House. Of the all the presidents to date, only the
first—George Washington—didn't live there. The White
House rooms and grounds have continuously born witness to the
lives and times of some of America's most powerful and influential
personalities. According to a long list of eyewitness reports, the
storied building also continues to house the spirits of many of its
illustrious former occupants.

To the skeptic or purist, the celebrated White House might
not need supernatural tales to add to its mystique and legend. To
the supernatural buff or the neutral spectator, however, a little
psychic seasoning simply enhances the reputation of the White
House as one of the most interesting locations in America. After
all, what more appropriate place might there be to reverberate
with the echoes of the past?

LINGERING LINCOLN

The best known and most widely reported postmortem personality
still stalking the White House halls is good old Abraham "Honest
Abe" Lincoln himself. Many people have heard strange noises or
felt a spine-tingling presence in the White House in the years after
Lincoln's death. But Grace Coolidge, wife of Calvin Coolidge, was
the first person to report having *seen* Lincoln's ghost in the White
House. She said that he stood at a window of the Oval Office,
hands clasped behind his back, gazing out over the Potomac. After
this startling metaphysical breakthrough, Lincoln apparently began
to regularly revisit his old haunts in the White House.

Queen Wilhelmina of the Netherlands was a guest of the
White House when she heard a knock on her bedroom door in
the middle of the night. She answered it and was confronted by

---

Herbert Hoover was the first president to have a telephone on his desk.

Lincoln's bearded specter, wearing his famous top hat and all. The Queen fainted dead away. When she came to, he was gone.

Eleanor Roosevelt said she often felt the presence of the sixteenth president, and Mary Eben, Mrs. Roosevelt's secretary, reported seeing Lincoln sitting on the bed in the Lincoln Bedroom, pulling on his boots. Many other members of the White House staff during the Roosevelt era also reported seeing Lincoln lying on the bed at different times.

Harry S. Truman, who succeeded Roosevelt in office, once responded to a 3:00 a.m. knock on his door and found no one there. Poking fun at the rash of Honest Abe sightings that punctuated Roosevelt's eight years in office, Truman insisted upon attributing the knock to Lincoln. Continuing to make fun of the superstitious Roosevelts, Truman joked of the ghosts that inhabited the White House in letters to his wife, Bess, who was visiting family in Missouri; "The damned place is haunted, sure as shootin' . . . You and Margie had better come back and protect me before some of these ghosts carry me off."

The latest person to meet Lincoln's ghost was Maureen Reagan, the actor-turned-president's oldest daughter, who awoke in the Lincoln Bedroom to behold "a transparent person." Ronald Reagan was inclined to believe his daughter's story, describing how his dog would bark when passing the Lincoln Bedroom and refused to enter the room.

For all the important people who have stayed in the Lincoln Bedroom over the years, there is one who would not. Britain's famously droll prime minister, Winston Churchill, refused to sleep there after claiming that he had spotted President Abraham Lincoln's ghost "lurking about."

CURSING IN THE CORRIDORS

Long before her husband became the White House's most famous ghost, Mary Todd Lincoln was describing ghosts of her own. On more than one occasion she reported hearing the ghost of President Andrew Jackson stomping around the White House corridors and cursing. (President Jackson had been a tough, salty frontier general before he became president, and the coarse language he unapologetically brought with him into the highest

Franklin D. Roosevelt met with the press a record 998 times.

office stood in stark contrast to the clean image presented by most of the men who have won this job.) Though, for what Mary said she heard, some experts have a more rational explanation. Perhaps one of Lincoln's inner circle had too sharp a tongue for his wife's more delicate ears; her references to hearing "the ghost of Andrew Jackson" cursing in the halls was a subtle hint that he should curb his vocabulary in a lady's presence.

GRUMBLING IN THE ATTIC

Then there is the story of the unfortunate President Harrison, who caught a chill while delivering his long-winded inaugural address on a snowy day in 1841. The chill developed into full-blown pneumonia and killed him exactly a month into his presidency. He was the first president to die in the White House, which fired up people's imaginations with a guilty mixture of horror and amusement. When aging floorboards began to creak and wail in the attic, the story developed that the noises came from Harrison's ghost, grumbling and moaning through the ceiling at the unfairness of life. The fact that cold weather could be the true cause of the creaking, as well as the cause of Harrison's death, was perhaps one last, ironic coincidence orchestrated by the universe at the poor man's expense.

William Harrison is the subject of another ghostly story that also reads like a cruel joke. During his briefest of terms in office, a bodyguard to President Harrison was reportedly kept awake for several nights, trying to protect the president from mysterious footsteps he kept hearing in the hallway. The guard grew so tired and worried that he finally attended a séance to beg the restless spirits—which he believed were dead former presidents—to stop, so that he could get enough sleep to properly protect the living one!

DOLLEY IN THE ROSE GARDEN

During the time President James Madison and his wife, Dolley Madison, lived in the White House, she made many additions to the house, including a rose garden. As the story goes, a century later President Woodrow Wilson's second wife, Edith, had ordered gardeners to dig up the familiar White House rose garden that Dolley had planned and built. But the gardeners ended up running

---

Dwight D. Eisenhower liked to eat TV dinners while watching westerns.

away in terror when Dolley's ghost appeared to stop them from ruining her beloved garden. Not one flower was harmed, and Dolley's rose garden continues to bloom to this day. We may never know the true story. Perhaps Mrs. Wilson simply had a change of heart, perhaps her gardeners came up with an elaborate excuse to take the day off, or perhaps Dolley Madison did rise from the grave to fiercely protect her White House treasure.

ABIGAIL IN THE EAST ROOM
Everyone's heard the tale of Abigail Adams hanging her laundry to dry in the unfinished East Room of the White House. Laundry can be such a chore, and poor Abigail seems to have been condemned to hanging the washing for all eternity. The legend goes that to this day, Abigail Adams can be seen hurrying toward the East Room with her arms outstretched as if she were carrying a load of laundry. Abigail Adams enjoys the distinction of being the "oldest" ghost to be encountered in the White House today.

AND THE REST
The ghost of a British soldier from the War of 1812 is said to walk the White House grounds at night. Other creepy tales tell of a long-deceased White House usher still turning off lights in the building and a former White House doorman who remains on the job, opening and closing doors—to the consternation of residents who could swear that's not how they left them.

Cesar Carrera, valet to Franklin Delano Roosevelt, said he once heard someone calling in the Yellow Oval Room. The voice seemed to come from a distance, saying, "I'm Mr. Burns." A similar story arose during the Truman years when a guard heard a soft voice saying the same thing. In fact, the owner of the land given to the government for the White House was named Mr. Burns. Maybe he's just looking for a little recognition?

Nixon once worked at the Wheel of Fortune game booth at the Slippery Gulch Rodeo.

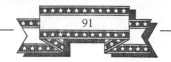
PRESIDENTIAL PREREQUISITES

*"Any man who has had the job I've had and didn't have a sense
of humor wouldn't still be here."—Harry S. Truman*

Ever wonder what might be the best career path to lead a starry-eyed dreamer into the highest office of the land? Among America's first forty-three presidents, there have been academics and actors, soldiers and farmers, not to mention enough lawyers to keep the country in court for more than two hundred years. Several presidents had no formal schooling at all. Very few had any background in economics or finance. George H. W. Bush was head of the CIA, and son George W. owned a baseball team. America's presidents have come from a wide variety of backgrounds. But is there any one thing that really turns a person into presidential material?

STRAIGHT-A STUDENTS?

A first rate education would seem to be requisite for the job. Thirty-two presidents went to college, and almost a quarter of those attended Harvard University. But many presidents never received any kind of formal education. They were tutored, home schooled, or just plain self-taught. The story of Lincoln teaching himself to read by dim firelight after finishing his chores in a meager log cabin is legendary, but Andrew Johnson, his successor, has a story that is even more unbelievable. Born into an extremely poor family, Johnson had little to no education until he was an adult. His wife, Eliza, taught Johnson the fundamentals of reading, grammar, and math. But if you're starting to think higher education isn't a must, you might want to think again. The last man to become president without having gone to college was Harry S. Truman.

Studying the law would probably be helpful. Twenty-six presidents were lawyers; however, only one president, Taft, chose to pursue a career in the judiciary and did rather well as a judge. Twice he was reputedly offered a position on the Supreme Court

---

John Quincy Adams suffered from insomnia, indigestion, and mental depression.

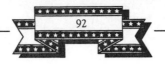

by Teddy Roosevelt, but turned down the offer both times. Taft decided he'd rather be president first before he accepted the Supreme Court gig. Six years after he left office, Taft became chief justice of the Supreme Court, a station he occupied for nine years.

SOLDIERING ON

Serving one's country in the armed services seems to carry a lot of weight. Thirty-one presidents served in the military in some capacity prior to becoming president. At least eight of those were considered to be war heroes. You might not know it, but Ulysses S. Grant was charged with insubordination and forced to resign from the military early in his career. (He was recommissioned during the Civil War because of the Union's desperate need for soldiers. The Union got lucky on that one!) There's always the danger of being captured, but luckily only one president was ever a prisoner of war. When he was fourteen, Jackson was captured, along with his brother, by British troops. Their mother secured their safe release.

PUBLIC (OFFICE) EXPOSURE

Experience in public office might also be a good idea. Fifteen presidents were governors of their home states before becoming president. Fifteen were U.S. senators, although one of those, James Garfield, never served in the Senate. He was elected president before he could take the congressional office. Only four presidents had never held an elected post before becoming president: Eisenhower, Hoover, Grant, and Taylor. In fact Taylor had never actually voted before becoming president.

EXECUTIVE BRANCH EXPERIENCE

Being in a previous president's cabinet might not hurt anyone's chances, but it probably won't help much either. Although five of the first seven presidents, after Washington, held the position of secretary of state, the last secretary of state to become president was James Buchanan. The fact that only one man ever held the position of secretary of commerce before becoming president might shed some light on the government's trouble with balancing budgets. However, that president happened to be Herbert Hoover, who

---

Rutherford B. Hayes was a major general in the Civil War.

is remembered—and often blamed for—the Great Depression, one of the lowest economic points in the nation's history.

So how about serving as the vice president? The odds are a little better, but not as good as one might think—unless death and disgrace are brought into the equation. Of the fourteen former vice presidents who went on to become president, more than half first ascended through no doing of their own. Eight became president after the elected chief died in office. (Four did so following assassinations and four after the elected president died of natural causes.) Only one veep, Gerald Ford, moved on up after a president's resignation. Only five of the eight—John Adams, Thomas Jefferson, Martin Van Buren, Richard Nixon, and George H. W. Bush—first came to the office of president as a result of being elected all by themselves.

Of course being elected isn't everything. Ford became president without ever winning a national election. He represented his hometown of Grand Rapids, Michigan, in Congress for almost twenty-five years and was chosen by his fellow Republican congressmen to be minority leader of the House. Nixon appointed Ford to the office of vice president when the guy who previously held the job, Spiro Agnew, resigned after being charged with tax evasion. It was from this appointed position that Ford ascended to the presidency upon Nixon's resignation.

THE PEOPLE LOVE A WORKIN' MAN

Some would say it doesn't quite matter what you do. Stories abound about Lincoln's getting his start by splitting rails, but he also piloted a ferry and owned a store. Before his political career began, James Garfield was a preacher and a canal worker. Chester Arthur, Garfield's successor, held down one of the toughest jobs known to man: he was a school principal. Among all the other activities that kept Teddy Roosevelt busy prior to his presidency, he was also an avid author, biographer, and historian. Herbert Hoover earned a fortune as an engineer.

So what kind of resume should a potential president have to qualify as presidential material? Who knows. But Truman was certainly onto something: a sense of humor is sure a good start for anyone who hopes to be president.

WAS HE OR WASN'T HE?

*The controversial theory that
President James Buchanan may have been gay.*

A re you sitting down? Good. Here's a taboo-busting hypo-
hesis: a man who once held the office of U.S. president
may just have been homosexual. Mind you, the jury's still
out on this one (and may be forever), but there's some evidence to
make a case that the first gay chief executive may have been the
fifteenth president, James Buchanan.

THE EVIDENCE
The strongest piece of evidence marshaled in support of the "he's
gay" argument is Buchanan's lifelong bachelorhood. He is to this
day, in fact, America's only bachelor president. (Cradle robber
Grover Cleveland was a bachelor when he was elected, but the
49-year-old Cleveland married 21-year-old Frances Folsom in the
second year of his first term.) During Buchanan's time in office,
the duties of hostess for the White House were taken up by his
niece, Harriet Lane.

The second main piece of evidence arguing for Buchanan's
homosexuality was his close relationship with the man who, perhaps not coincidentally, was America's only bachelor vice president, William Rufus King. King, who served as veep under
Franklin Pierce, is described in historical accounts as having a
fondness for silk scarves and showy stickpins. Buchanan and King
lived together in Washington for eight years when both of them
were senators (Buchanan from Pennsylvania and King from
Alabama). The two of them as a pair also had gossipy nicknames,
including Aunt Fancy and Miss Nancy, Siamese twins, and Mr.
and Mrs. Buchanan. When King was appointed to a post in
France in 1844, Buchanan wrote in a personal letter:

> I am now "solitary and alone," having no companion in
> the house with me. I have gone a wooing to several gen-

Gerald R. Ford once worked as a fashion model.

tlemen, but have not succeeded with any one of them. I feel that it is not good for man to be alone; and should not be astonished to find myself married to some old maid who can nurse me when I am sick, provide good dinners for me when I am well, and not expect from me any very ardent or romantic affection.

The relationship between them came to an end in 1853 when William Rufus King died of tuberculosis, shortly after he became vice president in the Pierce administration.

THE COUNTEREVIDENCE

Keep in mind though, that all of the pro-gay evidence is circumstantial. There's nothing more than innuendo and rumor to any sexual relationship between Buchanan and King. Their relationship may have been an entirely chaste friendship that just happened to be between two bachelors. In possibly the only mythologizing of James Buchanan ever to be written, John Updike presents his theory in his novel *Memories of the Ford Administration*. In the work the narrator, a scholar struggling to write a biography of Buchanan, theorizes that King and Buchanan may have had a very close, nonsexual relationship and preferred each other's company to the company of women (sort of like a nineteenth-century version of a no-girls-allowed club). In such a repressed time as the Victorian age, affection between men did not become physical in the way that such a relationship might today. In this view, which fits entirely with the known evidence, Buchanan and King were not homosexuals—just bachelors.

BUT WHAT ABOUT ANN?

Only adding fuel to the fire, Buchanan did have one significant heterosexual relationship early in his life. When he was a young lawyer in Pennsylvania, he courted and was engaged to a woman named Ann Coleman, the daughter of a millionaire and nearly an old maid at twenty-two. They were engaged in the summer of 1819. Tragically Ann died under mysterious circumstances that December, shortly after breaking off their engagement. Medical science not being then what it is today, the death was ascribed only to a fatal form of "hysteria."

When Zachary Taylor died, the First Lady allowed an Italian artist to sketch his corpse.

Ann's death raised a number of suspicions. Gossips at the time speculated that she had called off the engagement because Buchanan was not attentive enough to her and that she felt he was only after her for her money. Indeed, she seemed to have been a picture of health even on the day of her death, leading many to think that she may have committed suicide. Buchanan refused to speak about Ann for the rest of his life; he kept all his personal papers regarding her tightly sealed and instructed his executors to destroy them without breaking their seal after his death. The executors followed Buchanan's wishes, denying hordes of future historians the details of the breakup. As a result, all kinds of wild theories have proliferated—among them, that Buchanan had told her that he preferred men and that she had reacted melodramatically, breaking the engagement, then killing herself.

An equally plausible explanation of Ann's death could include no reference to Buchanan's sexual preference. Ann was known to be extremely emotional, even before the fit of "hysteria" that led to her death. One of Buchanan's biographers floats the possibility that Ann was still unmarried at twenty-two because she was "emotionally unstable." Perhaps Buchanan really had been inattentive to Ann because of a professional distraction in the months before she broke the engagement. Around the time of their breakup, Buchanan was involved in a large lawsuit that mandated he travel to Philadelphia several times to work on the case. On one of these visits he called on a friend whose unmarried sister-in-law happened to be present. When the excitable Ann heard about this meeting, she reportedly went mad with jealousy and wrote the official "breakup" letter. In the aftermath of her rash decision, she may have grown melancholy and decided to take her own life.

WHO KNOWS?

The truth is that both sides of the argument are based entirely on speculation and hearsay. Buchanan may have been gay, he may have been straight, or he may have been asexual. No one really knows since whatever proof there may have been went up in flames. Through the burning of his papers, Buchanan unwittingly started another cottage industry for historians who specialize in questions that can never be definitively answered.

NUMBER EIGHT: MARTIN VAN BUREN

Served from 1837 to 1841

Vital Stats: Born on December 5, 1782, in Kinderhook, New York. Died on July 24, 1862, in Kinderhook, New York.
Age at Inauguration: 54
Vice President: Richard M. Johnson
Political Affiliation: Democratic
Wife: Hannah Hoes (married 1807)
Kids: Abraham (1807–1873); John (1810–1866); Martin (1812–1855); Smith Thompson (1817–1876)
Education: Provincial schools. Studied law under William Van Ness
What he did before he was president: Lawyer; New York State Senator; Attorney General of New York; U.S. Senator; Governor of New York; Secretary of State; U.S. Vice President
Postpresidential Occupations: Politician

MEMORABLE QUOTE

"All the lessons of history and experience must be lost upon us if we are content to trust alone to the peculiar advantages we happen to possess. Position and climate and the bounteous resources that nature has scattered with so liberal a hand—even the diffused intelligence and elevated character of our people—will avail us nothing if we fail sacredly to uphold those political institutions that were wisely and deliberately formed."
—Martin Van Buren in his inaugural address, March 4, 1837

Abraham Lincoln loved Edgar Allan Poe's poem "The Raven."

A SEAWORTHY DESK FOR THE PRESIDENT

The story of how a British ship made it to the Oval Office.

E veryone remembers the famous photo of little John
Kennedy, Jr., in the Oval Office peeking out beneath a desk
as his father, the president, works above. What everyone
doesn't know is that the desk John-John called "My House"
started out as a British ship on her majesty's seafaring service.

RESOLUTE RESCUE

In 1854 the *Resolute*, a British vessel, became hopelessly trapped
in Arctic ice. Surviving crew members were forced to abandon
ship, but the HMS *Resolute* was stuck in the ice for a year. An
American whaler, the *George Henry*, was eventually able to free
the *Resolute* from the ice and tow it back to port. In a gesture of
international friendship, the ship was repaired and returned to
Queen Victoria by President Franklin Pierce on behalf of the
American people. The *Resolute* then served the British navy for
nearly two decades. When the ship was decommissioned, Queen
Victoria ordered that it be broken up, and its oak timbers were
then used to make a beautiful, elaborately carved desk. Queen
Victoria presented the desk to President Rutherford B. Hayes as a
symbol of goodwill between Great Britain and the United States.

Many presidents used the *Resolute* desk throughout the years.
Franklin D. Roosevelt admired the desk, but didn't like how an
open panel in the front allowed his lower body to be exposed. He
ordered the kneehole to be covered with a wooden cap bearing
the presidential coat of arms, reportedly to shield the braces on his
legs from visitors and reporters.

When First Lady Jacqueline Kennedy embarked on a historical
redecoration of the White House during the first years of her husband's administration, she discovered the historic desk with Queen
Victoria's original brass plaque that explained the *Resolute*'s history
still attached. Mrs. Kennedy had the desk refinished and brought to

Ulysses S. Grant smoked 20 cigars a day and eventually developed mouth cancer.

the Oval Office, where she made it the centerpiece of the room. President Kennedy used it throughout his administration, along with a specially made chair to ease his chronic back pain.

Jimmy Carter loaned the desk to the Smithsonian Institution to display for a time, so everyone could see and enjoy the desk. President Ronald Reagan brought it back to the White House, but had the desk raised by two inches, to accommodate his 6 feet 2 inches sized frame. George H. W. Bush preferred an even larger desk and moved the piece to a private study. But son President George W. Bush uses the *Resolute* desk in the Oval Office, where his recent predecessor Bill Clinton had returned it.

PANIC (BUTTON) ATTACK?

At some undisclosed point in time, a "panic button" was installed so that the president might use it to summon Secret Service agents in case of an emergency. The button is located at about knee level on the desk, a space just perfect for accidental brushings. A common experience for new presidents is to be startled by a rushing brigade of protectors when they inadvertently push the button with their legs.

★　★　★　★　★

STRANGE BEHAVIOR?

- Ulysses S. Grant began each day with a breakfast of cucumber soaked in vinegar.

- Chester A. Arthur owned over 80 pairs of pants, and changed his clothes several times during the day.

- Calvin Coolidge's family communicated in sign language when they were afraid of being overheard. Herbert Hoover's family spoke in Chinese for the same reason.

Rutherford B. Hayes was a spelling bee champion.

AILS OF THE CHIEFS

*We've all heard of playing sick, but it turns out that
presidents like to "play well" instead.*

The forty-two men who have held the office of chief executive have ranged in age from 42 to 77 while in office, middle- to old age. Unsurprisingly, then, the presidents have had a number of medical issues while in office. More surprisingly, perhaps, a large number of these episodes were hidden from the public to avoid a loss of confidence in their leader—even though such a loss of confidence may at times have been justified. Here's the low-down on some of the top-secret maladies of the presidents.

KEEP YOUR MOUTH SHUT

Grover Cleveland, during his second term in office, had a cancerous growth removed from his mouth in a surgical procedure conducted aboard a friend's yacht, the *Oneida*. The growth was a "gelatinous mass," which was also (in a rather unappetizing visual) referred to as a "cauliflower lesion." It may have resulted from Cleveland's heavy smoking—this president was known to enjoy his vices. He was a heavy smoker, drinker, and, especially eater. At 280 pounds, Cleveland was the largest president except for the famously portly William H. Taft.

Cleveland took his doctors' advice and arranged for the growth to be removed immediately. Meanwhile the country was ailing financially, with the disagreement about whether to continue basing the value of U.S. currency on silver reaching a fever pitch. Cleveland worried that the appearance of his failing health would be enough for a contagious unease to spread around the country and perhaps precipitate a financial panic even worse than the one already taking place. He called for a special session of Congress to convene in just over five weeks, when he expected to have recovered, to discuss the coinage issue. Then he traveled on the *Oneida* under the pretense of taking a vacation.

The surgeons cleared the saloon of the *Oneida* and settled

Cleveland into a deck chair. They began administering nitrous oxide and ether. The ether dose had to be alarmingly high to knock Cleveland out due to his high tolerance for alcohol that also made him resistant to the effects of ether. The surgeons removed two teeth and a huge portion of the upper left jawbone. A few weeks later a second operation was conducted to remove a little more tissue that looked suspicious and to fit the president with an artificial portion of jaw made of vulcanized rubber. Both operations were a complete success. After the implantation of the rubber jaw, Cleveland's appearance was indistinguishable from what it had been before the operation, and his speech was virtually unaffected.

The trouble now was keeping it quiet. Rumors leaked out that Cleveland was ill. The president's advisers fought back by blatantly lying, saying he was a little under the weather with rheumatism and a toothache, but would recover soon. Their story held fast. The truth only came out 24 years later, when his surgeon published his account of the episode in the *Saturday Evening Post*.

CAL FALLS SILENT

President Calvin Coolidge is remembered today as one of the more leisurely presidents in history. He famously slept between ten to eleven hours a day, which commonly included a two-hour nap in the afternoon between three hours of work in the morning and one in the afternoon. He is also remembered for being laconic, as in the anecdote about a White House guest who told Coolidge she had made a bet that she could get more than two words out of him. "You lose," said Coolidge.

His reputation while governor of Massachusetts, though, was quite the opposite of his as president. He regularly rose before 7:00 a.m. and worked throughout the day, even having meetings after dinner. These days, with the ability to look back with greater medical knowledge, it appears that Coolidge's sudden new idleness was due to clinical depression, instigated by the tragic death of his son.

Calvin and Calvin Junior faced off in a tennis match one summer day in 1924 on the White House grounds. Calvin Junior played wearing sneakers but wore no socks and developed a blister on his foot. He ignored the injury, which then became seriously

infected. Doctors were unable to save him, and Calvin Junior died of blood poisoning.

Coolidge fell into a deep funk, losing interest in politics and his presidential duties. He began to be obsessed with his own health and would take his pulse while sitting at his desk, looking for symptoms of heart disease. He became more compliant with people, trying to hide what he saw as intolerable personal faults, even though these faults were invisible to others, or at least not intolerable. In short he met all the textbook criteria for a major depressive episode. Coolidge died five years after leaving office, of what his doctors called, ironically, a "silent coronary."

PROFILE IN COURAGE

In spite of his image as a young and vigorous leader, John F. Kennedy may just have been the nation's sickliest president. His troubles started early in life, when he suffered from almost every childhood illness imaginable—plus a few more: scarlet fever, bronchitis, chicken pox, ear infections, German measles, measles, mumps, whooping cough, asthma, diphtheria, allergies, hives, an irritable colon, a weak stomach, and many bouts with colds and flu. He was in and out of the hospital throughout his life with one problem or another. In fact his medical condition twice became so grave that he received the last rites of the Roman Catholic Church. After graduating from college, Kennedy was only allowed to serve in the Navy when his father's influence helped him "pass" his physical.

In addition to his childhood ailments, Kennedy suffered from a bad back for most of his life. Although the source of the problem was probably congenital, Kennedy seriously aggravated it when he tried out for the football team at Harvard University. The injury was compounded, when, while in the navy during World War II, Kennedy's PT boat was rammed by a Japanese vessel and sunk. The jolt of the initial collision and the immense strain from rescuing his shipmates ruptured a spinal disk; in the years that followed the war, Kennedy underwent two surgeries to help ease the pain. He even took to wearing a back brace after he became president.

As if a bad back weren't problem enough, another major health problem that went undiagnosed for most of Kennedy's life

was Addison's disease, an autoimmune disorder that causes weight loss, muscle weakness, chronic fatigue, low blood pressure, and nausea. The Kennedys did their best to keep the illness a secret, especially during JFK's run for the White House.

During his campaign for the presidency in 1960, direct questions about whether Kennedy had Addison's were posed on both sides of the party divide. Republican congressman Walter Judd found a description of a case in a journal called *Archives of Surgery* that gave names of doctors and dates of surgery, but not the name of the patient. There was little doubt, though, that the patient in the article was Kennedy. Lyndon Johnson also made a public statement that Kennedy had Addison's when he and Kennedy were both candidates for the Democratic Party's nomination. The Kennedy camp's response to these allegations? Just to deny them. A statement issued by Robert Kennedy stated unequivocally, giving details from John's doctors, that John was not sick.

With all these medical problems, Kennedy submitted to a battery of injections and swallowed a handful of pills every day. To deal with pain, he received injections from a doctor named Max Jacobson, a.k.a. Dr. Feelgood, who one of his nurses described as "absolutely a quack." Jacobson actually did turn out to be a quack and lost his license in 1975 for manufacturing "adulterated drugs consisting in whole or in part of filthy, putrid, and/or decomposed substances." Kennedy insisted about his injections from Jacobson, "I don't care if it's horse piss. It works." It is awfully tough to argue with success.

★　★　★　★　★

JAMES WINS THE NAME GAME

More presidents have the name James than any other. Six in all, the Jameses are followed only by the Johns and Williams, both with four presidents apiece. The next closest are the Georges with three, followed by Andrews and Franklins with two each.

EDITH ROOSEVELT WINS THE WAITING GAME

Edith Roosevelt was hopelessly devoted to her husband Teddy—even when he was married to someone else.

Edith Carow was actually Teddy Roosevelt's second wife. She knew him just about all her life—literally from the time they were both toddlers. They played together, studied together, and went to social functions together. He wrote her letters from his boyhood trips to Europe, and she visited him at the Roosevelt summer home in Oyster Bay, Long Island.

After his father died in 1878, Teddy and Edith spent a lot of time together. So much time in fact that there were whispers that the two might be in love. Rumors abounded that Teddy might have popped the question, but Edith turned him down either because of her age or because she felt his family looked down on her family (her father had a drinking problem that hurt the Carows' reputation). Whatever the rumor mill spun out, there was little confirmation as to why the pair didn't tie the knot back then. It was a secret Teddy, Edith, and their parents took with them to the grave.

THE OTHER WOMAN

The following year while studying at Harvard University, Teddy fell in love with and proposed to another woman named Alice Lee. Teddy would write of her as "radiantly pure and good and beautiful." Edith was understandably shocked and disappointed at the news, but she did have her chance. She managed to keep it together and in a great display of graciousness and poise, she managed to dance up a storm at his wedding on October 27, 1880.

Though it's impossible to know what went through her mind for the next three years, some say Edith often skipped social events or just watched them from the sidelines to avoid running into her old flame. To make matters worse, her father's fortune dwindled away as his health declined, both of which diminished

---

Benjamin Harrison enjoyed billiards and duck hunting.

Edith's hopes for remaining a true member of Victorian New York's high society. She seemed to be heading directly for spinsterhood at the tender age of twenty. Yet somewhere in the back of her mind, she knew she was destined for more. One of her grandchildren later wrote that Edith had no doubt she would "someday, somehow" still marry Teddy Roosevelt.

And she was right. Three years later Alice Lee died tragically shortly after the birth of their daughter, Alice (on the same day Roosevelt's mother died, incidentally), leaving Teddy a widower at the age of twenty-five. A year and a half later, Edith and Teddy ran into each other unexpectedly in New York. Having already known each other for twenty-one years, the timing couldn't have been better for both of them. Three weeks later in November 1885, he asked her to marry him and she did not let this opportunity slip away and said yes. They kept the engagement a secret until the summer of 1886 and were married in December. Nine months later Edith had the first of their five children, Theodore Junior.

CHILDREN OF THE HOUSE
Four more boisterous children followed: Kermit, Ethel, Archie, and Quentin. Edith's five children together with Alice (Alice Lee's daughter) all moved into the White House in 1901 when their father became president. The family provided the press with countless stories of mischief for the next eight years. Known for riding bikes around the White House lawn, stilt-walking down the halls, roller-skating on a newly refurbished and polished East Room floor, and rough housing with their father in the mansion's bedrooms, the Roosevelt children kept Washington well amused.

The kids also kept the nation laughing with the antics of their many pets. There were escapades with Tom Quartz, the cat; a kangaroo rat who ate sugar at the breakfast table; Eli, the noisy blue macaw; Josiah, the badger; and Emily Spinach, a bright green snake that Alice would stick in her purse and take to parties. Quentin once even managed to get a 350-pound pony into the White House elevator and up to his brother Archie's room to cheer him up when he was sick!

LADY OF THE HOUSE
Edith was not only a wife and mother of six who abolished the

Calvin Coolidge liked to ride a mechanical horse that he kept in the White House.

post of official housekeeper and supervised everything herself, but also a full-time first lady of the land. She threw afternoon teas, garden parties, and lavish state dinners. She somehow managed to read huge volumes of mail, oversee all White House entertainment, organize lunches for cabinet members wives, take French lessons, go antique shopping, accompany her energetic husband on horseback rides in the park, and always read to and talk to her children before dinner.

Today's White House occupants can thank the Roosevelts for the White House's West Wing. It was due to that large and active family that Congress was finally persuaded to appropriate enough cash to redo the executive mansion (a task they had refused to fund under several previous administrations), and it was under Edith's watchful eye that the West Wing was built. She was tasteful yet frugal, both with her own money and the nation's.

Edith established the White House china collection by gathering up and completing an inventory of all previous administration's sets of dishes—many of which had been all too casually scattered about the nation. She also created a gallery of the First Ladies' portraits, making the not-so-subtle statement that presidential wives had played and continue to play an important role in the history of the nation.

Though Theodore Roosevelt died at the relatively young age of 60, Edith lived to see seventeen different presidents and died at the age of eighty-seven while Truman was campaigning for his second term.

★　★　★　★　★

EXCEPTIONAL EDITH

"Edith is very well this summer and looks so young and pretty. She rides with us a great deal . . . We also go out rowing together, taking our lunch and a book or two with us. The children fairly worship her, as they ought to, for a more devoted mother never was known."
—Teddy Roosevelt, 1903

An avid stamp collector, FDR's collection grew to 25,000 stamps by the 1930s.

NUMBER NINE: WILLIAM HENRY HARRISON

Served from March 4, 1841 to April 4, 1841

Vital Stats: Born on February 9, 1773, in Charles City County, Virginia. Died on April 4, 1841, in Washington, DC.
Age at Inauguration: 68
Vice President: John Tyler
Political Affiliation: Whig
Wife: Anna Tuthill Symmes (married in 1795)
Kids: Elizabeth Bassett (1796–1846); John Cleves Symmes (1798–1830); Lucy Singleton (1800–1826); William Henry (1802–1838); John Scott (1804–1878); Benjamin (1806–1840); Mary Symmes (1809–1842); Carter Bassett (1811–1839); Anna Tuthill (1813–1845); James Findlay (1814–1817)
Education: Hampden-Sidney College
What he did before he was president: Soldier; U.S. Congressman; Brigadier General in the U.S. Army; Governor of Indiana and Superintendent of Indian Affairs; Ohio State Senator; U.S. Senator
Postpresidential Occupations: None (died in office)

MEMORABLE QUOTE

"Gentlemen and fellow citizens . . . Perhaps this may be the last time I may have the pleasure of speaking to you on earth or seeing you. I will bid you farewell, if forever, fare thee well."
—William Henry Harrison speaking in Cincinatti, Ohio on January 26, 1841

Speed reader Jimmy Carter was clocked reading 2,000 words a minute.

THE SIMPSON TRIAL

*America's longest running animated series
has had its fair share of presidential gags.*

Fans of *The Simpsons* should have no trouble spotting the jokes made at the expense of the chief executives. Get out a pen and your sense of humor and see if you're the president of *The Simpsons* nation.

1. Which former president invites Homer Simpson over to watch football, eat nachos, and drink beer?
   A. George H. W. Bush
   B. Richard Nixon
   C. Gerald Ford
   D. Bill Clinton

2. According to Homer, which former president's dog now resides in Doggy Hell?
   A. Bill Clinton's dog Buddy
   B. Richard Nixon's dog Checkers
   C. George H. W. Bush's dog Millie
   D. Lyndon Johnson's dog Yuki

3. Which president moved in across the street from the Simpsons and gave Bart Simpson a spanking?
   A. Richard Nixon
   B. Gerald Ford
   C. Ronald Reagan
   D. George H. W. Bush

4. Abraham "Grandpa" Simpson has also been spanked by a president (on two nonconsecutive occasions). Which Chief Executive paddled Grandpa?
   A. William McKinley
   B. William Howard Taft
   C. Calvin Coolidge
   D. Grover Cleveland

Truman on education: "Kids should learn more fundamental reading, writing and arithmetic."

5. While leading his employees in morning calisthenics, the evil, aged owner of the nuclear power plant, C. Montgomery Burns wants them to pick up the pace. So he says he wants to see . . . (*pick the correct phrase to finish the sentence*)

    A. "more Teddy Roosevelts and less Franklin Roosevelts."
    B. "more Benjamin Harrisons and less William Henry Harrisons."
    C. "more George H. W. Bushes and less George W. Bushes."
    D. "more John Quincy Adamses and less John Adamses."

6. While studying to become a mall Santa Claus, Homer Simpson has to name the reindeer. He recites: "Dasher, Dancer, Prancer," and then swaps "Vixen" for the last name of this president. Who is it?
    A. Reagan
    B. Nixon
    C. Clinton
    D. Johnson

7. In an annual Halloween special aired during an election year, these two presidential candidates were kidnapped and replaced by aliens disguised as look-alikes. Nobody notices, even when one of them says: "It makes no difference which one of us you vote for. Either way, your planet is doomed. DOOMED!" Who were the two candidates?

    A. George H. W. Bush and Bill Clinton
    B. Al Gore and George W. Bush
    C. Bill Clinton and Bob Dole
    D. Ross Perot and Bob Dole

ANSWERS: 1. C, 2. B, 3. D, 4. D, 5. A, 6. B, 7. C

KEEPING UP APPEARANCES

The White House changes with the times and the presidents.

A longtime symbol of American freedom and power, the White House, at its heart, is really just a well-known family home. Each First Family has adapted the building and its furnishings to suit their own needs and tastes. And each family has left its mark on the White House.

LET THERE BE LIGHT . . . AND HOT WATER?

The early administrations didn't have much to work with. The executive mansion wasn't even completed when its first resident, John Adams, moved in to live out the last few months of his presidency. Since there was no indoor plumbing of any kind, water had to be hauled from nearly a mile away. Abigail Adams couldn't find enough wood to build a laundry line—and she couldn't find laborers to build one anyhow—so she hung the First Family's wet clothes out to dry in the East Room (now one of the most elegant state rooms).

To help the decorating process along, Congress allocated $14,000 (a princely sum in the early nineteenth century!) for furnishings during Adams's four months in the White House and gave his successor, Thomas Jefferson, $29,000. Much of this money went simply to painting and plastering. Even though Jefferson was only the second resident of the White House, during his stay he had to replace the roof, which had leaked almost as soon as it was up. What little furniture the Adamses had contributed had been ruined. Jefferson ended up bringing his own furnishings in from his estate, Monticello, to decorate the White House. He did temporarily solve the water problem; he smartly set up an attic cistern to catch the DC rainwater.

As the years went on White House residents continued to upgrade their home with modern conveniences and luxuries. In 1833, during Andrew Jackson's second term, pipes were installed

---

James A. Garfield was the only president to have been a preacher.

to bring in water for bathing. Jackson spent more than $45,000 on elegant additions to the mansion, including china and crystal from France. He rebuilt the East Room to make it impressive and grand. But critics argued that Andrew "Old Hickory" Jackson's cohorts were not suited to such finery. Many rugs *were* ruined by muddy boots and many curtains damaged by souvenir hunters who cut swatches from the window coverings. (Such rowdiness could have been predicted by the mob scene at Jackson's inaugural celebration, which forced the new president to jump out a White House window to escape.)

But the need for sufficient water, heat, and light had not abated. Martin Van Buren put in a basement reservoir for cooking and bathing needs. By 1853, there were bathtubs in the family quarters with hot and cold running water. In 1848, President James K. Polk installed gas lighting, to replace the oil lamps and candles. Millard Fillmore brought in a kitchen stove in the 1850s; before this the cooks had prepared elegant meals at an open fireplace. The first central furnace, a coal-fueled hot water and hot air system, was installed in 1853, after Franklin Pierce moved in. Benjamin Harrison brought in the first electrical lighting—but the Harrisons were afraid to turn the lights on and off for fear of getting shocked.

LINCOLNS MAKE IT OVER

During the Civil War, while her husband went about the business of saving the Union, Mrs. Mary Todd Lincoln took it upon herself to redecorate the White House. She first supervised scrubbing down the walls and floors, painting, and replastering the entire house. For the first time in years, the White House was actually *clean*.

Congress had been generous enough to allot $20,000 for new furnishings; the money had to last over the course of four years. This sum was more than four times President Lincoln's salary had been before he took office, and thus it seemed a fortune to Mrs. Lincoln. Nevertheless she managed spend it—and then some. She traveled to New York and Philadelphia and bought the best and most expensive of everything. Mary concentrated on the family quarters, especially the guest bedroom, which she furnished with

what is now known as the "Lincoln bed." (The president, in fact, probably never slept in it.)

Once everything was finished, Mrs. Lincoln's critics approved of the new elegant and refined look. But her husband, not so much. Abe was furious with her overspending and would not (initially) agree to her plan to ask Congress to approve a supplemental appropriation. "It would stink in the nostrils of the American people to have it said that the President of the United States had approved a bill overrunning an appropriation of $20,000 for *flub dubs* for this damned old house, when the soldiers cannot have blankets." He vowed he would pay the overdraft himself. But eventually Lincoln came to realize that he didn't have sufficient funds (almost $7,000) for this gesture and quietly agreed to let Congress cover the deficiency.

HUNTING TROPHIES
AND "HAUNTED" CHANDELIERS

The next major restructuring of the White House took place during Theodore Roosevelt's administration in 1902. Congress appropriated $540,641 to remodel the executive mansion, including $65,196 for a "temporary" office building to be known as the West Wing. Teddy Roosevelt was eager to make over the White House in his own testosterone-soaked image and happily declared, "Smash the glass houses!" (the conservatories that had been up since James Buchanan's time). He threw out Chester Arthur's Tiffany screens and William McKinley's potted palms and added moose heads and bear rugs. He had the modern West Wing built on the foundation of Jefferson's office buildings, and he added offices for reporters for the first time.

The West Wing went through several more renovations through the years. After a devastating fire on Christmas eve 1929, the offices needed another overhaul. In 1934 when construction was complete, the newly remodeled White House included three new stories of office space added to the East Building and a secret (at the time) underground bomb shelter in the basement of the Treasury Building, connected by an underground passageway to the White House. During his administration Franklin D. Roosevelt enlarged the West Wing and also arranged for the con-

---

So poor after leaving office, Tyler was unable to pay a bill for $1.25 until he sold his corn crop.

struction of the East Wing. During World War II military guards were stationed for the first time in the halls, and bulletproof glass was installed in the Oval Office windows.

Several years later in 1948, President Harry S. Truman noticed chandeliers swaying suspiciously in the White House and was alarmed when his daughter Margaret's grand piano leg punctured the floor of her room and some of the ceiling beneath. Truman ordered a study of the mansion structure at once. Horrified inspectors proclaimed that the White House was still standing "purely by habit." The first family was moved immediately to the Blair House, across the street on Pennsylvania Avenue. The interior of the White House was gutted and rebuilt, at a cost of $5,761,000; work was completed in 1952.

CH ... CH ... CHANGES

Style maven Jacqueline Kennedy sought to make the White House the nation's finest showplace, furnished with top-quality American antiques and accented by eighteenth- and nineteenth-century paintings. In 1961 she created the Fine Arts Committee for the White House and the Special Committee of Paintings, and she set about redoing the mansion. In 1962 she conducted a widely viewed TV tour of the White House, giving many Americans their first glimpse of the newly refurbished executive mansion. By the time of President John F. Kennedy's assassination in 1963, Mrs. Kennedy's committee had restored the state rooms on the first floor and several historic rooms on the second.

Thanks to Jackie Kennedy incoming First Ladies may now furnish and decorate the second- and third-floor residence quarters however they see fit. But the ground floor corridor and main public rooms must be maintained in their museum-like state, according to a law passed by Congress in 1961 to protect and continue the historical restoration begun during the Kennedy administration. Any proposed changes or additions in these public rooms have to be approved by the Committee for the Preservation of the White House.

First Ladies can make selections from furniture and artwork already in the White House and from a government warehouse containing pieces used by previous occupants of the executive

---

Millard Fillmore was the first president to have a stepmother.

mansion. If she still cannot find artwork that she likes, she may borrow additional pieces from the National Gallery. The artwork rotates throughout the executive mansion much like it rotates through a museum: the finest pieces are always on display but often finding new locations. (Presidents have been known to rearrange presidential portraits so that paintings of their partisan soul mates take center stage.)

THE TRADITION CONTINUES

Mrs. Kennedy's successors carried her torch and continued to work to make the White House a first-class representation of American style. Lady Bird Johnson appealed for donations of important paintings to the White House. Pat Nixon worked to bring back original American furniture pieces to replace the reproductions that were everywhere. Rosalynn Carter decided to follow in Jackie's footsteps by broadcasting White House concerts on national television so that the many Americans who wanted to visit the White House but could not could still enjoy the People's House. But Rosalynn's successor caused a minor scandal in her efforts to spruce up the place: Even though the Reagans raised more than one million dollars in private funds to redecorate the second- and third-floor family quarters, Nancy Reagan outraged her critics when she ordered new (and expensive!) state china in her favorite color, now known as Reagan Red. It seemed to be an extravagant indulgence given the state of the U.S. economy and the fact that the mansion owned dozens of sets of china by that time.

From 1980 to 1992, about forty layers of whitewash and paint were stripped from the façade of the White House, which allowed the decorative trim and scrollwork to show through. Toward the end of this process the Clintons (with private donations) redecorated the Lincoln Sitting Room and the Treaty Room, and the Oval Office was made over in striking golds and reds. The Clinton administration oversaw the final phase of the restoration and redecoration of the Blue Room as well. Hillary Clinton said that in their first few years in the White House, they woke not to alarm clocks in the morning but to the sound of hammers and power tools. President Bill Clinton brought in the Internet, and his administration was the first to use online services and to com-

---

Kennedy and Taft are the only presidents buried in Arlington National Cemetery.

municate via email. Hillary was the first First Lady to put her foot down about smoking in her home: starting in 1992 the White House was designated a no-smoking building. (President Clinton was known to step outside on the Truman Balcony to enjoy an occasional lit cigar, however.)

Early in George W. Bush's presidency First Lady Laura Bush redecorated the Oval Office in the subdued southwestern colors of her native Texas. But the September 11, 2001, attacks on the United States put a halt to renovations. The biggest changes in the White House during this time have been for security purposes. For more than two years the White House was closed to the public. In 2004, with added security in place, public tours were again offered—albeit to a restricted number of visitors. The style and creativity of the presidents and first families are again on display, and the White House remains the People's House.

★　★　★　★　★

THE GRATEFUL PRESIDENT

"To-morrow the National Convention meets, and barring a cataclysm I shall be nominated . . . How the election will turn out no man can tell. Of course I hope to be elected, but I realize to the full how very lucky I have been, not only to be President but to have been able to accomplish so much while President . . . It is a wonderful privilege to have been here and to have been given the chance to do this work, and I should regard myself as having a small and mean mind if in the event of defeat I felt soured at not having had more instead of being thankful for having had so much."
—Theodore Roosevelt in a letter to his son Kermit, June 21, 1904

Ronald Reagan was the first president to wear contact lenses.

GETTING DIRTY

*The Founding Fathers weren't any kinder
in their campaigns way back when.*

Modern voters are often shocked by the level to which political candidates will sink to make points against their opponents. During election season, TV commercials that accuse rival candidates of being soft on crime, amoral, and much, much worse are as common as fast food spots during the dinner hour. But if you think this is a modern phenomenon, you're dead wrong. Today's politicians can look to history for some dirty, low-down examples of below-the-belt campaigning. Uncle John's has amassed a mess of muck from some of the dirtiest campaigns ever. Put your waders on and jump right in.

WHY, MR. JEFFERSON!

The invective started flying during the very first presidential campaign of 1796, when John Adams ran against Thomas Jefferson just before George Washington's two terms were set to run out. They produced handbills and articles accusing each other of a range of misdeeds. But things really got vicious when the pair faced off again in 1800, with Jefferson angling to win the seat John Adams had held for four years.

The Adams-backing Federalists accused Jefferson of bilking creditors and business partners; giving in like a coward as governor of Virginia when the British invaded his state during the Revolutionary War; and cheating an old widow out of her husband's pension. They claimed Jefferson was a "howling atheist," and if he were elected he would confiscate and burn all the Bibles in America; tear down all the churches; put an end to the institution of marriage; and clap the country's women into bordellos. The Hartford *Connecticut Courant* darkly warned against Jefferson, claiming that if he became president "murder, robbery, rape, adultery, and incest will be openly taught and practiced. The air will be filled with the cries of the distressed, the soil will be soaked with blood, and the nation black with crimes."

Jefferson's followers were no kinder to Adams, calling him a hypocritical, bald, blind, crippled, and toothless old fool. In his bid to become "King of America" he would marry his children to those of King George III and would rule over the country like a tyrant. Not only was he a monarchist, he was a whoremaster, too, and had sent his running mate to Europe to procure prostitutes. In the end, as we all know, Jefferson won out. But Jefferson and Adams were political enemies for many years after their flagrant political scuffle.

LIKE FATHER, LIKE SON

Things were even nastier in 1828 when President John Quincy Adams (John's son) ran against Andrew Jackson. Adams acolytes claimed Jackson was an adulterer, a liar, a bigamist, and a murderous drunk who gambled on cockfights. In a pamphlet they produced they elucidated the candidate's many brawls and duels during which Jackson had "killed, slashed and clawed various American citizens." They went after Jackson's family, too, branding Jackson's dear old mom a prostitute who'd been imported by the British as comfort for the English Revolutionary War troops. Worst of all for Jackson, they picked on his dear wife Rachel, who was vulnerable due to a problem with her divorce from her former husband, which wasn't granted until after she'd married Jackson. They called Rachel an adulteress and a paramour, causing the Jacksons great personal pain.

Jackson followers struck back by terming President Adams an elitist tyrant who lived in a "presidential palace" in "kingly pomp and splendor." He traveled on Sunday instead of going to church; installed "gambling tables and furniture" in the White House on the public's bill; and had had premarital sex with wife Louisa. As minister to Russia, they claimed, Adams had pimped for Czar Alexander I, procuring a young American lady for his perverted pleasure.

The false charges slung on both sides were truly towering. But even though Jackson won the presidency he was forever embittered by the battle. Rachel died soon after the election of a heart attack, which Jackson forever after believed was caused by the slings and arrows she'd weathered during the 1828 campaign.

Ulysses S. Grant's favorite breakfast was a cucumber soaked in vinegar.

MORE PRESIDENTIAL MUDSLINGING

Of course, these two squalid campaigns weren't the last in which such sordid accusations were wielded as a tool: *Harper's Weekly* published a long list of the insults leveled against Abraham Lincoln in 1864 (Fiend? Butcher? Ignoramus Abe?!), while *The Nation* complained in 1872 that the Ulysses S. Grant and Horace Greeley race was "a shower of mud to a far greater extent than any other campaign within our remembrance."

Yes, mudslinging is not a thing of the past. Although charges of cockfighting may not be as prevalent these days, as long as a candidate can score political points by going negative, there are going to be those desperate enough to sink to it. If it was good enough for the presidents of our past, it's good enough for us, right?

★　★　★　★　★

I'M LATE, I'M LATE!

Taft had a punctuality problem of which he was well aware.

"Roosevelt could always keep ahead with his work, but I cannot do it, and I know it is a grievous fault, but it is too late to remedy it. The country must take me as it found me.

"Wasn't it your mother who had a servant girl who said . . . that she was a 'Sun-day chil' and no 'Sunday chil' could hurry? I don't think I am a Sunday child, but I ought to have been; then I would have had an excuse for always being late."

—William H. Taft, from a letter written November 21, 1909

NUMBER TEN: JOHN TYLER

Served from 1841 to 1845

Vital Stats: Born on March 29, 1790, in Charles City County, Virginia. Died on January 18, 1862, in Richmond, Virginia.
Age at Inauguration: 51
Vice President: None
Political Affiliation: Whig
First Wife: Letitia Christian (married in 1813. died in 1842)
Kids from First Marriage: Mary (1815-1848); Robert (1816–1877); John (1819–1848); Letitia (1821–1907); Elizabeth (1823–1850); Alice (1827–1854); Tazewell (1830–1874)
Second Wife: Julia Gardiner (married 1844)
Kids from Second Marriage: David Gardiner (1846–1871); John Alexander (1848–1883); Julia (1849–1871); Lachlan (1851–1902); Lyon Gardiner (1853–1935); Robert Fitzwater (1856–1927); Pearl (1860–1947)
Education: The College of William and Mary
What he did before he was president: Lawyer; U.S. Congressman; Governor of Virginia; U.S. Senator; Vice President
Postpresidential Occupations: Lawyer

MEMORABLE QUOTES

"On the same day I dined with Mr. Cary Selden, brother of Jas. Selden's. Several gentlemen were there, and after dinner Miss . . . and her brother danced a waltz—a dance which you have never seen, and which I do not desire to see you dance. It is rather vulgar, I think."
—John Tyler advising his daughter on the evils of waltzing, December 26, 1827

"My God! The president is dead."
—John Tyler's exclamation upon hearing the news of Harrison's death, April 4, 1841

NUMBER ELEVEN: JAMES KNOX POLK

Served from 1845 to 1849

Vital Stats: Born on November 2, 1795, in Mecklenburg County, North Carolina. Died on June 15, 1849, in Nashville, Tennessee.
Age at Inauguration: 49
Vice President: George M. Dallas
Political Affiliation: Democratic
Wife: Sarah Childress (married 1824)
Kids: None
Education: University of North Carolina
What he did before he was president: Lawyer; U.S. Congressman; Speaker of the House of Representatives; Governor of Tennessee
Postpresidential Occupations: Retired

MEMORABLE QUOTE

"None can fail to see the danger to our safety and future peace if Texas remains an independent state or becomes an ally or dependency of some foreign nation more powerful than herself . . . Whatever is good or evil in the local institutions of Texas will remain her own whether annexed to the United States or not.

"Perceiving no valid objection to the measure . . . I shall . . . endeavor by all constitutional, honorable, and appropriate means to consummate the expressed will of the people and Government of the United States by the reannexation of Texas to our Union at the earliest practicable period."

—James K. Polk wanted Texas for the U.S., from his inaugural address, March 4, 1845

ALL THE PRESIDENTS' GAFFES

Mistakes, as they say, were made.

Forty-two men have occupied the office of U.S. president; if each one made only one mistake or misspoke just once during his time in office, we'd already have a substantial collection of presidential faux pas. Fortunately for the cynics among us, most of these men have made more than a few boo-boos over the years. A few of our favorites bear special mention, however:

- Franklin Delano Roosevelt served hot dogs to the king and queen of England on their state visit. Here's hoping they served him bangers and mash the next time he crossed the pond!

- Harry S. Truman was known as a no-nonsense straight shooter whose desk bore a sign reading, "The buck stops here." While running for reelection, he told a campaign-stop crowd, "I don't give 'em hell, I just tell the truth and they think it's hell," which led to his nickname: "Give 'em hell Harry."

- Dwight D. Eisenhower was asked by a journalist what significant decisions his vice president, Richard Nixon, had helped him to make. "If you give me a week I might think of one," he replied. (He later apologized to Nixon.)

- John F. Kennedy wins the award for the "gaffe that never was," his famous "Ich bin ein Berliner" speech. For years the media and the public believed that Kennedy had misspoken, saying "I am a jelly doughnut" (a Berliner is indeed a type of Berlin jam-filled pastry) instead of "I am a citizen of Berlin." However experts now say that Kennedy did speak correctly, so there's a little jam on the face of his critics.

- On September 16, 1968, Richard Milhous Nixon, in an effort to appeal to the young people, made campaign history on *Rowan & Martin's Laugh-In*, the hippie-esque sketch comedy

---

6 presidents were southpaws: Garfield, Hoover, Truman, Ford, Reagan, & George H. W. Bush.

television show. During a fast-paced montage sequence, this president with the stuffed-shirt persona appeared and cried out the show's most famous catchphrase, "Sock it to me!"

- Gerald Ford was prone to all manner of physical gaffes, from locking himself out of the White House to tripping and falling down the steps of *Air Force One* during a visit to Austria. His clumsiness was famously parodied by comedian Chevy Chase on NBC's *Saturday Night Live*.

- Jimmy Carter caused a minor scandal when he admitted in a *Playboy* interview that he had "lusted after women" in his heart. Most *Playboy* readers instantly agreed that they had, too.

- Testing the microphone during what he thought was a sound check before a radio address, Ronald Reagan joked, "My fellow Americans, I'm pleased to tell you today that I've signed legislation that will outlaw Russia forever. We begin bombing in five minutes." Only he didn't realize that they were broadcasting. The joke fell flat with Cold War-era listeners.

- George H. W. Bush declared that he disliked broccoli and scores of irate farmers sent bushels of the green stuff his way. He stuck to his guns, saying "I'm the president and I don't have to eat broccoli if I don't want to."

- Bill Clinton created a minor scandal dubbed "Hair Force One." He received a $200 haircut from celeb stylist Christophe on *Air Force One*, reportedly shutting down two runways at Los Angeles International Airport for an hour, at an estimated cost to airlines of $76,000.

- George W. Bush has made plenty of grammatical gaffes, but one of his biggest missteps was when, believing his microphone was off, he turned to Vice President Dick Cheney and pointed out a reporter by calling him a "a major league a**hole." It's a good thing his mom Barbara Bush wasn't there, he'd have found his mouth filled with soap—in a major league way.

Abraham Lincoln was the only U.S. president to hold a patent on an invention.

SERENDIPITY SELECTS A PRESIDENT: THE ELECTION OF 1824

Fans of Uncle John's Great Big Bathroom Reader may remember this tale of the 1824 presidential election, when, depending on whose side you're on, good fortune or rotten stinking luck chose a president.

TIGHT SITUATION

The presidential election of 1824 was a four-way race. Andrew Jackson got the most votes—with John Quincy Adams close behind—but didn't receive a majority. That meant the election would be decided in the House of Representatives. According to law, the candidate with the most votes in each delegation would get the state's electoral vote.

The House met to pick a president on February 9, 1825. It was close, but Adams was the favorite. Although he'd come in second in the popular vote, he had put together almost enough support to win the presidency on the first ballot. However, if he *didn't* make it the first time around, his opponents felt sure that his support would begin slipping away. So the anti-Adams forces concentrated on keeping the election unresolved.

A CRUCIAL DECISION

As the vote approached, Adams was one state shy of victory, and there was only one state still undecided: New York. Their delegation was evenly split—half for Adams, half against. If it remained tied, New York's ballot wouldn't count, and the election would be forced into a second round. But there was a weak link in the anti-Adams camp. As Paul Boller writes in *Presidential Campaigns*:

> One of the New York votes [that anti-Adams forces] were counting on was that of General Stephen Van Rensselaer, the rich and pious Congressman from the Albany district ... The old General went to the Capitol on election day

---

In 1849, Lincoln was granted Patent No. 6469 for "A Device for Buoying Vessels over Shoals."

firmly resolved to vote against Adams, but on his arrival he was waylaid by Daniel Webster and Henry Clay. They took him into the Speaker's Room and painted a dismal picture of what would happen to the country if Adams wasn't chosen on the first ballot. Van Rensselaer was deeply upset by the encounter . . . "The election turns on my vote," he told a cohort. "*One* vote will give Adams the majority—this is a responsibility I cannot bear. What shall I do?"

His friend urged him to vote against Adams, as planned, and Van Rensselaer agreed. Boller continues:

But Van Rensselaer wasn't really resolved. He was still perplexed when he took his seat in the House Chamber. Profoundly religious, however, he decided to seek divine guidance while waiting to cast his [anti-Adams] ballot and bowed his head in prayer.

When he opened his eyes, the first thing he saw, lying on the floor, was a ballot with Adams's name on it. Van Rensselaer took this as a sign from God. He threw his other ballot away, picked the Adams ticket off the floor, and stuck it in the ballot box. As a result of this serendipitous moment, New York went for Adams, and "Adams was elected president on the first ballot."

★ ★ ★ ★ ★

PENNY FOR YOUR THOUGHTS?

Did you know that there are fifty-six steps to the top of the Lincoln Memorial, one step for each year that Lincoln lived? Most Americans carry a picture of this memorial in their pockets: it is depicted on the back of the penny, but you might be hard-pressed to count the steps there.

Thomas Jefferson walked to and from his inaugural ceremony.

A SITTING PRESIDENT'S MEMORIAL

FDR spent his entire presidency hiding the fact that he needed a wheelchair, and he wanted a memorial that would do the same. Future generations disagreed.

F our years before his death, Franklin Delano Roosevelt told Supreme Court Justice Felix Frankfurter that if he had to have a memorial, he wanted it to be about the size of his desk and placed on a patch of grass in front of the National Archives—anything more would be too showy and costly a remembrance (a granite tablet fitting this description was placed there in his honor in 1965). Frankfurter may have heard what FDR wanted, but Congress didn't seem to have been listening. One year after Roosevelt's death in 1945, Congress felt the need to commemorate him on a larger scale and passed a resolution authorizing the creation of a grander memorial, one comparable to the other presidential memorials located around the Tidal Basin. There was just one problem: FDR's wheelchair.

POWERFUL MAN, INVISIBLE CHAIR

Despite being completely unable to walk, President Roosevelt led the country out of the Great Depression and through World War II during his unprecedented four terms in office. He was the first disabled leader to be elected in American history, but most Americans of the 1930s and 1940s didn't even know their president required a wheelchair. They were aware that Roosevelt had contracted polio in 1921 and were under the impression that he wore braces or used a wheelchair occasionally for convenience. And that's just what FDR wanted them to believe because he was afraid that otherwise the world would perceive him as weak.

Roosevelt went to great lengths to deceive the public regarding his paralysis—he even created a method to make it appear he was walking. With his legs in locked braces, he would lean heavily on a cane with one hand and on someone else's hand with the

other. Then he'd swing each leg forward while leaning on the opposite hand, throwing his upper body forward. When he sat down the braces had to be unlocked. The braces caused Roosevelt to fall in public three different times, but the cooperative press never reported these incidents. In fact they never photographed him in his wheelchair at all. Of the 125,000 photos housed in the FDR library in Hyde Park, New York, only two private photos show the president seated in his wheelchair.

The Secret Service built permanent ramps at all the places he visited often. They'd get him into cars by putting his back to the door and helping him vault himself with the strength of his arms; so it would appear he was getting in on his own steam. The act even included events at the White House. Dinner guests were first escorted upstairs and greeted by FDR seated in front of drinks. Then Mrs. Roosevelt would lead them downstairs for a tour of the house. By the time they arrived in the dining room for dinner, FDR would already be seated in his chair, ready to eat. At outdoor receptions, gardeners would set up a tall seat, like a bicycle seat, for FDR to lean against and appear to be standing. Then they'd hide it with ferns. With all this help, Roosevelt managed to maintain his active image—both politically and in bearing, with a constant broad smile and a strong voice.

A WHEELCHAIR FOR EVERYONE TO SEE

More than fifty years after FDR's death, President Bill Clinton finally dedicated the FDR Memorial in 1997. Located between the Lincoln and Jefferson memorials along the famous Cherry Tree Walk surrounding the Tidal Basin, the memorial consists of a red South Dakota granite plaza with a series of outdoor galleries that each depict the chronological events of one of Roosevelt's four terms. Alcoves, shady trees, plants, and soft water cascades give the statues and educational engravings the feel of an expansive, reflective garden. The memorial includes a larger-than-life statue of Roosevelt covered with his characteristic cloak as he sits in a chair with an oversized sculpture of his beloved Scottie dog, Fala, beside him. If you look closely, you can see two tiny wheels in the back of the chair, just visible beneath the cloak's edge.

Theodore Roosevelt's 1901 inaugural oath was the only one not sworn on a Bible.

Even though the monument had officially opened, the controversy over FDR's wheelchair continued. By depicting the wheelchair subtly, rendering it almost invisible in the memorial, the FDR Memorial Commission decided to underplay the president's infirmity. They did this despite angry complaints that doing so was a denial of the achievements of people with disabilities and a harmful continuation of the fiction President Roosevelt felt forced to maintain because of the prevailing attitudes of his time. The commission and its supporters argued it would be wrong to revise history and portray what FDR went to such great lengths to actively hide from the world. Activists for the disabled argued that his tremendous achievements in spite of his condition couldn't be properly celebrated or understood without accurately portraying it. Many observers pointed out that the fight was largely symbolic: FDR was one of the greatest American presidents and potentially the greatest hero disabled Americans ever had. A memorial recognizing FDR's own private struggle with his paralysis could never undermine the greatness of his personal and public achievements.

After six years of protests and debate, groups championing those with disabilities finally won approval from the National Park Service to add a new statue, and they raised $1.65 million to do it. Placed near the entrance of the memorial in July 1998, the life-size, bronze statue features FDR sitting in the wheelchair he himself designed and lived in for more than twenty years. In this statue the president wears his customary fedora and gazes upward. Positioned low enough so that those in wheelchairs can touch it, the statue is the first ever to depict a world leader seated in a wheelchair.

★　★　★　★　★

SOCKS-ESS STORY

In 1991, Chelsea Clinton found a black-and-white kitty underneath the porch of her piano teacher and took him home to be the family pet. The cat, christened Socks after his four white paws, became a White House inhabitant when Chelsea's dad became president. In 1999, the 25th Annual Westchester Cat Show nominated Socks for Cat of the Year for "elevating the status of the feline as a household pet."

Ronald Reagan saved 77 people when he worked as a lifeguard.

NUMBER TWELVE:
ZACHARY TAYLOR

Served from 1849 to 1850

Vital Stats: Born on November 24, 1784, in Orange County, Virginia. Died on July 9, 1850, in Washington, DC.
Age at Inauguration: 64
Vice President: Millard Fillmore
Political Affiliation: Whig
Wife: Margaret Mackall Smith (married 1810)
Kids: Anne Margaret Mackall (1811–1875); Sarah Knox (1814–1835); Octavia Pannill (1816–1820); Margaret Smith (1819–1820); Mary Elizabeth (1824–1909); Richard (1826–1879)
Education: Private tutors
What he did before he was president: Farmer; Soldier: Rose from 1st Lieutenant to Major General in the U.S. Army (1808–1849)
Postpresidential Occupations: None (died in office)

MEMORABLE QUOTES

"I will engage in no schemes—no combinations, no intrigues. If the American people have not confidence in me they ought not to give me their suffrages—If they do not, you know me well enough to believe me when I declare that I shall be content—I am too old a soldier to murmur against such high authority."
—Zachary Taylor in a letter offering himself as a presidential candidate, April 22, 1848

"The appointing power vested in the President imposes delicate and onerous duties. So far as it is possible to be informed, I shall make honesty, capacity, and fidelity indispensable prerequisites to the bestowal of office, and the absence of either of these qualities shall be deemed sufficient cause for removal."
—Zachary Taylor in his inaugural address, March 5, 1849

NUMBER THIRTEEN: MILLARD FILLMORE

Served from 1850 to 1853

Vital Stats: Born on January 7, 1800, in Cayuga County, New York. Died on March 8, 1874, in Buffalo, New York.
Age at Inauguration: 50
Vice President: None
Political Affiliation: Whig
First Wife: Abigail Powers (married 1826. died 1853)
Kids from first marriage: Millard Powers (1828–1889); Mary Abigail (1832–1854)
Second Wife: Caroline Carmichael McIntosh (married 1858)
Kids from second marriage: None
Education: Some formal schooling. Studied law in Cayuga County and Buffalo, New York.
What he did before he was president: Lawyer; U.S. Congressman; U.S. Vice President
Postpresidential Occupations: Politician; Chancellor of the University of Buffalo

MEMORABLE QUOTES

"These are the only objects for which I have sent Commodore Perry, with a powerful squadron, to pay a visit to your imperial majesty's renowned city of Yedo: friendship, commerce, a supply of coal and provisions, and protection for our shipwrecked people."
—President Fillmore's letter to the Japanese Emperor, July 1853

"I have not the advantage of a classical education and no man should, in my judgment, accept a degree he cannot read."
—Millard Fillmore declines an honorary degree from Oxford University, 1855

President Garfield juggled Indian clubs to build his muscles.

ILL-STARRED SON

*Robert Todd Lincoln not only had the great misfortune of
losing his father to an assassin's bullet, but he also had the ill luck
to be present when two other presidents fell.*

I t barely seems possible for a single person to be closely connected with three presidential assassinations, given that there
have only been four in the nation's history. However Robert
Todd Lincoln, son of Abraham Lincoln, had this unlucky distinction. He was either present at or quickly arrived at the scenes of the
killings of his own father, James Garfield, and William McKinley.
And if you accept the stretch, he could be distantly associated with
the fourth: Robert Lincoln was buried in Arlington National
Cemetery, which would also become Kennedy's final resting place.

THE FIRST ONE

On the morning of his assassination, Abraham Lincoln had breakfast with his son, Captain Robert Lincoln, recently returned from
the battlefields of the Civil War. Robert E. Lee had surrendered at
Appomattox Courthouse, Virginia, only five days before, an event
at which Robert Lincoln had been present. He had even been
introduced to General Robert E. Lee. At breakfast Robert and
Abe talked about the war, about a picture of Lee that Robert had
with him, and about the "era of good feeling" that the president
saw blooming for the United States in the early 1865 spring. The
Lincolns were attending the theater that night to see the play *Our
American Cousin*; possibly Robert was invited to come along, but
he declined the invitation.

That fateful evening John Wilkes Booth shot President
Lincoln in the back of the head and leapt from the Lincolns' box
to the stage and a temporary escape. After hearing about the incident, a guard at the White House tracked down Robert, who had
spent the evening with his friend John Hay, then a private secretary to the president. The guard informed them that something
terrible had happened to the president. Robert and Hay rushed
immediately to the theater, where their way was blocked. Robert

desperately shouted, "It's my father! My father! I'm Robert Lincoln!" and was finally let through. President Lincoln was being kept in a small room, surrounded by friends, family, and government officials. As the night passed, the president's health slipped away, and by the next morning he was dead. At age twenty-one Robert had become the head of the Lincoln family.

In a bizarre coincidence Robert Lincoln's life had been saved shortly before his father's assassination by Edwin Booth, the brother of Abraham's assassin. The incident occurred in Jersey City while Robert was traveling from New York to Washington. He was standing in the late evening on an overcrowded train platform filled with people purchasing space in the sleeping car. The crowd pushed so hard that he was pressed up against the side of the stopped train. While he was stuck there, the train began to move and spun Lincoln off his feet. He had started to fall into the small space between the platform and the moving train when his coat collar was suddenly grabbed by Edwin, who yanked him back up to safety on the platform. Neither Robert nor Edwin ever forgot the incident, and Edwin was able to take some solace in it after his brother's deplorable crime.

THE SECOND ONE

Under President James Garfield, Robert Lincoln was appointed the secretary of war. Lincoln had been practicing law very successfully in Chicago when he was tapped for the job. Only a few months after beginning his service under President Garfield, he and a few other secretaries were to accompany the president on a trip from Washington, DC, to see Garfield's ailing wife in Elberon, New Jersey. On the train platform, the disgruntled and mentally ill office seeker Charles Guiteau shot Garfield in the back. There was a great commotion and shouts that the president had been shot. Lincoln came running and found the ashen-faced president lying on his back. Lincoln sent his driver to find a doctor and stayed with the fallen president. Garfield's color returned, his eyes opened, and he reached out calmly for Lincoln's hand. Lincoln would later say of Garfield's calm that it made him the coolest man in the crowd.

In the days that followed, Lincoln fielded countless inquiries about Garfield's condition and, like the other members of the cab-

---

Jefferson ate meat only "as a condiment to the vegetables which constitute my principal diet."

inet, ran the War Department and assured the ailing Garfield that nothing required his attention. In public Lincoln stated that he thought the president would recover, but in private he gave voice to his doubts. Two and a half months later, Garfield died. Lincoln submitted his resignation to incoming president Chester A. Arthur, who refused to accept it. Lincoln graciously continued to serve until the end of Arthur's term.

THE THIRD ONE
In 1901 the Pan-American Exposition in Buffalo, New York, attracted visitors from all over the world. Robert Lincoln, now president of the Pullman Company, a manufacturer of luxury railroad cars, was no exception. As he and his family exited the train in Buffalo, they heard the news that President McKinley had been shot. McKinley had been greeting a crowd of people all trying to shake his hand when anarchist Leon Czolgosz shot him. Lincoln went directly to visit the wounded president, who died eight days later.

AVOIDING A FOURTH ONE
In the years to follow, Lincoln repeatedly declined invitations to events where the current president would be appearing. Despite all he had been through, though, Lincoln, managed to keep a sense of humor about the subject and was heard to say that "there is a certain fatality about presidential functions when I am present."

★   ★   ★   ★   ★

CARTER'S CULPABILITY COMMENTS
"I personally think that he did violate the law, that he committed impeachable offenses. But I don't think that he thinks he did."
—President Jimmy Carter on former President Nixon, 1977

PRESIDENT FOR A DAY?

Were there really forty-four presidents or is the claim that David Rice Atchison was in charge for a day just full of hot air?

Born on August 11, 1807, in a place named Frogtown, Kentucky (today known as Kirklevington), David Rice Atchison was just a senator from Missouri. But one Kansas City, Missouri, statue dedicated to him has an inscription that reads, "David Rice Atchison, 1807-1886, President of the U.S. [for] one day." The day of President Atchison's presumed presidency occurred on March 4, 1849. This would then make Atchison our twelfth president, falling between James K. Polk and Zachary Taylor. Do we have one more U.S. president than we thought we did?

SUNDAY MORNING, STEPPING DOWN

At age thirty-six, Atchison was appointed to the U.S. Senate to replace a Missouri senator who had died. The Democratic senator remained in office from 1843 to 1855. Well-respected, his colleagues elected him president pro tempore on thirteen occasions. The president pro tempore's job? Why, to fill in for the vice president when he was not in attendance of Senate sessions. Consequently the Senate chose a president pro tempore to serve only during brief vice-presidential absences.

The year 1849 was an unusual one for the presidency. First James Polk, the outgoing president, was stepping down rather than running for reelection after what had been a successful term in office. Polk would be stepping down at noon on inauguration day. The second reason it was unusual was that inauguration day, March 4, fell on a Sunday that year, a relatively rare occasion. President-elect Zachary Taylor, a devout Christian, refused to be sworn in on his Sabbath and insisted on waiting until the following day. Thus the question arose: who acted as president from noon on March 4 until the following day's inauguration?

Vice President George M. Dallas had resigned on Friday, March 2nd. If the president were removed from office and there were no vice president to step up, back then the powers of the

. . . former president Ronald Reagan. There were 28 lines devoted to his wife, Nancy.

presidency went to the president pro tempore of the Senate. (Nowadays, thanks to the Presidential Succession Act of 1947, the Speaker of the House comes after the veep.) Senator Atchison was technically the next in line, right?

THE VACANT CHAIR

While it would be awfully fun to think that someone had held such a powerful office for such a short time, it seems that no one actually did. In 1849 nothing in the Constitution specified when a president's term officially began and ended (The Thirty-third Amendment does that now); so even though Polk had stepped down at noon on March 4, Taylor technically stepped up into his new office. Also, nothing in the Constitution says that a president-elect must be sworn in before officially becoming president; he must only take the oath of office before executing the powers of the presidency.

Another major point is that Atchison was technically no longer president pro tempore of the Senate on March 4, 1849. The Thirtieth Congress, whose session closed at midnight on March 3, had appointed Atchison to that role. But the office of president pro tempore didn't carry over from one session of Congress to the next. No one was president pro tempore on Sunday, March 4.

THE DEBATE GOES ON

Many, including Atchison, continued to question whether or not he was actually president. Atchison did polish his own legend though and called his administration the "honestest" the country had ever had. When asked what he did on this day, Atchison commented, "I went to bed. There had been two or three busy nights finishing up the work of the Senate, and I slept most of that Sunday." At least he was honest.

WANT A RIDE?

"When they fly you on Air Force One,
you know you're the president."
—Gerald Ford, 1974

So much more than a 1997 movie starring Harrison Ford, *Air Force One* is the vehicle that jets the American president all over the world in comfort and safety. Hearing the name typically brings to mind a picture of a massive blue and white airplane emblazoned with the presidential seal alongside its nose and the American flag tattooed on its tail. But Uncle John has gone inside to get you the scoop on the president's sweet ride.

THE PRESIDENT CAN FLY

Franklin Roosevelt, who was the first acting president to fly on any type of aircraft, was also the very first president to commission a fleet of planes for his exclusive use. Roosevelt flew on a modified C-54 Skymaster that was known as the *Sacred Cow.* Later, President Truman flew on the *Independence* and Ike liked *Columbine II* and *Columbine III.* So how did we get from the colorful *Sacred Cow* and *Independence* to the more official-sounding moniker?

Air Force One is actually the call sign for any air force plane that has the president on board. (The vice president's plane is called, you guessed it, *Air Force Two.*) The name came into use in the 1950s after an Eastern Airlines aircraft and President Dwight D. Eisenhower's plane entered the same air space with the same exact call sign. *Air Force One* now refers only to the president's plane. In fact Richard Nixon was flying cross-country on *Air Force One* when his formal resignation was read and Gerald Ford was sworn in as president. The call sign for Nixon's plane was changed midflight—the moment he ceased to be president.

THE PLANES BEHIND THE NAME

A mental picture of the most famous presidential transport is probably the first airplane to be popularly known as *Air Force One*: a Boeing 707, tail number 26000, which carried John F. Kennedy.

Wanting an external design to reflect the spirit of America, Kennedy actually commissioned the paint scheme for the exterior of SAM 26000 (SAM stands for Special Air Missions and was the commonly used prefix for the plane). He hired Raymond Loewy, the man responsible for the design of the Coca-Cola bottle, to come up with the plane's new look. SAM 26000 was the first jet-propelled aircraft designated for exclusive use by the president. The interior of this plane served as the backdrop for Lyndon Johnson's being sworn in as president after Kennedy's death. SAM 26000 officially retired in 1998. It can now be seen on display at the U.S. Air Force Museum on Wright-Patterson Air Force Base near Dayton, Ohio.

Even though SAM 26000 remained in service, its twin 27000 took over as the primary presidential aircraft at the end of Nixon's first term; SAM 27000 retired in August 2001 and was replaced by two specially configured Boeing 747-200B aircraft, tail numbers 28000 and 29000, which currently serve the president.

NO SIDE AIRBAGS BUT . . .

Air Force One is generally considered to be the safest aircraft in the world. The plane can travel at speeds of up to 630 miles an hour, can reach heights of 45,100 feet, and has a range of 7,800 miles. It can fly halfway around the world before refueling but can also be refueled in flight. The plane is equipped with antimissile defenses, and all the wiring and electronic equipment is shielded from the possible effects of an electromagnetic pulse. Surprisingly enough *Air Force One* is not equipped with parachutes because the huge slipstream it creates would render them useless.

THIS PLACE HAS GOT EVERYTHING

Air Force One is truly a presidential home away from home. The plane can carry up to 70 passengers plus 23 crew members. There are two galleys on board that can serve up to 100 gourmet meals at a time. The president can relax and work in style in the executive suite that includes a bedroom, a bathroom, and an "Oval Office." There is a workout room, a conference room/dining room, as well as office space for the senior staff. One office can even be converted into a medical facility if necessary. The press has its own

work and rest area! There are 19 televisions and 85 telephones, which can be set up for normal air-to-ground connections, as well as for secure communications. Maybe the only thing *Air Force One* doesn't have is an ornamental fountain—which King Fahd of Saudi Arabia is reported to have on his private aircraft. If the plane did have a fountain, you can bet the presidential seal would be on it. It adorns everything else on board: seat belt buckles, shaving kits, pillows, blankets, towels, cups, and even window shades.

Air Force One is aptly referred to as the Flying White House, and like the White House, the interior typically changes with each administration. Presidents have special amenities installed or spaces rearranged to suit them. Johnson rearranged the seats to face the rear of the aircraft toward the president's quarters, supposedly so he could keep a better eye on the passengers. He also had a large desk and chair put in that could rise or sink at the touch of a button. When Nixon took office, he sent the aircraft back to the Boeing factory for a major overhaul. Many of the features of Johnson's plane were simply redesigned. But Nixon also eliminated a few—like a tape-recording system that recorded all incoming and outgoing calls.

★　　★　　★　　★　　★

IKE GOES UNDER

Although Dwight Eisenhower had submerged two times in a submarine before, he was the first president to ride in an atomic-powered submarine. On September 26, 1957, President Eisenhower was aboard the *Seawolf* when it dove sixty feet below the surface of the ocean and stayed there for fifteen minutes. Before the voyage ended, Eisenhower addressed the crew: "Everything was of interest to me—all of the gadgets and the machines . . . It's a memorable experience. I hope to see you all again. Thank you all for making this trip so pleasant."

NUMBER FOURTEEN: FRANKLIN PIERCE

Served from 1853 to 1857

Vital Stats: Born on November 23, 1804, in Hillsboro, New Hampshire. Died on October 8, 1869, in Concord, New Hampshire.
Age at Inauguration: 48
Vice President: William Rufus King
Political Affiliation: Democratic
Wife: Jane Means Appleton (married 1834)
Kids: Franklin (b. and d. 1836); Frank Robert (1839–1843); Benjamin (1841–1853)
Education: Bowdoin College
What he did before he was president: Lawyer; Soldier; Brigadier General in the U.S. Army; U.S. Congressman; U.S. Senator
Postpresidential Occupations: Retired

MEMORABLE QUOTE

"With an experience thus suggestive and cheering, the policy of my Administration will not be controlled by any timid forebodings of evil from expansion. Indeed, it is not to be disguised that our attitude as a nation and our position on the globe render the acquisition of certain possessions not within our jurisdiction eminently important for our protection, if not in the future essential for the preservation of the rights of commerce and the peace of the world.

"Should they be obtained, it will be through no grasping spirit, but with a view to obvious national interest and security, and in a manner entirely consistent with the strictest observance of national faith."
—Franklin Pierce's inaugural address, March 4, 1853

CLOSE CALLS II

Just imagine—the Great Depression without Fireside Chats.
A Cold War with no Truman Doctrine. It almost happened.

I f not for bad aim and bad planning, two of the shapers of the twentieth century might never have had the chance.

GIUSEPPE ZANGARA: FRANKLIN D. ROOSEVELT
In 1932 Franklin D. Roosevelt was elected president for the first time. The country was mired in the midst of the Great Depression, war was brewing in Europe, and Roosevelt's supporters saw him as the hope of the nation. It is no surprise then that ten thousand people showed up in Miami's Bay Front Park on February 15, 1933, to hear the president-elect speak. The planned speech was short, though, so much of the press didn't bother to attend.

FDR rose from his open car and spoke for less than a minute, telling a few fishing jokes, and sat down again. As he sat back down, Giuseppe Zangara, a barely 5-foot-tall Italian immigrant, jumped onto a rickety wooden chair and fired five shots toward the car, hitting five bystanders, but missing Roosevelt completely.

A Real Lifesaver
Who or what could have saved Roosevelt? Depending on whose story you believe, it was either a housewife or a rickety chair. Mrs. W. F. Cross, who was standing on a chair next to Zangara, claimed to have forced his arm up. She was close enough to the muzzle of the gun for powder to burn her face, but Zangara insisted no woman grabbed him. Thomas Armour, standing behind Zangara, claimed to have grabbed him after the first shot was fired. The press immediately named the 100-pound housewife, Cross, as the president's savior, but Armour wanted his share of the limelight. As Cross continued to get radio appearances and accolades, Armour sent avalanches of affidavits and witness testimonials to Congress demanding that he be given the Congressional Medal of Honor. Witness accounts vary—some saw Cross grab Zangara, some say she strangled him, some say she just fell off her chair and

knocked into him. Zangara said no one interfered while he was shooting; the chair shook and spoiled his aim.

Shortly after the shots were fired, police jumped on top of Zangara, but an angry crowd seemed intent on doing him harm. Afraid the crowd would beat Zangara to death, policemen cuffed him to the trunk rack of a car and drove him to prison. Roosevelt waved to the crowd, to assure them he was okay. Unfortunately, Mayor Anton Cermak of Chicago had been hit in the abdomen. In critical condition, Cermak was taken to the hospital

Just five days after the shooting, Zangara was tried and sentenced to eighty years. When he heard this, Zangara said, "Oh, judge, don't be stingy. Give me hundred years!" Perhaps he should have kept quiet. But Zangara tempted fate, who quickly responded. Mayor Cermak died of his wounds and Zangara went back on trial for murder this time.

Back On Trial

The mayor's death put Zangara back on trial. This time, it was for murder. Even his defense lawyers seemed eager to convict him. One of his attorneys even advocated the electric chair in his closing. The judge took this under advisement and sentenced Zangara to death.

In the press, conspiracy theories abounded. Zangara was a Fascist, an anti-Fascist terrorist, a Communist, a Socialist, an anarchist. He'd sent letter bombs, and tried to kill Italian dictator Benito Mussolini. Some even believed he was a hit man hired by the Chicago mob to kill Cermak. Zangara denied all this. He was part of no groups, believed in no religion, and had come up with his idea to kill the president all by himself.

Born in southern Italy in 1900, Zangara was pulled from school by his father and forced to do hard labor at six years old. Ever since then he suffered from a burning pain in his stomach that he blamed on the capitalists that sent him to work. He served in the Italian army and claims to have tried to kill King Victor Emmanuel III of Italy. He failed because he was too short to see over the guards. He immigrated to the United States and became a naturalized citizen. In 1933 he bought a gun intent on killing president Hoover in Washington. When he saw in the papers that

FDR would appear in Miami, he decided to kill Roosevelt instead. Either way he figured he was getting even for his stomach pain.

Zangara was executed fewer than five weeks after he jumped on a chair in Miami's Bay Front Park—the swiftest legal execution in twentieth-century America. When taken to the electric chair, he became enraged that there were no photographers there to immortalize his death. His last words are reported to be, "Go ahead! Push the button!"

OSCAR COLLAZO AND GRISELIO TORRESOLA: HARRY S. TRUMAN

Oscar Collazo and Griselio Torresola were born (twelve years apart) in the same small town in Puerto Rico. Collazo moved to New York when he was twelve, working there in later years to help immigrants from Puerto Rico learn English and settle into their new home. Torresola moved to New York in 1948, when he was twenty-one and lived mostly in poverty. They knew each other, but were not friends. They had only one thing in common: a firm belief in Puerto Rican independence.

The Nationalist Party of Puerto Rico staged a revolt on October 30, 1950. The insurrection was quickly put down, but Collazo and Torresola decided that the revolt signified a time to help the cause. Originally planning to travel to Puerto Rico, Collazo decided that the real problem was the American press. Most Americans didn't know where Puerto Rico was, or that the independence movement was fighting against American imperialism, not just their own government. Collazo convinced Torresola that they needed to gain the attention of the press so they could publicize their cause. And in America, there's one sure way to get everyone's attention— kill the president.

Targeting Truman

Torresola bought a gun for Collazo, who had never fired one before, and they traveled to Washington. Totally unfamiliar with the town, they hired a cabbie to show them Blair House, the president's temporary residence while the White House was being remodeled. They knew nothing of the president's schedule or of his security, but they were undeterred.

On November 1, President Truman lay down for his customary after-lunch nap. Oscar Collazo, without the benefit of the glasses he needed, approached Blair House and fired on the guard, only he forgot to remove the safety. Private Birdzell, the White House guard, heard the click and looked up to see the barrel of a semiautomatic gun. He ran out into the street to draw fire away from the house. Collazo struggled with the safety, and the gun accidentally went off, shooting Birdzell in the leg. As other guards rushed forward, Torresola swooped in from the west, killing a guard before he himself was killed. Collazo was shot in the chest while trying to reload but survived the encounter.

Truman awoke to the sounds of battle on the front lawn and looked out his window. A policeman yelled at him to get back. In a few seconds it was over: one policeman dead, two more injured, and the surviving assailant in custody. It certainly drew the attention of the press—a carful of photographers from the Associated Press, who were less than a block away at the time, filled the papers with lurid photos of the attack.

Not the Best Laid Plans

In retrospect, Collazo and Torresola's assault was remarkably ill conceived. If they had only waited a half an hour, President Truman would have walked right past them on his way back to work. As it was, they would have had to shoot past twenty guards to reach the president.

Collazo was found guilty of the murder of the guard and sentenced to death, but President Truman commuted his sentence to life imprisonment. Jimmy Carter again commuted Collazo's sentence to time already served in 1979, freeing the sixty-four-year-old assassin. Collazo appeared before a cheering crowd in front of the United Nations building in New York, announcing that he would continue to fight for Puerto Rican independence. He returned to Puerto Rico, and shortly thereafter, Puerto Rican Nationalists attacked a U.S. Navy bus, killing two and wounding ten others. This was the first attack on American personnel in more than ten years. Coincidence or Collazo?

WHAT A SWELL PARTY THIS IS!

*A little bored of the major political parties?
Here are some wacky alternatives that might tickle your fancy.*

You may not know it, but there are plenty of other options out there besides the usual Democrats, Greens, Libertarians, Reformers, and Republicans. Uncle John has done some serious research on some not-so-serious political parties. Have a look!

PARTY NAME: American Beer Drinkers Party
MOTTO: "America's premium political party, committed to the ideology founded on the simple logic, developed when men (& women) sit down, talk, and have a beer."
FOUNDED IN: 1997, by two guys at the Around the Corner bar in Lakewood, Ohio.
PLATFORM: While exuberantly in favor of both the Iraq war and Bush's tax cuts, the party has yet to issue an official platform. (The rough draft is illegibly scrawled on a buffalo wing sauce-smudged bar napkin.) Instead they offer us this bit of wisdom: "On most issues, both sides are wrong, and even if one side seems right, they probably have ulterior motives."
MEMBERSHIP: Just visit their web site to sign up. It's free and only takes a few steps: "1. Go to your fridge. 2. Get a Beer. 3. Open it. 4. Enjoy. 5. Click on 'Membership Card' below. 6. Right Click and Select 'Save Picture As . . . ' 7. Print out, cut and proudly put in your wallet. 8. That's it."
ORGANIZATION: Central Committee: Buddy Pilsner (Chairman, Dictator, Co-Founder), Thirsty Lager (Vice Chairman & Chief Financial Officer), and Malt Liquor (Co-Founder).
ELECTION HISTORY: Have yet to field a candidate.

PARTY NAME: The Birthday Party
MOTTO: "Live and let live is the Birthdayan way."

. . . The Sherwood Forest Plantation is still owned by the Tyler family.

FOUNDED IN: 1999, by R.J. Sargent and Tyson Schritter, two students from Highland High School in Pocatello, Idaho. The party was created on February 12, Lincoln's Birthday, hence the party's name.

PLATFORM: While stressing personal freedom and small government, their actual platform is very specific to high school, where football tends to dominate life: "We want all activities to be recognized equally."

MEMBERSHIP: N/A

ORGANIZATION: N/A

ELECTION HISTORY: In the 2000 student body election at Highland High, the Birthday Party almost swept, winning 16 of 18 possible seats.

PARTY NAME: The Pansexual Peace Party

MOTTO: "An it harm none, do as thou wilt."

FOUNDED IN: c. 1996

PLATFORM: "To promote positive political progress and the partnership paradigm through prurient propaganda . . . The basic underlying ethic is maximization of peace, freedom, creative expression, and the glorification of human sexuality." This Wiccan-based party is pro-hemp, pro-women's rights, and unabashedly pro-sex: "Sex is good! Sex is great! Yea, Sex!"

MEMBERSHIP: The party boasts 444 members.

ORGANIZATION: There is intentionally no hierarchical structure to the party.

ELECTION HISTORY: Have yet to field any candidates.

PARTY NAME: The Feline Party

MOTTO: "Instead of donkeys or elephants, vote for cats!"

FOUNDED IN: c. 2001

PLATFORM: The candidates' owner states, "today I ask for *peace toward all creatures*. Cats, dogs, birds, fish, kangaroos, everyone." The cats are prorecycling and decidedly self-sacrificing, advocating the spaying and neutering of pets.

MEMBERSHIP: Cats Tabby and Goldie seem to be the only party members— it's not clear whether humans can join.

ELECTION HISTORY: In the 2004 election, Tabby is a write-in candidate for president, with his litter mate Goldie also doubling as his running mate.

PARTY NAME: The Guns and Dope Party
MOTTO: "Like what you like, enjoy what you enjoy, don't be afraid to make slurping sounds, and don't take crap from anybody."
FOUNDED IN: N/A
PLATFORM: The party advocates: "1. Guns for those who want them, no guns forced on those who don't want them (pacfists [sic], Quakers etc.); 2. Drugs for those who want them, no drugs forced on those who don't want them (Christian Scientists etc.); 3. An end to Tsarism and a return to constitutional democracy; 4. Equal rights for ostriches." Their first act upon entering office would be to fire one third of Congress and replace them with ostriches, "whose mysterious and awesome dignity will elevate the . . . barbarity long established there."
MEMBERSHIP: N/A
ELECTION HISTORY: Have not fielded a candidate. The party suggests you write in your own name.

PARTY NAME: The Monster Raving Loony Party
MOTTO: "Insanity . . . It makes perfect sense."
FOUNDED IN: 1963, by English rocker Screaming Lord Sutch.
PLATFORM: Intent on spurring people to action by making them laugh, the MRLP proposes programs such as the Federal Approaching Hurricane Relief Team (FAHRT), in which everyone near the coast is given a fan, so they can collectively blow hurricanes back out to sea.
MEMBERSHIP: $10.00 for a lifetime membership
ELECTION HISTORY: The American wing of the party has yet to score a victory. However, in England—where the party actually fields candidates with names like Flash Gordon Approaching and Dancing Ken Hanks—it's a different story: history was made in 2001 when Loony candidate Alan Hope won a council seat in Devon.

NEGATIVE REVIEWS

Political campaigns get down and dirty on television.

Turn on the TV during an election year and you'll be faced with a slew of political advertisements. Maybe the ads are positive, sticking to the issues and communicating just why you need to vote for this person or that one. But chances are most ads seen and remembered are the negative ones—the nasty, sniping attacks meant to discredit the "other guy" and sway voters to the opposing side.

It may seem like there are more negative ads than ever before, but the advent of TV did not create them. Even George Washington at one time had to deal with accusations that he had an affair with a washerwoman's daughter. (Going negative doesn't always work: Washington would win his first presidential election unanimously.) But TV has given negative campaigning its broadest reach.

GOING NEGATIVE ON THE AIR
Republican candidate Dwight Eisenhower ran the first presidential TV ads in 1952, and the first negative presidential ad appeared just four years later in 1956. That year President Eisenhower's opponent, Adlai E. Stevenson, attempted to show in a TV ad how Eisenhower had not followed through on a pledge to keep corruption out of the White House. Voters still reelected Eisenhower that year, so the first foray into negative TV advertising wasn't a success.

DAISY DROPS THE BOMB
Years later Lyndon Johnson's advisers created probably the most famous and successful negative ad. The 1964 "Daisy" commercial became an icon of President Lyndon B. Johnson's run against his Republican opponent, Barry Goldwater. It showed a little girl counting the petals of a daisy as she plucked them. Then a narrator's voice started counting backward from ten, as is done in a rocket or missile launch. When the narrator reached one, the

camera zoomed in to a close-up of the girl's face before cutting to a picture of a nuclear explosion and mushroom cloud. Johnson's voice is then heard saying, "The stakes of the election are high."

The thrust of the ad was to imply that Goldwater—who had said, "I'd love to lob an A-bomb into the men's room at the Kremlin"—could not be trusted with the awesome nuclear responsibility that comes with being president. Surprisingly the Democrats only ran the ad once because it was so controversial. However TV news programs seized the controversy and replayed "Daisy" so many times that about forty million Americans ended up seeing it. Johnson went on to win the 1964 election by a landslide.

BUSH BEATS ON DUKAKIS
Another memorable negative ad was the "Willie Horton" ad that Republican presidential candidate George H. W. Bush ran against Massachusetts governor and Democratic presidential nominee Michael Dukakis in 1988. Willie Horton was a convicted murderer who, shortly after being furloughed from a Massachusetts prison, kidnapped and raped a woman. The Bush camp ran ads showing a line of convicts going into a prison via one door but coming out another. It did not mention the name of Willie Horton at all, but because the Horton case had been greatly discussed in the press, viewers watching the ad no doubt thought of him. The ad was the Republican way of saying that Dukakis's criminal justice policy in Massachusetts was nothing but a revolving door and soft on crime. (It did not mention the fact that the state's furlough policy was set up by Dukakis's Republican predecessor.) The damage was done, and Bush won the election convincingly.

WHY GO NEGATIVE?
Some political strategists use negative campaigning as a way of steering the debate away from meatier, more important issues. Political observers, pointing to the decline in voter turnout, say that mean and nasty advertising can cause many in the electorate to throw up their hands in disgust and decide not to participate. Some political managers use this to their advantage if they think their candidate might fare better with a smaller voter turnout.

They hardly worry at all if their ads make voters so disheartened and apathetic that they stay home on Election Day.

But the most obvious reasons are the ones that keep negative advertisements on the air. It is widely accepted by those who manage political campaigns that negative ads often work well. They are the ads that evoke the most emotion; they are the ads that charge up one's supporters; they are the ads that people remember. Especially near the end of a campaign, if a candidate is trailing by a large margin, turning to negative advertising always offers one last chance at catching up. But candidates need to be wary of being too negative: studies show that excessive, mean-spirited attacks as well as false and misleading negative ads can derail a campaign and doom a candidacy.

★　★　★　★　★

NON-PARTISAN POLITICS

Democrat Woodrow Wilson had great things to say about Republican Abraham Lincoln.

"A great nation is not led by a man who simply repeats the talk of the street-corners or the opinions of the newspapers. A nation is led by a man who . . . hearing those things, understands them better, unites them, puts them into a common meaning; speaks, not the rumors of the street, but a new principle for a new age; a man in whose ears the voices of the nation . . . [are] concurrent and concordant like the united voices of a chorus, whose many meanings, spoken by melodious tongues, unite in his understanding . . . and reveal to him a single vision, so that he can speak what no man else knows, the common meaning of the common voice. Such is the man who leads a great, free, democratic nation."

—Woodrow Wilson, "Abraham Lincoln: A Man of the People," February 12, 1909

George Washington loved crabmeat soup and his favorite drink was eggnog.

NUMBER FIFTEEN: JAMES BUCHANAN

Served from 1857 to 1861

Vital Stats: Born on April 23, 1791, in Cove Gap, Pennsylvania. Died on June 1, 1868, in Lancaster, Pennsylvania.
Age at Inauguration: 65
Vice President: John C. Breckenridge
Political Affiliation: Democratic
Wife: None
Education: Dickinson College
What he did before he was president: Lawyer; Member of the Pennsylvania Legislature; U.S. Congressman; Minister to Russia; U.S. Senator; Secretary of State; Minister to Great Britain
Postpresidential Occupations: Retired

MEMORABLE QUOTES

"Having determined not to become a candidate for reelection, I shall have no motive to influence my conduct in administering the Government except the desire ably and faithfully to serve my country and to live in grateful memory of my countrymen."
—James Buchanan in his inaugural address, March 4, 1857

"As a natural consequence, Congress has also prescribed that when the Territory of Kansas shall be admitted as a State it 'shall be received into the Union with or without slavery, as their constitution may prescribe at the time of their admission.' A difference of opinion has arisen in regard to the point of time when the people of a Territory shall decide this question for themselves. This is, happily, a matter of but little practical importance."
—James Buchanan in his inaugural address, March 4, 1857

SWEARIN' AND SPEECHIFYIN'

The ins and outs of Inauguration Day.

SWEAR ME IN ALREADY!

- The oath of office is found at the end of Article II, Section 1, of the U.S. Constitution. After taking the oath at his 1789 inauguration, George Washington added, "So help me, God" to the end. Every subsequent president has followed his example and added that phrase too.

- Each president takes the oath of office with one hand placed on a Bible open to a passage of his choosing. No two presidents have chosen the same passage.

- Calvin Coolidge was sworn in by a notary public and justice of the peace on August 3, 1923, after Warren Harding's death. The man doing the swearing was also his father, John Calvin Coolidge.

- Sarah Tilghman Hughes, district judge of the North District of Texas, is the only woman to have administered the oath. She swore in President Lyndon Johnson after the Kennedy assassination.

I'D LIKE TO SAY A FEW WORDS . . .

- The shortest inaugural address was George Washington's second at just 135 words The longest? Why, that honor belongs to William Henry Harrison whose long speech (8,495 words) foretold nothing about his short term of office (only 30 days!).

- Five presidents (Tyler, Fillmore, Andrew Johnson, Arthur, and Ford) did not give inaugural addresses. They weren't suffering from performance anxiety; they were just taking over for a deceased or resigned president and only served out that one term.

JEFFERSON UNIFIES
"But every difference of opinion is not a difference of principle. We have called by different names brethren of the same principle. We are all Republicans, we are all Federalists. If there be any among us who would wish to dissolve this Union or to change its republican form, let them stand undisturbed as monuments of the safety with which error of opinion may be tolerated where reason is left free to combat it."
—Thomas Jefferson's first inaugural address, March 4, 1801

FDR FIGHTS A WAR
"On each national day of inauguration since 1789, the people have renewed their sense of dedication to the United States. In Washington's day the task of the people was to create and weld together a nation. In Lincoln's day the task of the people was to preserve that Nation from disruption from within. In this day the task of the people is to save that Nation and its institutions from disruption from without.

"To us there has come a time, in the midst of swift happenings, to pause for a moment and take stock—to recall what our place in history has been, and to rediscover what we are and what we may be. If we do not, we risk the real peril of inaction."
—Franklin Roosevelt's third inaugural address, March 4, 1941

THE GIPPER LOOKS AHEAD
"These will be years when Americans have restored their confidence and tradition of progress; when our values of faith, family, work, and neighborhood were restated for a modern age; when our economy was finally freed from government's grip; when we made sincere efforts at meaningful arms reduction, rebuilding our defenses, our economy, and developing new technologies, and helped preserve peace in a troubled world; when Americans courageously supported the struggle for liberty, self-government, and free enterprise throughout the world, and turned the tide of history away from totalitarian darkness and into the warm sunlight of human freedom."
—Ronald Reagan's second inaugural address, January 21, 1985

Thomas Jefferson thought seating dinner guests around a circular table was "democratic."

THE HITCHING POST

Uncle John puts on his top hat and tails to get the gilded dish on White House weddings.

THE FIRST WEDDING

The dish: President James Madison was only the third president to occupy the White House and the first president to host a wedding there. The bride was Lucy Payne, the sister of First Lady Dolley Madison; it was Lucy's second time at the altar. Lucy was a widow who accepted the proposal of Supreme Court Justice Thomas Todd. The 1812 ceremony wasn't as grand as later White House weddings, but the event was carried off with typical aplomb by Mrs. Madison, perhaps the most consummate Washington hostess of all the First Ladies.

Some deep dish: Guests at the wedding were treated to a pinch of snuff from Dolley's own snuffbox. The first lady loved her habit and very generously shared it with her company. A-choo!

THE MOST EXCLUSIVE WEDDING

The dish: In 1820 James Monroe was the first president to see his daughter marry in the White House—but he sure got a lot of grief for it. Held in what is now known as the Blue Room, the wedding was an elegant, candlelit affair that honored a young, romantic couple. The bride was a shy seventeen-year-old poet, Maria Monroe; the groom was her handsome cousin, Sammuel Gouvernor, a presidential secretary. So why did the ceremony generate so much criticism?

Though Maria and Sammuel were the stars of the show, they didn't get to run it—Eliza wouldn't let them. Eliza was Maria's older sister and the acting First Lady because Mrs. Monroe was often very ill. Eliza had been educated with royals in France and she considered her presidential family too elevated to entertain mere Washington society. Over Maria's objections Eliza pared down the guest list until not even members of the president's cabinet received an invitation. An offended Washington, DC, considered itself thoroughly snubbed.

Four presidents (Reagan, Ford, Harding, & Jackson) married divorced women.

Some deep dish: Maria and Sammuel wanted to smooth things over. They planned to attend balls held in their honor where everyone could celebrate. Their first ball was hosted by Commodore Stephen Decatur, a beloved naval hero. Unfortunately he was killed in a duel the very next day and Washington went into mourning over Decatur's demise. All partying ended, and the capital continued to resent the Monroe wedding and the newlyweds. For their part Sammuel and Maria resented Eliza for dominating their big day, and the sisters became estranged.

THE MOST AWKWARD WEDDING

The dish: The only president to see his son married in the White House was John Quincy Adams. But he was unhappy because this was a wedding he'd done his best to prevent. First Lady Louisa Adams couldn't enjoy herself because she was sure that the groom, her son, John, "looked quite sick." The source of all this angst? It was John's bride, Mary Catherine Hellen, a nineteenth-century femme fatal who took the Adams family by storm.

It all started when the First Lady invited her lively niece to live with her at the White House. Mary's beauty and flirtatious personality soon captured the attentions of all three of the president's sons. First Mary snared the heart of her cousin Charles. They were an item until Mary met her Cousin George and forgot all about Charles. Mary and George were engaged (though President Adams didn't approve and was doing his best to break it up) when Cousin John arrived to the White House after being expelled from school. George was soon forgotten and then Mary and John became a hot item. Mama Louisa was forced to spruce up the Blue Room and let the pair marry for fear the couple would cause a scandal.

Some deep dish: Neither Charles nor George attended their brother's wedding. Mama Louisa took to her sick bed after the whole ordeal. Sensitive, poetic George plunged into a depression, took up drinking, and died less than two years later. The cause was said to be accidental drowning. But some whispered it was a suicide and blamed fickle Mary.

The Library of Congress started from Thomas Jefferson's library of some 6,000 books.

THE MAY–DECEMBER WEDDING

The dish: She was twenty-one and gorgeous. He was fair, fat, and well past forty. But their union caught the public fancy. Everyone knew that the president doted on the daughter of his former law partner, and rumors had been circulated about their engagement for months. When President Grover Cleveland married Frances Folsom in 1886, happy crowds filled the White House grounds. Sounds of music coming from the Blue Room told the public that John Philip Sousa was leading the Marine Band in the wedding march.

President Cleveland and Frances tried to keep the wedding as simple and private as possible. There were no attendants, and guests reported their amazement at Frances's ability to manage a dress with a fifteen-foot train all by herself. (It was her first triumph as one of America's most popular First Ladies.) When the short wedding was over the White House crowds heard a twenty-one-gun salute from a local navy yard, and church bells rang throughout Washington.

Some deep dish: Trying to protect his bride from publicity, President Cleveland released no public photos. But he couldn't protect Frances during the honeymoon. Newsmen staked out the presidential honeymoon cottage and watched it with spyglasses. The horrified president railed to the papers about immoral journalistic standards. The more things change, the more they stay the same.

THE MOST CROWDED WEDDING

The dish: President Theodore Roosevelt's oldest daughter Alice was beautiful, witty, spirited, and adored by the American public. Over Pop's presidential protests Alice managed to smoke, drive fast cars, and travel without a chaperone—and it didn't hurt her popularity a bit. Admiring Americans sang songs such as "Alice Blue Gown" in her honor. European royalty gave her gifts. The world worshipped "Princess" Alice, and she graciously allowed them the privilege. When Roosevelt announced that his daughter would marry Ohio congressman Nicholas Longworth at the White House, Alice watched the "loot" pour in. She received everything from a hand-carved teak chest containing jewels and furs from the dowager empress of China to a barrel of popcorn from the U.S. citizens.

Jefferson's epitaph, which he wrote, does not mention that he served as president.

Despite the president's announcement that he planned a small family affair, demands for invitations poured in. When the wedding day came on February 17, 1906, the ballroom-sized East Room couldn't hold all the guests. They overflowed into adjoining rooms and hallways. One woman even fainted in the crush of bodies. A staff of 101—including policemen, maids, and butlers—was barely adequate to handle the crowd. Meanwhile thousands of people gathered outside the White House in celebration of America's greatest wedding.

Some deep dish: The bride soon discovered that her new husband was both an alcoholic and a playboy. She would have divorced him, but felt that would hurt her father's political chances of staying in the White House. According to Alice's family, her marriage was as great a failure as the wedding had been a fabulous success.

★　★　★　★　★

BARNEY CAMS IT UP

George W. Bush's pup is a real star.

Just as FDR was rarely seen without his loyal Scottie dog, Fala, President George W. Bush is especially fond of his high-spirited Scottish terrier Barney, whom he received as a gift from former Environmental Protection Agency Director Christine Whitman. (Her Scottish terrier, Coors is Barney's mother.) In addition to being a cute pup, Barney has become a celebrity in his own right.

Check out the White House web site and you'll see that this little superstar has a whole section devoted entirely to him and his antics. Every day, a new Barney picture is posted, so viewers can keep track of playtime, naptime, and suppertime. Even better, Barney stars in three motion pictures—*Barney Cam, Barney Cam II: Barney Reloaded*, and *Barney and Spot's Winter Wonderland*—that show his personal dog's eye view of the White House.

Presidents Jefferson, Garfield, and Hayes all liked to play chess.

NUMBER SIXTEEN: ABRAHAM LINCOLN

Served from 1861 to 1865

Vital Stats: Born on February 12, 1809, in Hardin County, Kentucky. Died on April 15, 1865, in Washington, DC.
Age at Inauguration: 52
Vice President: Hannibal Hamlin (first term); Andrew Johnson (second term)
Political Affiliation: Republican
Wife: Mary Todd (married 1842)
Kids: Robert Todd (1843–1926); Edward Baker (1846–1850); William Wallace (1850–1862); Thomas "Tad" (1853–1871)
Education: Local tutors
What he did before he was president: Store Clerk; Store Owner; Ferry Pilot; Surveyor; Postmaster; Lawyer; U.S. Congressman
Postpresidential Occupations: None. Died in office.

MEMORABLE QUOTES

"A house divided against itself cannot stand. I believe this government cannot endure permanently half slave and half free. I do not expect the Union to be dissolved—I do not expect the house to fall—but I do expect it will cease to be divided. It will become all one thing, or all the other."
—Abraham Lincoln's "A House Divided" speech, delivered on June 16, 1858

"With malice toward none, with charity for all, with firmness in the right as God gives us to see the right, let us strive on to finish the work we are in, to bind up the nation's wounds, to care for him who shall have borne the battle and for his widow and his orphan, to do all which may achieve and cherish a just and lasting peace among ourselves and with all nations."
—Abraham Lincoln's second inaugural address, March 4, 1865

George Washington was stricken with smallpox on a trip to the West Indies in 1751.

WHAT ARE YOU, A COMEDIAN?

Turns out that presidents can be pretty funny guys too.
Here's just a short sampling of their comedic stylings.

"It's a damn poor mind that can only think
of one way to spell a word."
—Andrew Jackson

"People who like this sort of thing
will find this the sort of thing they like."
—Abraham Lincoln

"If I were two-faced, would I be wearing this one?"
—Abraham Lincoln

"How many legs does a dog have if you call the tail a leg?"
"Four. Calling a tail a leg doesn't make it a leg."
—Abraham Lincoln

"I know but two tunes;
one of them is Yankee Doodle and the other isn't."
Ulysses S. Grant

"About the time we think we can make ends meet,
somebody moves the ends."
—Herbert Hoover

"Blessed are the young, for they shall inherit the national debt."
—Herbert Hoover

"Always be sincere, even if you don't mean it."
—Harry S. Truman

Calvin Coolidge played the harmonica.

"Things are more like they are now than they ever were before."
—Dwight D. Eisenhower

(At a White House dinner honoring Nobel prize winners):
"I think this is the most extraordinary collection of talent,
of human knowledge, that has ever been gathered
together at the White House—with the possible exception
of when Thomas Jefferson dined alone."
—John F. Kennedy

"Did you ever think that making a speech on
economics is a lot like pissing down your leg?
It seems hot to you, but it never does to anyone else."
—Lyndon Johnson

"Politics would be a helluva good business
if it weren't for the goddamned people."
—Richard Nixon

"I know I am getting better at golf
because I am hitting fewer spectators."
—Gerald Ford

"It's true hard work never killed anybody,
but I figure why take the chance?"
—Ronald Reagan

"A lot of presidential memoirs are, they say, dull and
self-serving. I hope mine are interesting and self-serving."
—Bill Clinton

"A low voter turnout is an indication of
fewer people going to the polls."
—George W. Bush

"It's clearly a budget. It's got a lot of numbers in it."
—George W. Bush

IT'S TOUGH TO SMILE WITH FALSE TEETH

The falsehoods told about George Washington are seemingly without number. Not only did he not chop down a cherry tree and rat himself out, he never wore wooden dentures. Here's the sad tale of Georgie's dental woes.

Perhaps George Washington considered his bad teeth his cross to bear. The Father of Our Country was a sickly lad, afflicted first with smallpox at age nineteen then with bouts of pleurisy, dysentery, dengue fever, malaria, flu, and rheumatism. Doctors diagnosed big doses of the typical treatment of the day, the sinister calomel (mercurous chloride), which was known to weaken the teeth. Poor Washington. He began complaining of toothaches, inflamed gums, and infections at age twenty-two, despite brushing his teeth daily (a relative rarity in his time).

OUT THEY COME
Naturally, Washington sought medical help. Dentists responded by yanking out his rotten teeth one by one. Washington lost his teeth at the rate of about one a year, and he suffered almost constantly with throbbing pain. Is it little wonder that his compatriots described him as having a quick and fierce temper? You might feel a little cranky, too, if you had a toothache that lasted more than thirty years! By the time Washington was elected president in 1789 he had two teeth left in his mouth. And it was soon down to just one.

DENTURE DEMENTIA
Washington consulted noted New York City dentist Peter Greenwood, who fashioned a creative pair of dentures for the president. These designer choppers were carved out of ivory from hippopotamus teeth, and also contained a cow's tooth, human teeth (some from Washington himself), and metal springs to hold the upper and lower plates together. The lower plate was equipped with a hole that fit over the resident's sole remaining tooth.

Washington was fond of Greenwood's dentures though they didn't fit or function perfectly, and was dismayed when the teeth began coming loose. He sent them back to Greenwood with an admonition to repair them quickly, as the pair he was forced to wear in the meantime "are uneasy in my mouth and bulge my lips out in such a manner as to make them appear considerably swelled."

This look was most memorably captured by Gilbert Stuart, the man who painted the portrait of Washington now seen on the dollar bill. Compared to other artists' renderings, Stuart placed a lot of emphasis the president's jaw and puffy mouth. Some historians have speculated that Stuart had developed a distaste for the president and thus meanly played up Washington's facial flaws. Others say that the president's denture problems led to a sunken jaw that Stuart padded with cotton to give a more natural appearance.

FAREWELL TEETH!

By 1796 Washington's last tooth was merely a memory. Greenwood consoled the president by suspending the final tooth on a piece of wire, allowing him to wear it on his watch chain if he desired to do so.

Washington had trouble with his various sets of dentures until the day he died. He complained that they hurt, pursed his lips out, and made it difficult to chew. He especially carped about the tendency of one pair to turn black after he drank his nightly port, as he told Greenwood in letters. Greenwood advised the president to either take them out when drinking or to brush his teeth with chalk afterward.

DENTURES ON DISPLAY

Today you can get a look at George's false choppers at the Baltimore College of Dental Surgery and at Mount Vernon, Washington's estate in Virginia. Joseph R. Greenwood, John's descendant, has both Washington's last tooth (enclosed in a gold locket) and the final set of his dentures.

THE LAST FIRST COW

Here's the story of President Taft's famous bovine, Pauline Wayne.

President William Howard Taft was a portly man, to say the least, weighing in excess of 330 pounds. Yet surprisingly he was a robust sportsman: he loved horseback riding, and was the first president to take up the game of golf. He simply wanted to enjoy himself, whether he was in the kitchen or on the links. In light of this, his love of baseball makes perfect sense: he could throw out the first pitch and moments later tear into a bag of peanuts.

His girth didn't make his wife, Helen, all that happy, however. An ambitious, take-charge kind of woman, she was largely responsible for shaping her husband's political career; now she wanted to reshape her husband's body as well. Mrs. Taft relied on a tactic she learned when typhus broke out in Manila, during her husband's tenure as governor-general of the Philippines; she brought in cows so that he could have fresh milk. Mr. Taft loved to drink the fresh milk, and Mrs. Taft thought it did a body good to drink fresh milk, so it only made sense to have a cow when the Tafts took up residence at the White House.

GOT MILK?
The first First Cow of the Taft presidency was affectionately called Mooly Wooly. The Tafts had planned on her supplying milk daily to the White House kitchen; however, poor Mooly's milk was bad. Their affections for her quickly dried up, and they sent her packing. Her replacement was a beautiful Holstein named Pauline Wayne, who could be seen grazing on the White House lawn throughout the day. Taft valued the milk from Miss Wayne so much that he hired a servant whose only job was to look after her and deliver the frothy pails full of her milk to the kitchen.

In 1910, the old stable where Pauline slept was to be torn down. So the cow was moved but allowed to graze on the lawn of the Navy Building right next door (now known as the Eisenhower Executive Office Building) for the rest of her days.

The oldest presidential candidate: Peter Cooper who was 85 when nominated in 1876.

NUMBER SEVENTEEN: ANDREW JOHNSON

Served from 1865 to 1869

Vital Stats: Born on December 29, 1808, in Raleigh, North Carolina. Died on July 31, 1875, in Carter County, Tennessee.
Age at Inauguration: 56
Vice President: None
Political Affiliation: Republican
Wife: Eliza McCardle (married 1827)
Kids: Martha (1828–1901); Charles (1830–1863); Mary (1832–1883); Robert (1834–1869)
Education: Self-taught
What he did before he was president: Tailor; Alderman; Mayor; U.S. Congressman; Governor of Tennessee; U.S. Senator; U.S. Vice President
Postpresidential Occupations: U.S. Senator

MEMORABLE QUOTES

"Amendments to the Constitution ought to not be too frequently made . . . [if] continually tinkered with it would lose all its prestige and dignity, and the old instrument would be lost sight of altogether in a short time."
—Andrew Johnson in a speech, given February 22, 1866

"I have been drawn into this long speech, while I intended simply to make acknowledgments for the cordial welcome; but if I am insulted while civilities are going on I will resent it in a proper manner."
—Andrew Johnson speaking in Cleveland, Ohio, September 3, 1866. Johnson had been heckled mercilessly throughout this speech by political opponents.

Lyndon Johnson was the first Southerner to hold office since Andrew Johnson.

NUMBER EIGHTEEN: ULYSSES S. GRANT

Served from 1869 to 1877

Vital Stats: Born on August 27, 1822, in Point Pleasant, Ohio. Died on July 23, 1885, in Mount McGregor, New York.
Age at Inauguration: 46
Vice President: Schuyler Colfax (first term); Henry Wilson (second term)
Political Affiliation: Republican
Wife: Julia Boggs Dent (married 1848)
Kids: Frederick Dent (1850–1912); Ulysses Simpson (1852–1929); Nellie Wrenshall (1855–1922); Jesse Root (1858–1934)
Education: U.S. Military Academy, West Point, New York
What he did before he was president: Farmer; Real Estate Agent; Leather Store Clerk; Soldier; General in Chief of Union Army
Postpresidential Occupations: Businessman; Writer

MEMORABLE QUOTES

"Let us have peace."
—Ulysses S. Grant's words on accepting the nomination for resident, May 29, 1868

"It is a national humiliation that we are now compelled to pay from twenty to thirty million dollars annually (exclusive of passage money which we should share with vessels of other nations) to foreigners for doing the work which should be done by American vessels American built, American owned, and American manned. This is a direct drain upon the resources of the country of just so much money; equal to casting it into the sea, so far as this nation is concerned."
—Ulysses S. Grant in a message to Congress, March 23, 1870

Both Harry Truman and Richard Nixon played the piano.

SHE SAID WHAT?

Match the quotation to the First Lady of the nation.

Rosalynn Carter, wife of Jimmy Carter, said: "First Ladies have enormous influence just because of their proximity to power." Whether exerting that influence to further political causes, defend husbands, or decorate the White House, all have had a lot to say about their husbands and life with the president. Can you tell who said what?

1. "The First Lady is an unpaid public servant elected by one person—her husband."

2. "It was always, music in my ears, both before and after our marriage, when my husband, told me, that I was the only one, he had ever thought of, cared for."

3. "If you vote for him, you get me."

4. "It is only the hope that you can live through (the campaign) that gives me a prospect of enjoyment."

5. "If your husband is a political figure, you have to be thick-skinned. There's always going to be a lot of criticism. It comes with the office and you have to ignore it."

6. "I tell him what I think."

7. "Always be on time. Do as little talking as humanly possible. Remember to lean back in the parade car so everybody can see the President. Be sure not to get too fat, because you'll have to sit there in the back seat."

8. "We want more men of deeds, and fewer of words."

9. "The ugly scapegoating that divides our country is the problem, not the solution."

10. "I always managed the money affairs of the family."

Thomas Jefferson thought the Carnation cherry was the best sort. It was . . .

11. "Of course he has matured through the years. But he wouldn't be worth his salt if he hadn't."

12. "You'll be glad to know that the President is practicing safe snacks."

13. "I'm saying that if you're a casual drug user, you are an accomplice to murder."

14. "The greater part of our happiness or misery depends on our dispositions and not our circumstances. "

15. "When Harvard men say they have graduated from Radcliffe, then we've made it."

A. Mary Todd Lincoln
B. Laura Bush
C. Nancy Reagan
D. Jacqueline Kennedy
E. Hillary Rodham Clinton
F. Elizabeth "Betty" Ford
G. Martha Washington
H. Patricia "Pat" Nixon

I. Claudia "Lady Bird" Johnson
J. Rosalynn Carter
K. Eleanor Roosevelt
L. Abigail Adams
M. Sarah Childress Polk
N. Mamie Eisenhower
O. Barbara Bush

ANSWERS: 1. I, 2. A, 3. E, 4. M, 5. F, 6. J, 7. K, 8. L, 9. O, 10. N, 11. H, 12. B, 13. C, 14. G, 15. D

• • • "so superior to all others that no other deserves the name of cherry," he said.

PRESIDENTIAL PLAYGROUND

If the president cannot go to the gym,
then the gym must come to the president.

Think you're too busy to find the time to work out? Think again. If the chief executive can do it, so can you. While in office, Dwight Eisenhower, John F. Kennedy, Gerald Ford, and Bill Clinton were avid golfers—with varying degrees of success. Herbert Hoover worked out with a medicine ball. Even the less physically active presidents have found some way to work up a sweat and relieve the stress of their office. Sometimes all it takes is a little creative thinking—and a staff of several hundred whose job it is to accommodate your every whim!

Life in the White House in recent years has left even less free time for the presidents and their families. Security concerns have made it all but impossible for them to take advantage of most recreational activities in the outside world. So presidents have had to modify the White House to suit their sporting preferences. What has resulted is a surprising collection of athletic additions to the executive mansion.

WHAT THE DEUCE?
Theodore Roosevelt built a tennis court and reportedly used it rain or shine, even in the worst of the DC summer swelter. Teddy was an avid tennis player and few could—or would—best him. He chose his opponents from a select group of young government officials, and this group came to be known as his Tennis Cabinet. Calvin Coolidge enjoyed a good game, too, up until tragedy struck on the courts. Coolidge's 16-year-old son Calvin Junior died as a result of an infected blister he got on his foot while playing tennis.

More recent presidents have donned their tennis whites as well. Gerald Ford and his family made heavy use of the court, and Jimmy and Rosalyn Carter were always up for a love match. During modern presidencies, it was an honor coveted by staffers

---

Richard Nixon was the first president to visit China.

and political VIPs alike to play on the White House court, and court times are scheduled on the weekends from early morning until twilight.

JUST A QUICK DIP

Both John Quincy Adams and Teddy Roosevelt liked to swim in the Potomac River. But as time went on and the Potomac became more sullied, using it as a swimming hole wasn't the best idea. It's a good thing that Franklin Roosevelt had an indoor pool built, which he used regularly for several years to strengthen his polio-stricken limbs. But as the rigors of the Great Depression and the war took their toll on his health, FDR was no longer able to swim by early into his third term.

John F. Kennedy, who suffered from back pain throughout his adult life, rediscovered the pool. He swam in the nude at least once every day while he was in the White House—often twice a day. But Richard Nixon, apparently not a skinny-dipper himself, had the pool filled in and ordered that the new Press Briefing Room be built over the top of it. Nixon *was* known to enjoy the one-lane bowling alley located under the North Portico—though presumably while clothed.

It seems like his successor, Gerald Ford, didn't exactly agree with Nixon's decision to nix the pool. Although most famous for his erratic golf playing (he hit several bystanders with wild balls), Ford was a great athlete; he played football in college and still loved to ski, play tennis, and swim on a regular basis. During his administration Ford raised private funds to build an outdoor swimming pool near the Oval Office. Not to be outdone, Bill Clinton later added a hot tub next to the pool. Take that, Nixon!

STICKY WICKETS AND REPLACING DIVOTS

Presidents have also been big fans of playing outside on the grass. Rutherford B. Hayes had a croquet court installed near the South Portico and was said to engage in a competitive, cutthroat game with anyone who was willing. George H. W. Bush installed a horseshoe pit and a basketball half-court. He also put in an artificial green on the South Lawn, so he was never more than a few steps away from a little putting practice.

Ronald Reagan was an economics major at Eureka College in Illinois.

Probably the most famous presidential golfer of all, Eisenhower made the first putting green on the lawn outside the Oval Office; Secret Service agents allegedly waited until the First Duffer was out of sight before they replaced his divots. Legend has it that the numerous pits in the hardwood floors of the Oval Office were made by Ike's spikes. Golf was Eisenhower's passion, and scoring a hole in one in 1968 was, he claimed, a highlight of his life.

Bill Clinton was not so serious about his golf game. When he did make it out to a course, Clinton had the reputation of taking frequent mulligans, better known as free shots or do-overs. The president himself admitted that this habit didn't improve his score much. Clinton said he liked to play golf because it was the only thing that made him feel "normal."

GETTING PHYSICAL
Teddy Roosevelt installed a small gym where he lifted weights. The tradition continued during Ronald Reagan's administration, when the Gipper pumped iron. George W. Bush also gets in a few sets whenever he can. But what is weight lifting without a little cardio to balance it out? Thanks to President Clinton, presidential jogging became a whole lot easier. Clinton installed a special cushioned running track that follows the perimeter of the South Lawn; this addition turned out to be cost-effective for John Q. Taxpayer, because it was cheaper to install the track than it was to pay for the Secret Service detail that was necessary when Clinton went out into the city to jog. But after injuring his knee during his second term, Clinton abandoned the track. George W. Bush is said to have thrown partisan prejudice out the window and uses the Clinton track several times a week.

SUMMER CAMP (DAVID)

Hello Mudda. Hello Fadda. Greetings from Camp . . . David?

While Americans frequently hear Camp David mentioned on the news, most often when the president is going there for a weekend retreat, few know the detailed history of this Maryland mountain enclave. Located seventy miles from Washington, DC, Camp David is meant to be a quiet place where the president can just get away from it all. Here are a few quick facts about the president's home away from home:

- Catoctin Mountain Park began as a Depression-era Work Projects Administration project to create a park out of unused agricultural land. A few years later, it became a camp for the families of federal employees and was renamed Hi-Catoctin.

- When Franklin Roosevelt's doctors suggested he find a place to rest away from Washington, DC, he chose Hi-Catoctin and requested that a main lodge be constructed to resemble his winter home in Warm Springs, Georgia. He then renamed the camp Shangri-La.

- Although Harry Truman didn't visit Shangri-La often (apparently Bess Truman thought it was dull), his successor Dwight Eisenhower was a frequent visitor and renamed it Camp David in honor of his grandson David. During Eisenhower's presidency, the first cabinet meeting was held here. Eisenhower did much to improve the property: refurbishing most of the cabins, adding a large flagstone terrace, a picnic and outdoor cooking area, and (how Ike can you get?) a golf green.

- President Richard Nixon used Camp David quite often, hosting family and foreign leaders. He updated the compound with

". . . never to read translations where I can read the original."

additional modern conveniences while preserving its rustic architecture.

- Camp David probably got the most attention under Jimmy Carter, who hosted the 1978 Camp David Summit between Egyptian president Anwar al-Sadat and Israeli prime minister Menachem Begin. The resulting Camp David Accords proclaimed peace between Egypt and Israel.

- Bill Clinton also tried to use Camp David as a venue for peace, hosting Israeli prime minister Ehud Barak and Palestinian leader Yasser Arafat there near the end of his term. Unfortunately the meeting ended without concrete results—but you can't blame a guy for trying.

★ ★ ★ ★ ★

PRESIDENTIAL FIRSTS

- First to marry a widow: George Washington
- First vice president to be elected president: John Adams
- First to lead the country into war: James Madison
- First to ride on a steamboat: James Monroe
- First son of a former president to be elected: John Quincy Adams
- First president born an American citizen: Martin Van Buren
- First to arrive by train to his inaugural: William Henry Harrison
- First to marry on his birthday: John Tyler
- First to be born in the nineteenth century: Franklin Pierce
- First to wear a beard: Abraham Lincoln
- First to be left-handed: James Garfield

Abraham Lincoln gave the eulogy at Zachary Taylor's funeral.

ONE BOURBON, ONE SCOTCH, ONE PRESIDENT

What do powerful presidents drink at the White House Happy Hour?

Beating the British and founding a new nation is hard work. No wonder many of our Founding Fathers liked to kick back to enjoy a few stiff drinks. Many Americans would be surprised to learn that the Father of Our Country George Washington, spent 7 percent of his $25,000 presidential salary on alcohol. Thomas Jefferson reportedly spent an extravagant $10,000 on wine during his two terms in office. Although John Adams favored temperance while in office, when he retired to his Quincy, Massachusetts, farm, the third president of the United States began each day with hard cider.

WHISKEY REBELLION

James Buchanan loved to drink, and his legendary stamina meant that he rarely showed the effects of his drinking. On his Sunday carriage ride to church, he often stopped at Jacob Baer's distillery, where he would be a ten-gallon cask of his favorite alcoholic drink, whiskey. During Prohibition, one president didn't let the law of the land stop him from enjoying his drink of choice. Warren Harding, whose term coincided with Prohibition, enjoyed tumblers of whiskey while playing poker.

Scotch and soda was a favorite of many presidents including Bill Clinton and Lyndon Johnson. On *Air Force One*, Johnson would throw his glass of Scotch and soda on the floor when it wasn't mixed to his taste—three quarters of the glass filled with liquor. He also drank scotch and soda in a plastic cup while driving around his Texas ranch in a convertible. Although Richard Nixon was also a fan of scotch, he drank martinis during his final flight on *Air Force One* the day he resigned from the presidency.

"No two men can differ on a principle of trigonometry," said Thomas Jefferson.

HOW DRY THEY WERE

While there's no evidence that these gentlemen battled the bottle, the same can't be said for some of their predecessors. Both Pierce and Grant battled alcoholism while in office. Andrew Johnson was reportedly drunk at his 1865 inauguration as Lincoln's vice president. He was battling typhoid fever and reportedly drank a few whiskeys to fortify himself. "The inauguration went off very well except that the Vice President Elect was too drunk to perform his duties & disgraced himself & the Senate by making a drunken foolish speech," Michigan Republican Senator Zachariah Chandler wrote home to his wife about the scene Johnson made.

Some presidents didn't imbibe at all. Sarah Polk, a devout Presbyterian, banned alcohol from her husband's White House for religious reasons. Rutherford B. Hayes's wife Lucy was notorious for serving no alcohol at the White House. A century later the trend continued as President Jimmy Carter, a born-again Christian, rarely drank. George W. Bush gave up drinking on his fortieth birthday, fearing that it was becoming a problem. He says he hasn't had a drop since.

★ ★ ★ ★ ★

PARTING SHOTS

Bill Clinton's farewell address has advice for all Americans.

"[W]e must remember that America cannot lead in the world unless here at home we weave the threads of our coat of many colors into the fabric of one America. As we become ever more diverse, we must work harder to unite around our common values and our common humanity. We must work harder to overcome our differences, in our hearts and in our laws. We must treat all our people with fairness and dignity, regardless of their race, religion, gender or sexual orientation, and regardless of when they arrived in our country; always moving toward the more perfect union of our founders' dreams."

—Bill Clinton, January 18, 2001

Herbert Hoover was the last president whose term ended on March 3rd.

THE ELECTION OF 1876: THE YEAR THEY STOLE THE PRESIDENCY

*This election was certainly close, corrupt,
and too interesting for Uncle John's scholars to ignore.
This "Too Close to Call" appeared in the* The Best of Uncle
John's Bathroom Reader *and we've brought it back.*

CHANGING COURSE

Eighteen seventy-six was a watershed year in American political
history. It was a "reunion" of sorts: The Civil War had been over
for just eleven years, and citizens of the former Confederate states
were going to be voting in the presidential election for the first
time since then. Would the North and South—so recently bitter
enemies—be able to pick a president without going to war? The
future of American democracy depended on it.

THE CHOICES

Republican nominee: Ohio governor Rutherford B. Hayes, a
"colorless" man who "fell like a wet blanket on the party." He was
picked as a compromise candidate after President U.S. Grant with-
drew from the race over corruption charges, and the party dead-
locked on several more popular candidates at their convention.
Democratic nominee: New York governor Samuel J. Tilden—a
crime-fighting prosecutor famous for busting the Boss Tweed Ring
and convicting its founder on charges of fraud, bribery, and graft.
America desperately wanted clean government, and Tilden, who
ran on the slogan "Tilden and Reform," promised to deliver it.

THE CAMPAIGN

Hayes and Tilden both ran extremely negative campaigns. "The
campaign, focusing on personalities, became bitter and dirty,"
historian Norman J. Ornstein recounted in *Roll Call* magazine in
1992. "Each side hurled insults and lies at the other. Hayes was
accused of stealing the pay of dead soldiers in the Civil War and

shooting his mother in a fit of insanity, while Tilden, among other things, was called a drunkard, thief, syphilitic, liar, and swindler." The Republicans placed particular emphasis on reopening the wounds of the Civil War by painting the Democrats as the party of treason. And they weren't too subtle about it, either. "Every enemy this great republic has had for twenty years has been a Democrat," Union Colonel Robert B. Ingersoll proclaimed at one particularly nasty campaign stop:

> Every man that shot Union soldiers . . . was a Democrat. Every man that loved slavery better than liberty was a Democrat. The man that assassinated Abraham Lincoln was a Democrat . . . Every scar you have got on your heroic bodies was given to you by a Democrat . . . Every arm that is lacking, every limb that is gone . . . is a souvenir of a Democrat!

DOWN TO THE WIRE
The election had one of the highest turnouts in American history and one of the closest votes: Tilden won the popular vote by 51 percent to 47.9 percent, or by a margin of about 250,000 votes. When the nation went to bed on the night of the election, it seemed certain that by the end of the next day Tilden would be declared the first Democratic president in over 20 years.

STEALING THE ELECTION
And that might well have happened, if John C. Reid, managing editor of the *New York Times* (then a pro-Republican paper), had not received a telegram from Democratic headquarters:

> PLEASE GIVE YOUR ESTIMATE OF ELECTORAL VOTES FOR TILDEN. ANSWER AT ONCE.

The telegram also asked specifically for the returns from Florida, Louisiana, and South Carolina, the only three states in the South still ruled by the Republican "carpetbagger" governments imposed by the North following the Civil War. Preliminary returns showed that Tilden had carried all three states, giving him 204 electoral votes to Hayes's 165, making him the clear winner. But the returns still had to be verified.

THE NUMBERS GAME

As Reid mulled over the surprisingly urgent tone of the telegram, he went over the electoral college votes in his head. Not counting the three states mentioned in the telegram, Tilden appeared to have only 184 votes, 1 vote shy of the 185 he needed to win. Hayes had only 165 votes—but Florida, Louisiana, and South Carolina together made 19 votes, and Oregon had 1 contested vote that was up for grabs—so if all of these votes could be swung in Hayes's favor, he could still beat Tilden, 185 to 184.

But was such a maneuver even possible? Reid thought it was. The Oregon vote was a sure thing, since it was (illegally) held by a Republican appointee who stood to lose his job if the Democrats won. And because the governments of the three contested states were controlled by Republicans, if the vote tallies were contested, Republican-stacked certification boards would be called in to resolve the dispute. They had the power to disqualify "fraudulent" votes and adjust the official accounts accordingly, throwing the election to Hayes. The board members weren't exactly Puritans, either, as historian Roy Morris relates:

> South Carolina's board included three Republicans who were themselves candidates for office. Florida's board was Republican by a two-to-one margin, the swing vote in the hands of a former Confederate deserter. Louisiana's board consisted of an undertaker, a saloonkeeper, and two thoroughly disreputable carpetbaggers—all of whom would be indicted for fraud the following year.

GETTING THE WORD OUT

As soon as Reid realized the election was still up for grabs, he rushed over to the Republican headquarters at the Fifth Avenue Hotel, woke up several senior party officials, and explained the situation. Republican National Committee chair Zachariah Chandler reportedly told Reid to do "whatever he thought was best," and that's exactly what he did—he took a carriage down to the Western Union office and dashed off identical telegrams to Republican leaders in each of the three contested states:

Lou Hoover, wife of President Herbert Hoover, spoke 5 languages.

HAYES IS ELECTED IF WE HAVE CARRIED
SOUTH CAROLINA, FLORIDA, AND
LOUISIANA. CAN YOU HOLD YOUR
STATE? ANSWER IMMEDIATELY.

When each state cabled back in the affirmative, Reid immediately
dispatched "visiting statesmen" to the three contested states to
make sure that the vote counting went according to plan.

ELECTION SURPRISE

On the afternoon of November 8, 1876, Republican Party chairman Zachariah Chandler announced to the press that Rutherford
B. Hayes had received the 185 votes needed to win the election.
The shocking announcement sent the country into an uproar.
Riots broke out, and President Grant had to dispatch federal
troops to maintain order. Sure enough, the Republican-controlled
election committees had "reviewed" the unofficial totals and
"corrected" them in favor of Hayes, making him the new winner
of the election.

FIGHTING BACK

The Democrats, however, refused to concede the 20 disputed electoral votes. New Democratic governors had just been elected to
replace the outgoing "carpetbagger" governments in all three contested states, and though they would not take office for several
weeks, they protested the final returns and submitted their own
versions to the Electoral College showing Tilden as the winner.
Confronted with multiple sets of returns, the College was unable
to declare a victor.

A CONSTITUTIONAL CRISIS

Some vague wording in the U.S. Constitution made the situation
even worse. William McFeely writes in his biography of Ulysses S.
Grant,

> The Constitution calls for the electoral votes to be
> opened in the presence of both houses of Congress,
> but it does not say *who* should do the counting. If the
> Republican Senate majority decided the count went
> one way, the Democratic majority of the House of

Representatives might decide it went the other. Another possibility was a Senate filibuster, begun before the count could be made, that might extend past Grant's last day in office, leaving the United States without a president.

CIVIL WAR II?

As the stalemate dragged into December, the mood in the country turned increasingly hostile. Rumors circulated that Tilden sympathizers were preparing to install him as president by force, and "Tilden Minutemen" militia groups sprang up in a number of states. Even the Democratic sergeant-at-arms of the House was causing trouble, threatening to deputize 100,000 men and use them to guarantee Tilden's election. Violence actually did erupt in a few instances in Louisiana, where the Republican candidate for governor was shot and wounded by an outraged Democrat, and in Ohio someone fired a shot through the window of the Hayes family home while they were sitting down for dinner.

President Grant took these threats seriously—he ordered several artillery companies into the capital and he issued a statement warning the public that "any demonstrations or warlike concentration of men threatening the peace of the city or endangering the security of public property would be summarily dealt with by a declaration of martial law." Tilden urged his supporters to remain calm. "It will not do to fight," he told his allies. "We have just emerged from one civil war, and it will never do to engage another."

A COMPROMISE

Finally, in January 1877, both houses of Congress agreed to appoint an independent electoral commission, composed of five senators, five congressional representatives, and five Supreme Court justices, to decide the election. It was hoped the commission would be impartial. Seven of the members would be Democrats, seven would be Republicans, and the 15th and tie-breaking member would be Supreme Court Justice David Davis of Illinois, whom both sides considered to be independent.

At the last minute, however, the Republican-controlled Illinois legislature elected Justice Davis to the U.S. Senate, which disqualified him from serving on the committee. This turned out

to be a master stroke. He was replaced by Justice Joseph P. Bradley, a Republican considered the least partisan of the remaining Supreme Court Justices.

THE END OF THE LINE

On February 1, 1877, both houses of Congress met to count the electoral votes. When the role call got to "Florida," the 15-man electoral commission paused for nine days' worth of hearings to decide who would get Florida's votes. In the end, Justice Bradley voted with his fellow Republicans to award Florida's four electoral votes to Hayes. When he did it again with Louisiana's votes, Tilden and the Democrats knew the game was up.

Meanwhile, Southern Democrats—who didn't particularly like Tilden to begin with—had been in secret talks with Hayes's people for weeks—and on February 26 they cut a deal: in exchange for not protesting Hayes's election, Hayes agreed to appoint a Southerner to his cabinet and speed Southern "home rule" by removing all federal troops from the three remaining "carpetbagger" states.

LAST GASP

But that didn't stop Tilden's allies from fighting to the bitter end. "The House session on March 1 was one of the stormiest in history," Roy Morris writes,

> Members roared with disapproval as House Speaker
> Samuel Randall, a former Tilden supporter, stymied all
> efforts to stop the vote. Some congressmen waved pistols,
> one climbed atop his desk, screaming with anger . . .
> Oaths and insults filled the air. Finally, after 18 tumul-
> tuous hours, the session ended with a telegram from
> Tilden graciously requesting that the vote be completed.
> He knew he must accept the electoral commission's
> results or risk the nation erupting into civil war.

The inevitable became official just after four in the morning on March 2, 1877, as the final votes were counted. Governor Hayes got 185 votes, Governor Tilden got 184. Hayes, denounced as "His Fraudulency" and "Rutherfraud" B. Hayes, became the 19th president of the United States.

Abigail Adams, the second First Lady, often expressed her political views openly . . .

NUMBER NINETEEN: RUTHERFORD B. HAYES

Served from 1877 to 1881

Vital Stats: Born on October 4, 1822, in Delaware, Ohio. Died on January 17, 1893, in Fremont, Ohio.
Age at Inauguration: 54
Vice President: William A. Wheeler
Political Affiliation: Republican
Wife: Lucy Webb (married 1852)
Kids: Birchard Austin (1853–1926); Webb Cook (1856–1934); Rutherford Platt (1858–1927); Joseph (1861–1863)
Education: Kenyon College; Harvard Law School
What he did before he was president: Lawyer; Major General in 23rd Ohio Volunteers; U.S. Congressman; Governor of Ohio
Postpresidential Occupations: Philanthropist

MEMORABLE QUOTES

"I am too far along in experience and years both for this business. I do not go into [it] with the zest of old times. Races, baseball, and politics are for the youngsters."
—Rutherford B. Hayes in a letter to his wife, Lucy, on August 14, 1875

"But at the basis of all prosperity, for that as well as for every other part of the country, lies the improvement of the intellectual and moral condition of the people. Universal suffrage should rest upon universal education. To this end, liberal and permanent provision should be made for the support of free schools by the State governments, and, if need be, supplemented by legitimate aid from national authority."
—Rutherford B. Hayes in his inaugural address, March 5, 1877

. . . for which she was widely criticized as unladylike.

WIN THIS OFFICE
FOR A SONG

Songs have been around as long as there have been humans.
Politics and music have long made a powerful marriage.

Anyone who grew up watching *Schoolhouse Rock* knows the power of a good ditty. If a smart little tune can make a generation remember what a conjunction is, it shouldn't come as any surprise that a catchy campaign song could brand a presidential candidate in the consciousness of the America public too. If it had a good beat and you could dance to it, chances are voters might be humming your tune in November.

ALL TOGETHER NOW
In colonial America, patriotic songs were highly popular. There were songs about important battles and the exploits of famous generals. These tunes were seldom original—they just added new lyrics to already popular melodies and published the resulting combination in newspapers. Thus the average citizen was quickly able to catch on to the issues of the day and easily remember them. Mr. and Mrs. Average-Colonial-Joe and their friends would gather around the old piano and belt out the tunes of the moment, a happening evening's entertainment in those days—sort of an early version of karaoke night at the local bar.

REEL POLITIC
The multitalented Thomas Jefferson made use of a popular tune of his day for the election of 1800. His campaign used a song called "For Jefferson and Liberty," set to an old Scottish reel. It marked the first use of an official campaign song. It included the lyrics:

Rejoice, Columbia's sons, rejoice!
To tyrants never bend the knee,
But join with heart, and soul, and voice,
For Jefferson and Liberty.

While attending the U.S. Naval Academy in Annapolis, Maryland, . . .

In 1824 John Quincy Adams's supporters took the campaign song to extremes. Set to a Scottish melody, the song, "Little Know Ye Who's Coming," catalogued all the terrible things that would befall the nation if Adams were not elected. The list included those three pesky p's: plague, pestilence, and plunder, as well as fire, slavery, and knavery. Although John Quincy Adams did win the presidency, it isn't known whether the song had anything to do with it.

CAMPAIGN SONGS GROW UP

It was with the election of 1840 that campaign songs became an important tool. That year William Henry Harrison roundly defeated his predecessor, Martin Van Buren. This outcome is widely believed to have been influenced by (you guessed it) campaign songs.

Thirty years earlier, at the Battle of Tippecanoe, General Harrison had led a small army of one thousand men to victory over Shawnee forces led by Chief Tecumseh and his brother. This victory resonated with Americans, and Harrison's name became associated with the battle. In 1840 Harrison's supporters published an anthology of campaign songs called, *The Tippecanoe Songbook*. The most famous of these is called "Tip and Tye," referring to Harrison's nickname of Tippecanoe and that of his running mate, John Tyler. (Van Buren, his opponent, is dismissively referred to as "Little Van.")

> What has caus'd this great commotion,
> motion, motion our county through,
> It is the ball that's rolling on,
> For Tippecanoe, and Tyler too,
> For Tippecanoe, and Tyler too,
> And with them we'll beat Little Van, Van,
> Van is a us'd up man,
> And with them we'll beat Little Van.

Another popular favorite from the same songbook was called "Little Vanny," whose partial lyrics went as follows:

> You can't make a song to Van Buren
> Because his long name will not do;
> There's nothing about him allurin',
> As there is about Tippecanoe!

He never was seen in a battle,
Where bullet and cannon shot flew;
His nerves would be shocked with the rattle
Of a contest like Tippecanoe!

And after all the fuss, it's a bit ironic that Harrison's term lasted no more than one month, and his slogans and songs have hung around.

U-G-L-Y, ABE AINT GOT NO ALIBI

It seems campaign songs became no better than playground teasing in the election of 1860. Abraham Lincoln's opponents had songs that were real doozies and regularly referred to Lincoln as "the lying baboon" and poked fun at his lanky stature. Stephen A. Douglas, Lincoln's opponent in 1860, is mostly remembered for being the other participant in the lofty Lincoln–Douglas debates. Yet one of his campaign songs included the cruel words:

Tell us any lie you want to,
In any kind of mixture,
But we pray you, God we pray you,
Don't show us his picture.

Lincoln supporters, on the other hand, used rousing, rollicking songs filled with patriotic fervor. One, "Roll on the Republican Ball" went in part:

Old Abe, he is honest and truthful,
A live representative man;
He's neither too old nor too youthful,
So Democrats beat if you can.

CAMPAIGN SONGS THAT FELL FLAT

Though well-meaning, some campaign songs have had unintended consequences. Often they remind the public of things the composers did not anticipate. Take, for instance, a campaign song for William Howard Taft. Campaign songs have to be simple and catchy, and songwriters love it when they can use the candidate's name in some sort of rhyming scheme. When Taft ran for president in 1908, they came up with a simple ditty called, "Get on a Raft with Taft."

In 1841, three presidents served in the same year: Van Buren, Taylor, and Tyler.

The only problem was that Taft weighed more than 330 pounds (it is rumored that nobody knew his exact weight because scales didn't register any higher). The image of Taft on a raft made most people think about sinking ships—not exactly the image of a candidate one wants to convey.

NOT QUITE WHAT IT SEEMS

Ronald Reagan's campaign liked the patriotic ring of the title of Bruce Springsteen's "Born in the USA," and chose it as their campaign song. Clearly none of Reagan's advisers had actually bothered to listen to the lyrics, which tell the story of an unemployed Vietnam veteran. According to Geoff Boucher of the *Los Angeles Times*, the song "is actually a dark essay on the fractured American dream."

Boucher notes another campaign song that somehow evoked unexpected associations in the public mind. Senator John McCain's (R-AZ) supporters chose the rousing John Philip Sousa march "The Liberty Bell." It seemed well suited to McCain's image as a war hero. What they didn't realize was that this particular march had been used as the theme song of the popular British television comedy series, *Monty Python's Flying Circus*. Unless McCain wanted to be connected with dead parrots, cheese shops, and lumberjacks, he might have been better off with another Sousa tune.

★　★　★　★　★

PRESIDENTIAL TRIVIA

Did you know:

- George H. W. Bush was one of the youngest aviators in the Navy during World War II?
- Thomas Jefferson's favorite vegetable was the pea?
- President Harding's powder blue silk pajamas are house in the Smithsonian?
- Laura Bush is the first First Lady to have given birth to twins?

Mary Todd Lincoln did not attend her husband's funeral.

NUMBER TWENTY: JAMES GARFIELD

Served 1881

Vital Stats: Born on November 19, 1831, in Orange, Ohio.
Died on September 19, 1881, in Elberon, New Jersey.
Age at Inauguration: 49
Vice President: Chester A. Arthur
Political Affiliation: Republican
Wife: Lucretia Rudolph (married 1858)
Kids: Eliza Arabella (1860–1863); Harry Augustus (1863–1942);
James Rudolph (1865–1950); Mary (1867–1947); Irvin McDonnell
(1870–1951); Abram (1872–1958); Edward (1874–1876)
Education: Williams College
What he did before he was president: Schoolteacher; College
Professor; Preacher; Canal Worker; Brigadier General of 42nd
Ohio Volunteers; Member of Ohio Senate; U.S. Congressman;
Postpresidential Occupations: None. Died in office.

MEMORABLE QUOTES

"It is now three days more than a hundred years since the adoption
of the first written constitution of the United States . . . Under this
Constitution twenty-five States have been added to the Union . . .
The jurisdiction . . . now covers an area fifty times greater than that
of the original thirteen States and a population twenty times greater
than that of 1780."
—James Garfield in his inaugural address, March 4, 1881

Life's race well run,
Life's work well done,
Life's victory won,
Now cometh rest.
—*Funeral Ode on James A. Garfield* by Edward Hazan Parker, M.D.

Thomas Jefferson used dumbbells and a wrist cushion to support and strengthen his wrists.

NUMBER TWENTY-ONE: CHESTER A. ARTHUR

Served from 1881 to 1885

Vital Stats: Born on October 5, 1829, in Fairfield, Vermont. Died on November 17, 1886, in New York City, New York.
Age at Inauguration: 51
Vice President: None
Political Affiliation: Republican
Wife: Ellen Lewis Herndon (married 1859)
Kids: William Lewis Herndon (1860–1863); Chester Alan (1864–1937); Ellen (1871–1915)
Education: Union College
What he did before he was president: Teacher; School Principal; Lawyer; Quartermaster General of New York State; U.S. Vice President
Postpresidential Occupations: Lawyer

MEMORABLE QUOTES

"Men may die, but the fabric of our free institutions remains unshaken."
—Chester A. Arthur speaking on the death of President Garfield, 1881

"Madam, I may be President of the United States, but my private life is nobody's damn business."
—Chester A. Arthur speaking to a temperance reformer, 1881

"There doesn't seem to be anything else for an ex-president to do but go into the country and raise big pumpkins."
—Chester A. Arthur speaking after his defeat for renomination, 1884

A BACHELOR'S FIRST LADY

Popular as a hostess and a woman of influence?

James Buchanan came to office in 1857 as the only bachelor president in the nation's history. To this day he still holds that title, one of dubious distinction. He brought with him Harriet "Hal" Lane, his twenty-seven-year-old niece, to serve as official White House hostess. Though she was young and his bachelorhood unique, she wasn't the first nonspouse to take on official White House duties. From 1829 to 1869, a series of young "substitutes" for presidential wives took on what we now consider the role of First Lady because, although most presidential wives did accompany their husbands to Washington, they often delegated official hosting responsibilities to someone else.

NO NIECE LEFT BEHIND

Harriet was the logical choice for Bachelor Buchanan, who had been her guardian since she was orphaned at the age of eleven. He had looked after her education in elite private schools, including two years at a convent in Georgetown. When he became secretary of state, he introduced her to all the members of high Washington society. She went with him to London in 1853 when he was appointed as envoy to Great Britain, where she was even able to count Queen Victoria among her admirers.

At Buchanan's inauguration, Harriet was hailed as the Democratic Queen, and she indeed was often treated that way. She won the hearts of American society with her lighthearted manner, her style, and the lavish parties she threw often to help promote her goals. Miss Lane was devoted to the arts. She frequently invited talented artists to important White House dinners to mix with the day's most powerful politicians— and hopefully future patrons.

The dinner table also proved to be quite the battlefield when Harriet had to invite guests with differing political opinions. As

national tensions leading up to the Civil War grew, those seating arrangements must have been nearly impossible to navigate. Harriet spent a lot of time working them out with the utmost diplomacy, so as to give everyone their "proper," honorable place and yet keep political opposites as far away from each other as necessary.

TWO FOR THE PRICE OF ONE?
But Harriet was more than just a pretty hostess. Having grown up alongside her uncle during his years of public service in the nation's capital, she was well versed in the ways of Washington. She knew who the influential people were and worked hard to help her uncle succeed politically. People who needed help knew to come to her for assistance and for access to the president, which she always generously tried to give. There were many rumors that she influenced her uncle, and perhaps she did. She was sharp and politically observant, so many believed that Buchanan listened to her counsel and used her as his confidante. Given her education, intelligence, and savvy, those were probably not bad ideas. After seven states seceded at the tail end of his administration, Buchanan needed all the help he could get.

FINALLY A BRIDE
Harriet waited until she was almost thirty-six before marrying—an almost spinsterly age for a bride of the mid-1800s. She eventually married Henry Elliot Johnston, a banker from Baltimore. They split time living in both Maryland and Pennsylvania. Many years later she moved to back to Washington, DC, to live among the people she had known as a happy, young First Hostess. When Harriet died in 1903, she left her sizable art collection to the government and a large amount of money to endow a center for children with disabilities at Johns Hopkins University. It became the Harriet Lane Outpatient Clinic. Today it continues to serve thousands of children every year.

THE MAN BEHIND THE MOUNT (RUSHMORE)

The monument of four presidents carved into
Mount Rushmore was the dream of one eccentric egotistical
genius, and he moved an entire nation to make it work.

On October 1, 1925, a flamboyant sculptor named Gutzon Borglum stood in front of a remote mountain in the Black Hills of South Dakota to announce that he was going to build the greatest American monument ever. The stone of Mount Rushmore would serve as his medium as he turned its face into thirty-stories-tall sculptures of four American presidents. It would be a monument big and showy enough to match America's new status as a world power. And he told the skeptical people of South Dakota he wouldn't need their money to do it. Right after the ceremony, Borglum met with the business elite of nearby Rapid City and told them he'd be needing *their* money, about $50,000 of it.

PORTRAIT OF THE ARTIST AS A YOUNG MAN

So who was this artist with the larger-than-life ambitions? An American, Borglum was born in an Idaho log cabin in 1867 to a polygamous Danish Mormon family. Claiming he would be famous by age thirty, young Borglum had dreams of being an artist. He often ran away from home and did eventually make it all the way to Paris by that age, although he struggled financially during his education. During his time in Paris, he struck up a friendship with an artist he idolized, the modern-art sculptor Auguste Rodin, whose ideas and style inspired Borglum to return to America to break through the old guard of the art world.

In 1901, Borglum settled in New York City. With new determination and momentum, Borglum saw his career take off as he began making large works of public sculpture and zealously self-promoting his art every step of the way. Within ten years, he had reinvented himself as a successful but temperamental artist, who

grew even more famous for his personality than for his artwork. Despite his difficult reputation, Borglum did work his way in to high society of the early 1900s, befriending everyone from the Wright brothers to Teddy Roosevelt. Borglum hadn't yet found a way to make his sculpture as large and famous as his own outsized personality, but that would soon change.

MOVING MOUNTAINS, TAKE ONE

In 1915 the Daughters of the Confederacy (DOC) invited Borglum to carve a bust of General Robert E. Lee on Stone Mountain, just outside Atlanta, Georgia. This wouldn't be just any old bust. Borglum felt it would be the eighth wonder of the world—a 1.33-acre monument featuring an enormous relief of Robert E. Lee on horseback carved directly into the granite face of the mountain. Undaunted by the fact the DOC didn't have a lot of money to back such a huge project (they had envisioned something a little smaller than what Borglum had in mind), he mortgaged his 500-acre estate in Connecticut and set to work on his first foray into mountain carving.

His first time out of the gate, Borglum's project went pretty poorly. It suffered chronically from a lack of funds and constant infighting stirred up by Borglum himself, who was irritated at those who refused to bow before his genius and demands. After ten years and completion of less than one tenth of the carving, Borglum was tossed off the project and run out of town in a hail of gunfire (according to him). He did manage to destroy all his models for the colossal sculpture prior to his departure. So, soon afterward the owners of the mountain blasted away Borglum's entire carving. They eventually hired another sculptor to complete the project.

MOVING MOUNTAINS, TAKE TWO

Luckily for Borglum the state historian of South Dakota, Doane Robinson, wanted to drum up some tourism dollars for his state. He had heard about all the Stone Mountain hubbub and thought his state could use a mountain sculpture too. Robinson invited Borglum to undertake the work and gave him creative control. Robinson was glad to let Borglum take charge—"After all," he

---

Early Riser: In a 50-year period, Thomas Jefferson said, the sun "never caught him in bed."

said, "God only makes a Michelangelo or a Borglum once every thousand years."

Luckily for Robinson, Borglum's grand vision fit in with the plans for South Dakota. "American art ought to be monumental, in keeping with American life," Borglum said. But instead of creating a regional piece, Borglum wanted to devote this sculpture to the power and might of the office of the president; this undertaking would be a national monument, not a provincial one, whose subject would be the "founding, preservation and expansion of the United States." From left to right, the faces would be George Washington, Thomas Jefferson, Theodore Roosevelt, and Abraham Lincoln. Washington would represent the fight for independence; Thomas Jefferson the idea of government by the people; Abraham Lincoln the preservation of the Union; and Theodore Roosevelt the rise of America as an international player. "The faces are in the mountain. All I have to do is bring them out," Borglum said.

At first, South Dakotans were skeptical and hostile to the project; huge, expensive (and somewhat pointless) monuments didn't exactly fit with the rugged, practical, frontier spirit. A year after Borglum's plea for $50,000, he had only raised $5,000. Newspapers across the country mocked his efforts "to destroy" another mountain and were glad it was tucked away in South Dakota.

All looked lost until South Dakota senator Peter Norbeck, the financial hero of the Rushmore fight, came to the rescue. He convinced President Calvin Coolidge to spend the summer vacationing in the Black Hills. By the time Coolidge had arrived, the excitement he brought with him had helped the Rushmore association to raise an additional $42,000. With the president's support, Senator Norbeck got a bill passed authorizing federal matching funds for every private dollar raised for Rushmore.

JACK-HAMMERING OUT THE FINE DETAILS
Carving officially began on August 10, 1927, and would continue on and off for the next fourteen years. Dangling from 3/8-inch cables 500 feet above the ground, the workers did most of the carving with dynamite and heavy pneumatic drills. First, they

John F. Kennedy was the first president born in the twentieth century (May 29, 1917).

blasted off the surface rock in the shape of an egg for Washington's face. Then they set to work replicating the proportions of the studio models onto the size of the mountain. Borglum and his workers used techniques pioneered by the ancient Greeks. First they drilled holes in the granite and inserted beams that corresponded to the location of pegs on the smaller-scaled studio models. They used the beams to hang plumb lines and extrapolated the correct points where features should lay on the mountain before chiseling away.

By 1930 Washington's face was finished. Newsreels and newspapers across the nation celebrated the amazingly mammoth construction. Workers spent the next eighteen months working on Jefferson's face, just to the right of Washington's visage. Unfortunately they found the granite there was too soft, forcing them to blast it off and start over on Washington's left. Borglum's difficult personality didn't make things any easier. Often impatient and angry, he fired his loyal workers only to have his son Lincoln rehire them behind his father's back.

RUSH MORE MONEY!

As the project ran into logistical problems, it hit hard financial times as well. The country was in a terrible depression, but that didn't phase Borglum, who had no problems about asking Congress for more money. Borglum never let up on his networking either, wiring "collect" to everyone he could think of—from William Randolph Hearst to the Duke of Windsor—in the hopes that their checks would roll on in.

Ironically it was the deepening Depression that saved the Rushmore monument. By 1932 President Herbert Hoover had started disbursing relief money, and Senator Norbeck was there to snag $100,000 for jobs on Mount Rushmore. By convincing the National Park Service to take over the site, Norbeck also guaranteed even more funding to finish the project. Meanwhile, Borglum continued to cultivate his imposing, difficult personality while managing the massive engineering project, threatening to walk away from it repeatedly and forcing Senator Norbeck to placate him time and time again.

At Choate prep school Kennedy was nicknamed Rat Face for his scrawny appearance.

IS IT DONE YET?

Construction on the monument continued for fourteen years, until 1941 when World War II forced Congress to cut all funding. The project wasn't nearly finished: the artist had meant to carve entire busts all the way down to the presidents' waists instead of just sculpting their heads. Sadly a week later, Borglum died from complications following surgery. Lincoln would be forced to put the finishing touches on his father's most famous work.

Altogether the monument cost $989,992.32, funded almost entirely from the U.S. Treasury. Workers technically worked on the sculpture for fourteen years. But between weather delays and lack of funds, however, they only spent about six and a half years actually carving Mount Rushmore.

Interestingly enough, Borglum's finished product has yet to be seen, and if you believe his planning, it shouldn't be available for a few hundred thousand millennia. "I am allowing an extra three inches on all the features of the various Presidents in order to provide stone for the wear and tear of the elements, which cuts the granite down one inch every hundred thousand years," said Borglum. In other words, if you want to see the end of the Mt. Rushmore story, it'll be about 300,000 years from now.

★　　★　　★　　★　　★

IT'S A LITTLE KNOWN FACT THAT . . .

- The four faces in Mt. Rushmore are scaled to men who would stand 465 feet tall.
- 450,000 tons of rock were cut away and still lie at the base of the mountain.
- Each head is 60 feet high, each nose 20 feet long, each mouth 18 feet wide, each eye 11 feet across.
- There are two-foot shafts cut in the center of each pupil in order to catch the light to make a glint.
- Some grumbled about Borglum's choice of Roosevelt since Teddy was a personal friend of the artist.

CLOSING REMARKS

*Presidents choose their words carefully, apparently even
on their deathbeds. Here are some of their last words—
many of them profound, and a few not so much.*

GEORGE WASHINGTON: Upon learning that his burial in-
structions would be followed, our first president muttered, *"Tis well."*

JOHN ADAMS: On July 4, 1826, the fiftieth anniversary of U.S.
independence, a dying President Adams was comforted by the
thought that another Founding Father would live on, exclaiming,
"Thomas Jefferson still survives." Adams passed away unaware that
Jefferson had died just a few hours earlier.

THOMAS JEFFERSON: *"Is it the fourth?"* Jefferson asked. When
told that it was, he then died peacefully.

JAMES MADISON: *"I always talk better lying down."*

JAMES MONROE: He told a friend, *"I regret that I should leave this
world without again beholding him,"* the him in this case being James
Madison.

JOHN QUINCY ADAMS: *"This is the last of earth. I am content."*

ANDREW JACKSON: To his family who had gathered around
him, Jackson said, *"Oh, do not cry. Be good children, and we shall all
meet in Heaven."*

MARTIN VAN BUREN: *"There is but one reliance."*

WILLIAM HENRY HARRISON: As a cold brought him to the
brink of death only one month after his inauguration, Harrison's
thoughts drifted to those who would succeed him. *"I wish you to
understand the true principles of government. I wish them carried out,
and ask for nothing more."*

JOHN TYLER: *"I am going . . . perhaps it is for the best."*

JAMES K. POLK: To his wife, who sat comforting him at his bedside, Polk whispered, *"I love you Sarah. I love you."* He smiled warmly, told her what provisions he had made for her, and then passed away.

ZACHARY TAYLOR: *"I regret nothing, but I am sorry that I am about to leave my friends."*

MILLARD FILLMORE: *"The nourishment is palatable."*

JAMES BUCHANAN: *"O Lord God Almighty, as Thou wilt!"*

ABRAHAM LINCOLN: When the First Lady asked him what people would think of them holding hands during the play, Lincoln replied, *"They won't think anything about it."* Moments later Booth's gun went off.

ANDREW JOHNSON: After falling out of his chair, Johnson said to his distraught granddaughter, *"My right side is paralyzed . . . I need no doctor. I can overcome my troubles."*

ULYSSES S. GRANT: *"Water."* Yet that wasn't going to help Grant's sore throat: he had cancer of the tongue.

RUTHERFORD B. HAYES: With his wife having died several years earlier, death had a silver lining for Hayes: *"I know that I am going where Lucy is."*

JAMES GARFIELD: Garfield was technically killed by an assassin's bullet, but it took quite a while. For eighty hot summer days doctors probed and prodded him to try to extract the bullet. Alexander Graham Bell even got in on the act, searching for the lead bullet with a crude metal detector. Finally, Garfield had had enough, and pleaded to his chief of staff, *"Swaim, can't you stop this? Oh, Swaim!"*

GROVER CLEVELAND: *"I have tried so hard to do right."*

BENJAMIN HARRISON: *"Doctor . . . my lungs."*

Thomas Jefferson described himself as having a "canine appetite for reading."

WILLIAM MCKINLEY: After being shot by an anarchist at the Pan-American Exposition in Buffalo, *"We are all going; we are all going; we are all going . . . Oh, dear."*

TEDDY ROOSEVELT: *"Please put out the light."*

WOODROW WILSON: Wilson is purported to have said, *"I am a broken piece of machinery. When the machinery is broken . . . I am ready."* Yet another account of his final moments is as poignant as it is short, with the President simply saying *"Edith,"* his wife's name.

WARREN HARDING: As he rested comfortably in a hotel bed in San Francisco, Harding's wife read out loud to him an article from the *Saturday Evening Post*. It was titled "A Calm View of a Calm Man," and was full of praise for the president, which he obviously liked. *"That's good. Go on. Read some more,"* he said to her and then suddenly went into convulsions and died.

CALVIN COOLIDGE: *"Good morning, Robert,"* Coolidge said to his handyman as the former president headed upstairs for his morning shave. But it wasn't a good morning for Calvin: a little while later Mrs. Coolidge discovered him dead on the bathroom floor.

HERBERT HOOVER: When told that Admiral Strauss had come to pay him a visit, Hoover was already speaking in the past tense: *"Lewis Strauss was one of my best friends."*

FRANKLIN ROOSEVELT: While sitting for a portrait painting, Roosevelt suddenly exclaimed, *"I have a terrific headache!"*

DWIGHT EISENHOWER: With this wife, Mamie, holding his hand, Eisenhower bravely said, *"I'm ready to go, God take me."*

LYNDON JOHNSON: After a sudden heart attack at his Texas ranch, President Johnson was still able to get to his intercom, where he pleaded for help: *"Send for Mike immediately!"*

Young Calvin Coolidge earned spare cash selling apples and popcorn balls at town meetings.

TAD AND WILLIE'S WILD RIDE

How Tad and Willie ran the White House (ragged)
during the Lincoln presidency.

Hooligans and tyrants and brats! (Oh my!) Those were just some of the kinder, gentler terms folks used to describe young Willie and Tad Lincoln, the two youngest sons of the sixteenth president. Brave souls who dared to visit the Lincoln White House might find themselves doused with a fire hose or faced with a goat-drawn chair as it roared at them at top speed. The culprits? Those two Lincoln boys! Luckily the irrepressible, tenderhearted sons could charm as well as terrify the public. And during the tragic Civil War years their high jinks brought welcome comic relief to a somber White House and a melancholy president.

A DEATH IN THE FAMILY
Both the president and Mrs. Lincoln lost their mothers early on in their childhoods, and both suffered through harsh parental relationships after their mothers' deaths. Abraham struggled to connect with his rough and distant father while Mary toiled with an unloving stepmother. After the couple married and had children of their own, they knew they wanted their kids to have the happy, carefree childhoods they'd never known. So the Lincolns raised their boys, Robert, Eddie, Willie, and Thomas (otherwise known as Tad)—with lots of affection and few rules. Willie and Tad first caused a ruckus while the family still lived in Springfield, Illinois. One pastime that they never tired of was visiting their Pa's law office and knocking all the leather-bound law volumes off the shelves. The two youngest boys continued to run wild even when dear old dad became president of the United States.

THE FIRST BRAT PACK?
In 1861 Abraham Lincoln moved his family (excluding Robert, who spent most of his time studying at Harvard, and Eddie, who

---

George H. W. Bush has a scar on his forehead from a prep school soccer accident . . .

had died in 1850 from what was believed to be tuberculosis) into the White House. Even though ten-year-old Willie and seven-year-old Tad were now in new territory, they didn't let that stop their antics! Their brand-new home provided endless opportunities for make-believe and mischief. The roof of the White House became their playground. It served at different times as a pretend circus (which the staff was made to attend), a ship (with sheets nailed up as sails), and a makeshift fort. Among other mishaps the boys broke a large White House mirror with their ball; took the paint tubes belonging to a presidential portrait artist and smeared paint all over the wall; and pounded nails into a secretary's desk. Not even the presidential office was immune from Willie- and Tadism. The boys pummeled each other through war conferences, and Tad famously opened fire on the important cabinet members with his toy cannon.

BROTHERS IN ARMS
Though Willie and Tad were inseparable pals, they were very different people. Willie was said to be the son most like his father. He had the same love of learning and the same kindly, magnetic personality. When a family friend died in battle, eleven-year-old Willie wrote a heartfelt poem that was good enough to be published in a Washington newspaper. The pride and comfort of his father, Willie was often seen walking hand in hand with the president.

Tad (his nickname was derived from Abe's observation that his newborn son resembled a tadpole) had problems concentrating and a severe lisp that made it difficult for him to be understood. He had no patience with lessons and never did learn to read much while in the White House. He spent most of his time inventing adventures and pranks—and pulling Willie into the fun. Yet Tad could also be warmhearted, bringing visitors with problems to the president and demanding that his father help them.

White House aides not only found Lincoln unwilling to rebuke his boys for their tricks, but they also fretted that he might join in with the two boys. A passenger who traveled on the same train as the Lincoln family noted sourly that while his "brats" upset the entire train, "Lincoln looked pleased as Punch [and] aided and abetted the older one in his mischief."

HONEST ABE THE DOGNAPPER

The man known as Honest Abe even entered into the crime of dognapping for the sake of Tad and Willie. When a handsome, black pointer followed their carriage, the president gave in to his sons' demands and allowed them to keep it. The president even denied seeing the dog when the anxious owner sent out inquiries about his lost black pointer. Only after the owner read about the first family's new canine acquisition in the newspapers and stormed into the White House did Lincoln agree to return the dog—in exchange for its pup.

Lincoln felt his sons should enjoy playing while they were young, that sorrow would arrive soon enough. In fact, Willie was only eleven years old when he contracted a fever—many historians think it was typhoid—and died. The grieving president, whose hysterical wife could offer little support, turned to Tad for comfort. Father and son soon became inseparable. Tad developed his own special code for entering Pa's office: three quick taps and two slow bangs. Presidential business was always interrupted for Tad and dignitaries might be forced to wait if he wanted help with his pet goat, a trip to the toy store, or just a hug. Aides even complained they couldn't trust the president with war secrets because he would blab to Tad!

Tad lost his best friend when Lincoln was murdered a few days after the boy's birthday in 1865. Trying to be brave Tad vowed to be good so he could see his brother and father in heaven. He became the mainstay of Mary Lincoln's life until he died of tuberculosis at eighteen. Tragedy, as their parents had feared, ended Tad and Willie's wild ride all too soon.

★　★　★　★　★

MODEST ABE

"I do not think myself fit for the Presidency. I certainly am flattered, and grateful that some partial friends think of me in that connection."
—Abraham Lincoln, April 16, 1859

NUMBER TWENTY-TWO & TWENTY-FOUR: GROVER CLEVELAND

Served from 1885 to 1889 and 1893 to 1897

Vital Stats: Born on March 18, 1837, in Caldwell, New Jersey. Died on June 24, 1908, in Princeton, New Jersey.
Age at First Inauguration: 47
Vice President: Thomas A. Hendricks (first term); Adlai E. Stevenson (second term)
Political Affiliation: Democratic
Wife: Francis Folsom (married 1886)
Kids: Ruth (1891–1904); Esther (1893–1980); Marion (1895–1995); Richard Folsom (1897–1974); Francis Grover (1903–1977)
Education: Public Schools
What he did before he was president: Lawyer; Erie County Assistant District Attorney; Sheriff of Erie County; Mayor of Buffalo, Governor of New York
Postpresidential Occupations: Lawyer

MEMORABLE QUOTES

"The lessons of paternalism ought to be unlearned and the better lesson taught that while the people should patriotically and cheerfully support their Government its functions do not include the support of the people."
—Grover Cleveland in his second inaugural address, March 4, 1893

"And still the question, 'What shall be done with our ex-Presidents?' is not laid at rest; and I sometimes think Watterson's solution of it, 'Take them out and shoot them,' is worthy of attention."
—Grover Cleveland, from a letter dated April 19, 1889

NUMBER TWENTY-THREE: <u>BENJAMIN HARRISON</u>

Served from 1889 to 1893

Vital Stats: Born on August 20, 1833, in North Bend, Ohio. Died on March 13, 1901, in Indianapolis, Indiana.
Age at First Inauguration: 55
Vice President: Levi P. Morton
Political Affiliation: Republican
First Wife: Caroline Lavinia Scott (married 1853. died in 1892)
Kids from First Marriage: Russell Benjamin (1854–1936); Mary Scott (1858–1930)
Second Wife: Mary Scott Lord Dimmick (married 1896)
Kids from Second Marriage: Elizabeth (1897–1955)
Education: Miami University
What he did before he was president: Lawyer; Notary Public; Brigadier General in 70th Indiana Volunteers; U.S. Senator
Postpresidential Occupations: Lawyer

MEMORABLE QUOTES

"The death of William Tecumseh Sherman . . . is an event that will bring sorrow to the heart of every patriotic citizen. No living American was so loved and venerated as he."
—Benjamin Harrison delivers a special message to Congress, February 14, 1891. Harrison fought under Sherman's command during the Civil War.

"It is essential that none of the other great powers shall secure these islands [Hawaii]. Such a possession would not consist with our safety and with the peace of the world."
—Benjamin Harrison tries to convince Congress to annex Hawaii, February 15, 1893

PRESIDENT
AU NATUREL

The aristocratic son of former president John Adams, John Quincy Adams was a man ahead of his time—and out of his clothes.

Presion John Quincy Adams was the sort of forward thinking, public spirited man people should want running their country. Long before such projects became popular and were proved to have far-reaching social benefits, Adams's plans included "federally sponsored scientific expeditions, astronomical observatories, roads and canals, and a national university." The following centuries would confirm that all these inspirations were fantastic ideas for the good of America's development and evolution.

Unfortunately Adams was an awkward intellectual who lacked the charisma needed to get people excited about his thoughtful ideas. Worse yet, his controversial 1824 election victory against Andrew Jackson had been highly disputed; Adams's enemies used this controversy to undermine his presidential authority. His inspirational ideas were almost all voted down in Congress, and America would have to wait on the progress he had envisioned for her. Poor old Adams was distraught at this ongoing sabotage of his term in office. But he did discover one liberating way to relieve his frustrations. He would cast off the weight of the world—along with his clothes, his cares, and his stodgy, intellectual image—and go skinny-dipping in the Potomac River.

JOHN Q. NUDIST
Proving himself a modern thinker as well as a lofty one, Adams would rise before dawn every morning, slip out of the White House to go down to the river and enjoy some therapeutic bathing in the buff—in full public view. It was, after all, a different time. And Adams enjoyed far more freedom to come and go as he pleased than he would today. He didn't have a security detail dogging him at every step, plus Washington, DC, was less crowded with potential gawkers then. More importantly, camera use was

just in its infancy, so no paparazzi were lurking about in the bushes. Best of all, the Potomac's waters were still sparkly clean and inviting. All of which added up to the perfect set of conditions for Adams to indulge in his favorite predawn ritual. This entertaining hobby led to a number of amusing adventures for America's sixth president.

THE PRESIDENT'S NEW CLOTHES

On one occasion a passerby stole Adams's clothes from the riverbank while he swam. When he finished his swim and discovered the theft, Adams was forced to quickly get back into the river to hide his nakedness. Eventually, he persuaded a passing boy to run to the White House and fetch him a fresh outfit.

Adams met with a similar calamity when he changed up the routine one day. Fully clothed, he took a canoe out on the river in place of his usual dip. The jolly trip soon veered sharply downhill when the canoe sank. This downturn in events gathered momentum as Adams's waterlogged suit started to pull him under. And the shipwreck was complete when Adams was forced to discard his Sunday best (turned expensive ballast) to the fishes and return to shore in his birthday suit instead. Well, not quite his birthday suit—this time he at least had some pantaloons to cover his manhood and preserve a little dignity. They were a small comfort, however, as Adams was forced to make the trip back to the White House in nothing but his knickers.

A ROYALL PAIN IN THE REAR

Adams did have one paparazzi-esque experience during his nude excursions. Anne Royall (notable newspaperwoman and trailblazer for shameless, modern journalistic tactics) staked out Adams's favorite swimming spot one morning, watched the president strip naked and plunge into the Potomac waters. She then sat on his clothes until he would grant her an interview. Adamant that she would not lose her opportunity, she refused Adams's offer of a frank, clothed interview in exchange for his garments. Instead, she insisted that he would not get them back before she had her interview with him. She proceeded to quiz the most powerful man in the nation while he stood naked in a swirling river.

OLD MAN ELOQUENT

After his presidency a clothed Adams achieved more in the service of his country than he had been able to within the surprisingly constricting confines of the Highest Office. He was humble enough to accept his community's nomination for further political office and was subsequently elected to the House of Representatives. He spent the rest of his life in Congress, fighting to force his fellow politicians to recognize the problem of slavery and, therefore, to address it.

Adams's passionate pleas to his colleagues to face the slavery issue rather than hide from it earned him the nicknames Old Man Eloquent from admirers and the Madman from Massachusetts from detractors. After many years, his hard work, wisdom, and vision resulted in the government agreeing to hear petitions requesting the abolition of slavery. Adams's eloquent campaigning had also helped turn the tide of political opinion toward the day when these petitions would be acted upon.

LEGACY OF A PUBLIC ENEMY

A true patriot, Adams passionately believed in his vision for a better America—even in the face of indignant opponents who branded him a public enemy—which led him to make a pivotal contribution to the abolition of slavery. Though his other fine plans to better his country would have to wait for another champion, it was for this important cause that he truly made his stand and in this success that he left his legacy.

Adams died in the House, still toiling in the service of his beloved country. When he collapsed at his desk in 1848, Old Man Eloquent was fittingly immortalized by his peer, Thomas Benton: "Where could Death have found him but at the post of duty?"

CLOSE CALLS III

Sometimes all you have to be is famous to be a target.

SAMUEL BYCK: RICHARD NIXON

If you walked past the White House on Christmas eve, 1973, you would have seen a rather strange Santa Claus. Samuel Byck, dressed as Santa, picketed with a sign petitioning the government for his constitutional rights. He had been arrested for picketing without a permit twice before and this time wanted to see "if they had the guts to arrest Santa Claus." He was not arrested and spent most of the evening posing for photos by tourists.

A middle-aged, out-of-work tire salesman from Philadelphia, Byck blamed all of his life's failures on what he saw as a corrupt and oppressive government, led by one Richard Nixon. Byck had a history of mental illness and sought psychiatric help in 1969 when he was diagnosed as having a manic-depressive illness. Unfortunately, his seeking medical attention did not help Byck to overcome his problems. The Secret Service questioned him after he threatened the life of President Nixon in 1972, but released him, concluding that he just liked to talk big.

A Sinister Plan

Around the time of his Christmas eve picket, Sam Byck came up with a plan he called Operation: Pandora's Box. Believing that the Watergate scandal proved the corruption of the government, Byck wanted to incinerate not just President Nixon but also his entire administration. His plan was to hijack a plane and crash it into the White House—a plan that seems even more sinister today.

Intent on his motives' being understood, Byck recorded his plans on cassette tapes that were mailed to a wide variety of people: composer Leonard Bernstein, *Washington Post* columnist Jack Anderson, Senator Ribicoff, and other celebrities. Driving to Baltimore the morning of February 22, 1974, Byck recorded another eerie monologue on tape. In it, it seems one of his most pressing concerns is that he might run out of gas before reaching the airport.

At Baltimore/Washington International airport, Byck

approached the security gate for Delta Flight 523 carrying a
.22-caliber pistol and a homemade gasoline bomb. He shot the
security guard, killing him instantly. Byck ran onto the plane and
demanded that the pilots take off. When told that they couldn't
because the blocks were still in front of the wheels, he shot and
killed the copilot and threatened the few first class passengers that
had already boarded. Police massing outside the plane shot Byck
through the windows. Falling to the floor, Byck turned his gun on
himself and ended his life.

Richard Nixon was at home in the White House that night,
unaware that any attempt had been made on his life. Sam Byck
was the first man to attempt a hijacking in the United States
since the government started requiring security screening of all
airline passengers.

JOHN HINCKLEY: RONALD REAGAN

Within minutes of its happening, Americans watched on their
TVs as a blonde man fired six shots at the commander in chief.
John Hinckley, son of a Colorado oil executive, crouched among
the press corps outside the Washington Hilton Hotel on March
30, 1981. As President Reagan waved to the crowd, Hinckley
opened fire, hitting Reagan, Press Secretary James Brady, a policeman and a Secret Service agent, the first one to be injured while
protecting the president.

At first, Reagan thought he was unharmed. But as his limo
pulled away from the scene of the attack, his companions noticed
he had been shot. Despite a collapsed left lung, the seventy-year-
old Reagan walked under his own power into the emergency
room. He said to his wife, when she arrived at the hospital,
"Honey, I forgot to duck," quoting the boxer Jack Dempsey.
Apparently not even bullets could stop this presidential sense of
humor. While surgeons prepared him for emergency surgery,
Reagan quipped, "Please tell me you're Republicans." Later, in
the recovery room, unable to speak because of the tubes in his
body, he wrote, "All in all, I'd rather be in Philadelphia," stealing
a line from W. C. Fields.

Reagan made a full recovery, but James Brady suffered permanent brain damage and never recovered full use of his body. Brady

---

Franklin D. Roosevelt wore dresses until he was 5, then he was clad in kilts. Pants came at 8.

worked in later years to pass gun-control legislation. Finally, under President Bill Clinton, he pushed through a gun-control bill, requiring a five-day waiting period and background check on all handgun purchases, among other restrictions.

Not Your Everyday Motive

The entire attack had been caught on videotape, so there was no question as to who shot the president. The only thing on people's minds was why Hinckley shot Reagan. When his trial began, John Hinckley's lawyers presented an insanity defense and claimed that Hinckley's obsession with the actress Jodie Foster and the film *Taxi Driver* drove him to attack the president. Foster appears in the film whose unhinged main character Travis Bickle (based on the real-life George Wallace attacker, Arthur Bremer) became a role model for Hinckley.

Hinckley fixated on his need for Foster's love, and he decided to do something to get her attention. On March 30, 1981, he noticed in the paper that Reagan was to speak at the Hilton hotel in only a few hours. Hinckley returned to his hotel, loaded his .22, and wrote a letter to Foster. In it he wrote, "Jodie, I would abandon this idea of getting Reagan in a second if I could only win your heart and live out the rest of my life with you, whether it be in total obscurity or whatever."

At his trial Hinckley declared that he had accomplished all of his objectives by shooting the president. To the nation's horror, the jury at Hinckley's trial returned a verdict of not guilty by reason of insanity. The public outcry after this led to laws restricting the use of the insanity plea in most states and abolishing it entirely in Utah.

Hinckley currently resides in St. Elizabeth's Hospital in Washington, DC. In 2003, despite evidence of his continued obsession with Foster, and a similar stalking incident of one of the hospital staff, Hinckley won the right to unsupervised visits with his parents.

EMBETTERING THE LANGUAGE

When everything you say in public gets written down,
a few things stick.

The English language can be either friend or foe to the president. Abraham Lincoln and John F. Kennedy ascended to the office on the power of their speeches and coined phrases that are firmly lodged in the American oratorical imagination. On the other hand, George W. Bush and Warren G. Harding were elected to the presidency *despite* a reputation for mangling the language when speaking off-the-cuff. Below are a few of our presidents' most unusual, lasting, or humorous contributions to the English language.

OK?

A lot of false etymologies have been proposed for *OK*, one of the most ubiquitous utterances in English (and many other languages, for that matter). Some popular theories posited that *OK* came from French, a Scottish dialect of English, or the African language Wolof. For a while it was even spelled *okeh* on the theory that it came from the Native American language Choctaw. None of these theories can be backed up by documentary evidence. The theory that most linguists now believe is that the word arose out of an 1830s craze for intentional misspellings. The first known citation of *OK* from the *Boston Morning Post* in 1839, states that it stood for "oll korrect," the misspelled version of "all correct."

Most of the abbreviations of this crazy misspelling fad died a quick historico-linguistic death. *OK*, however, took off after its use in Martin Van Buren's 1840 reelection campaign. Van Buren was from Kinderhook, New York, so he took on the nickname Old Kinderhook during his campaign (maybe hoping that Andrew Jackson's success with the nickname Old Hickory would transfer to his "Old" nickname). They called him *OK* for short, and his supporters used *OK* all by itself as a campaign slogan. They would

---

A mining engineer, Herbert Hoover was a self-made millionaire by the age of 40.

also report success for Van Buren just by reporting "OK." Unfortunately, Van Buren's bid for reelection was not OK. He lost the election to William Henry Harrison.

ROORBACK

Roorback is a rare word with a very specialized meaning: a false or slanderous story that is meant to cause political harm. It came out of the presidential campaigns of 1844, when James K. Polk was running against Henry Clay. Their tactics were full of ad hominem attacks. In one episode, Polk's followers published a pamphlet that accused Clay of breaking every single one of the Ten Commandments.

Clay's supporters searched in vain for comparable skeletons in the closet with which to smear Polk, but they discovered that he was just too boring to find incriminating material on. So instead, they just made some up. They claimed that a book by the imaginary Baron von Roorback called *Roorback's Tour Through the Southern and Western States* proved that Polk was deeply involved in the slave trade. The allegation was quickly proved false, and the resulting backlash actually helped Polk in the polls.

BULLY PULPIT

Theodore Roosevelt coined the term *bully pulpit* to describe the power of the office of the presidency that allowed the person holding it to express his view on any topic and be listened to. Roosevelt believed strongly that he was able to shape American life most favorably through speaking to the people. He wrote all his own speeches and delivered them with evangelical fervor. His first recorded use of *bully pulpit* was in response to criticism of his speech making in 1909. He responded, "I suppose my critics will call that preaching, but I have got such a bully pulpit!" In coining the phrase he attached one of his favorite adjectives, bully, which means super or great, to pulpit, the place from which a minister delivers a sermon. The word has been extended in meaning since then to refer to all sorts of public offices and the opportunities they offer to communicate with the public.

The primary presidential helicopter is a Sikorsky VH-3D, called the Sea King.

TEDDY BEAR

Theodore Roosevelt is also famously responsible for the well-known phrase *teddy bear*. Roosevelt's interest in outdoor activities was notorious both during and after his presidency. On one of his hunting expeditions, nearing the end of the day, it looked as if he would have to go home without scoring a hit. His Mississippi hosts had prepared for this embarrassing contingency by catching a bear beforehand and tying it up so it couldn't escape. Roosevelt saw the poor trapped creature and refused to shoot it on the grounds that it was not sporting to kill the defenseless bear. His gesture of pity became legendary, spurring a stuffed-toy craze that eventually got so big that the capital *T* on *teddy bear* was dropped.

BLOVIATING HIS WAY TO NORMALCY

Warren G. Harding was known for being a great speaker—but not for saying anything while doing it. He liked to use lots of words to communicate to his audience but was very well aware of his tendency to maximum verbosity. Harding did have the ability to laugh at himself and used the term *Bloviate*, a mock-Latinate creation thought to arise from *blow*, to describe his own speech-making style. *Bloviate* can mean to speak pompously but not really say anything or to use a lot of words to not say very much. The term may have originated in the late 1800s, but Harding is credited with making it popular.

You may not know it now, but *normalcy* was not an accepted word when Harding used it in his campaign, when he ran promising a "return to normalcy" and saying that what America needed was "not nostrums but normalcy." The word *normality* was and is the accepted noun form of *normal*. Pedants responded with hostility to Harding's usage of *normalcy*—even six years after Harding's election Fowler's famous usage guide scorned it as a "spurious hybrid." *Normalcy* is not actually Harding's own coinage, being cited back as far as 1857 in a mathematics text. However, his influence surely brought about wide acceptance of the word in the United States. Most American dictionaries now consider it an acceptable alternative to *normality*, whereas British dictionaries still look down their noses at it.

SNOLLYGOSTER

Snollygoster, a word that appeared headed for the dustbin of history, was revived by Harry S. Truman in 1952 after a long period of dormancy. Strangely, though, Truman succeeded in reviving it without really knowing what it meant. He claimed that it meant "a person born out of wedlock," but previous references to the word showed that it had been used only to mean "a shrewd, unprincipled person, especially a politician." Research showed that an 1895 explanation of the word also stipulated that a snollygoster has attained his position "by the sheer force of monumental talknophical assumnacy." The origin of *snollygoster* unfortunately is unknown. One theory has that it's connected with *snallygaster*, a mythical half-bird, half-reptile that supposedly haunts Maryland and preys on poultry and children.

EMBETTERMENT, MISUNDERESTIMATE

President George W. Bush has had his difficulties with the English language in public. He has inadvertently invented the words *Hispanically*, *subliminable*, *resignate*, and *arbolist*, not to mention many other syntactical problems and laughable slips of the tongue. It's hard to say so soon which of these Bushisms stands a chance of catching on à la *bloviate*, but here are two likely candidates.

Embetterment is Bush's version of *betterment* that seems to have been influenced by *empowerment*. The root word *embetter*, though, unlike most of Bush's coinages, has an entry in the *Oxford English Dictionary*. Granted, its last citation is dated 1839, but *embetterment* could catch on in the same way that Truman was able to resuscitate *snollygoster*.

Misunderestimate, which Bush first said just before the 2000 election, has been cited more often than many of his other gaffes, and it has even become a kind of symbol for his verbal mix-ups. *They Misunderestimated Me!* was the title of a calendar of Bushisms that became a best seller, for instance. Bush has even cited it as one of his most well known neologisms. That is to say, he meant to. In a speech in March 2001 Bush said, "I've coined new words, like 'misunderstanding' and 'Hispanically.'" It was the first known example of a meta-Bushism.

Marine One is the call sign used when the president is on board the HMX-1 Marine helicopters.

HOUSE ON FIRE

*Dolley Madison earned the title First Lady
with her bravery . . . or was it the ice cream?*

One of the most popular and vivacious First Ladies of the early days of the Republic was Dolley Madison. Dolley reveled in her role as First Hostess, threw the very first inaugural ball, and quickly established that an invitation to the James Madison White House was always a hot ticket. In fact she began her career as official hostess of the White House in 1801, when widower Thomas Jefferson asked her to fill the position for him.

Many political critics, both then and now, maintain that Dolley's vigor and charm did much to enhance her husband's career. Dolley's sense of style captivated the young nation; she both held to traditions of Southern hospitality and thrilled to offer amusing novelties. She was the very first to serve ice cream in the White House, a delicacy introduced to her by Jefferson, who brought the French creation to the new nation. When Dolley died in 1849, President Zachary Taylor delivered her eulogy, which showed just how much the nation loved Mrs. Madison. Taylor's speech honored Dolley with a name that all future White House hostesses would come to be known as: "She will never be forgotten, because she truly was our First Lady for a half-century."

MADISON RESCUES WASHINGTON

While Dolley was a famous hostess, she is most famous for her heroism in the face of danger. During the War of 1812, Dolley faced down advancing enemy forces in an attempt to save her home. She was ultimately forced to run for her life, but thanks to her courage, priceless objects belonging to the American people were rescued.

The War of 1812 had been waging for two years. Washington, DC, was awash with rumors of a pending British invasion (and not just four cute mop-tops with guitars; it was redcoats back then). President James Madison had left his wife behind in the capital to join the defending forces in Maryland. On August 23, while the president was away, Dolley manned the White House as the

---

Millard Fillmore's wife Abigail established the White House library.

British troops approached Washington. She stood atop the White House roof with a spyglass for hours, watching the British troops advance on foot, all the while being urged by her friends and advisers to get out as quickly as she could. But she was reluctant to leave. She wrote to her sister Lucy, "I have pressed as many Cabinet Papers into trunks as will fill one carriage . . . Our private property must be sacrificed, as it is impossible to procure wagons for its transportation." She also wrote, "I am determined not to go myself until I see Mr. Madison safe, and he can accompany me."

When it became clear that she had to abandon her post, Dolley gathered the trunks of government papers, as much silver as she could carry, and—famously—the Gilbert Stuart portrait of George Washington. Contrary to popular legend, Dolley did *not* cut the painting from the frame; she had the frame broken up and removed the canvas intact. (The frame was apparently screwed to the wall and her stewards couldn't figure out how to get it down in a hurry.) Dolley loaded everything into a waiting carriage that sped her and the treasures to safety. She fled to Virginia, where she soon met up with her husband. The British burned down the White House the next day, along with the Capitol, the departmental buildings, and the navy yard. The fire could have been worse if not for a heavy rainstorm that quenched the flames before they spread further.

Ironically the French minister, Louis Barbe Sérurier, who had remained in the city after the approach of the British troops, sent a diplomatic request via messenger to the British commanding officer, General Robert Ross, to spare the mansion. General Ross received the message as he prepared to set the White House on fire; he sent the French minister his promise that the King's House, as he called it, would be spared. General Ross must have had an odd sense of humor: he burned it down anyway.

SPEND, SPEND, SPEND!

On August 27 the Madisons returned to the city and found the White House in ruins. They moved to the Octagon House, the second-largest residence in the city, and one year later they moved again to a house on the corner of 19th Street and Pennsylvania Avenue, NW.

Kennedy enjoyed collecting scrimshaw—carved or engraved ivory from whale or walrus tusks.

After the fire, the prevailing mood of U.S. citizens—with their general distaste for public spending for finery for the federal government—changed. It became a point of national honor to rebuild the city. There was a consensus that it should be bigger and better than ever. It turns out that the fire was actually "a blessing in disguise" according to the newspaper the *National Intelligencer*, the "Capitol, President's House, and Executive Offices will be rebuilt with additional splendor."

Original White House architect James Hoban oversaw the rebuilding of the mansion. By mid-September 1817 the White House was livable again. Congress appropriated $20,000 for furnishings so that Elizabeth Monroe, the next White House hostess, might entertain in style similar to her energetic predecessor. Luckily Mrs. Monroe would not have to replace the Gilbert Stuart portrait of Washington. It now hangs in the East Room and is the oldest original piece in the White House. The Madisons would eventually retire to Virginia after the end of their administration. After James died in 1836, Dolley returned to Washington, DC, to reign supreme as a hostess once more.

EMBERS AND ASHES

Incidentally, the fire of 1814 was not to be the last in the White House. A fire broke out in the West Wing on Christmas eve 1929 while President Herbert Hoover and his guests were dining. The president himself supervised the removing of papers from the Oval Office, but most everything else was lost to fire or damaged by smoke and water.

Reminders of the first fire remain to this day. Beneath the North Portico, in what is now the White House kitchen, there are several unpainted blocks of sandstone visible, still scorched and blackened from the flames. And when layers of old paint and whitewash were removed from the exterior of the White House—a process that was completed in 1992—there were still traces of soot and ash evident. These reminders are a testament to the enduring legacy of the energetic First Hostess who stood her ground to protect her home.

Lincoln's son Willie was the only presidential child to die in the White House.

NUMBER TWENTY-FIVE: WILLIAM MCKINLEY

Served from 1897 to 1901

Vital Stats: Born on January 29, 1843, in Niles, Ohio. Died on September 14, 1901, in Buffalo, New York.
Age at First Inauguration: 54
Vice President: Garrat A. Hobart (first term); Theodore Roosevelt (second term)
Political Affiliation: Republican
Wife: Ida Saxton (married 1871)
Kids: Katherine (1871–1875); Ida (born and died 1873)
Education: Allegheny College
What he did before he was president: Teacher; Soldier; Lawer; U.S. Congressman; Governor of Ohio
Postpresidential Occupations: None. Died in office.

MEMORABLE QUOTES

"With our near neighbors we must remain close friends . . . The transfer of American control to the new government is of such great importance, involving an obligation resulting from our intervention . . . The peace which we are pledged to leave . . . must carry with it the guaranties of permanence."
—William McKinley on Cuban-American relations, in his second inaugural address, March 4, 1901

"Expositions are the timekeepers of progress."
—William McKinley's last speech, given at the Pan-American Exposition, September 5, 1901

Harry S. Truman liked some artists—Rubens, Leonardo da Vinci—but hated Picasso.

STARRING
<u>THE PRESIDENT</u>

Presidents seem to have a knack for
finding their way to the silver screen.

I n a cinematic tribute to the presidents, we've put together a crafty little quiz to test how closely you were watching.

1. A little-known classic from 1946, *Magnificent Doll* stars Ginger Rogers as Dolley Madison, David Niven as the scheming Aaron Burr, and this future archfiend of Batman as James Madison. Can you name him?
   A. Vincent Price
   B. Burgess Meredith
   C. Cesar Romero
   D. Frank Gorshin

2. In the 1991 movie *Point Break*, four surfers rob banks and disguise themselves with rubber masks of the ex-presidents. Which presidents are they?
   A. Reagan, Carter, Ford, Nixon
   B. George H. W. Bush, Reagan, Carter, Nixon
   C. Reagan, Nixon, Lyndon Johnson, Kennedy
   D. Washington, Lincoln, Teddy Roosevelt, Jefferson

3. Everyone knows that Ronald Reagan was an actor before he went into politics, but do they know the names of his pictures? Pick the flick that Reagan did <u>not</u> appear in.
   A. *Hellcats of the Navy*
   B. *Bedtime for Bonzo*
   C. *Kings Row*
   D. *The Caine Mutiny*

He said, "Any kid can take an egg and a piece of ham and make more understandable pictures."

4. In the 1997 thriller *Air Force One*, the president, played by Harrison Ford, and his family tussle with hijackers aboard the famous plane while the vice president struggles in DC to take action. Who plays the vice president?
A. Scott Glenn
B. Glenn Close
C. Glenn Ford
D. Glen Campbell

5. Who can forget 1999's *Austin Powers: The Spy Who Shagged Me*? But we're wondering if you can remember who played the president that Dr. Evil demands "one billll-yun dollars" from in the 1960s?
A. Tim Conway
B. Tim Curry
C. Tim Robbins
D. Tim Roth

6. In 1999's *Dick*, a funny spin on the Watergate scandal, a teenage girl develops a crush on Nixon during her stint as an official White House dog walker. On Dick's personal tape recorder in the Oval Office, she uses an 18-1/2 minute song to tell him how she feels. What song does she sing?

A. "I Honestly Love You" by Olivia Newton John
B. "McArthur Park" by Richard Harris
C. "Knights in White Satin" by the Moody Blues
D. "I Think I Love You" by the Partridge Family

ANSWERS: 1. B, 2. A, 3. D, 4. B, 5. C, 6. A

Lyndon B. Johnson had a chopper seat refitted for use as his Oval Office desk chair.

OH, BROTHER!

Many people have a sibling they would rather no one knew about.
Why should presidents be any different?

Ah, those scandalous siblings!
It must have been difficult growing up in the same house as
the guy who would one day become the president of the United
States. The ambition, the drive, the smarts—all the characteristics
that make a person able to successfully run for the highest office
in the nation must be apparent in some form during childhood.
Pity the poor sibling who must share a room and parental attention with that shining star!

A lot of presidential siblings, particularly the brothers of presidents, seem to have had certain things in common. Growing up,
a lot of them became the family clown and used jokes, stunts, and
laughter to capture the attention—a direct contrast to their more
serious, goal-oriented brothers. Often when their siblings attain
the White House, these black sheep brothers capitalize on it,
often very lucratively. Maybe they feel that they are entitled to
something for having had to share their formative years with these
paragons of virtue. If nothing else, being the president's brother
certainly seems to open up some unique career opportunities.

PRISONER IN THE WHITE HOUSE

Growing up, Lyndon Baines Johnson and Sam Houston Johnson
shared a narrow bed in their modest Texas ranch house. They
were constant companions who mostly played together because
there were few other children in their dusty little hometown
along the banks of the Pedernales River. Together they took
elocution lessons from their mother Rebekah, who encouraged
the boys to imagine a crowd of people gathered in front of their
house as they stood on the porch to recite. Young Lyndon clearly
took a lot away from this practice, which served him well as he

Chester Arthur avoided reporters and granted few interviews.

entered politics. In fact, the first speech of his political career was given right on that same front porch, when he ran for Congress in 1937.

But how did younger brother Sam Houston use his elocution lessons? Not terribly well, it turns out. When compared to his larger-than-life brother, Sam Houston was more easygoing and far less ambitious. He is more well remembered for his world-class drinking than his world-class achievements. Sam Houston remained dependent on his older brother for most of his life and he lived with Lyndon and Lady Bird off and on throughout his life, including during their White House years.

The public, for the most part, was largely unaware of Sam Houston. He was kept squirreled away behind closed doors, and newspapers didn't report on Lyndon's private life. Nonetheless LBJ was concerned enough about his younger sibling that he ordered the Secret Service to keep a close eye on Sam Houston and follow him wherever he went. While living with Lyndon and Lady Bird, Sam Houston considered himself a virtual prisoner in the White House until Lyndon left office in 1969.

That same year Sam Houston Johnson burst onto the publishing scene with a tell-all book, *My Brother Lyndon*. Praised for its readable style and unflinching view of the president, Sam's portrayal of Lyndon is generally positive, if not downright admiring. A man concerned with privacy and control of his image, Lyndon Johnson considered the book a great betrayal by a family member he had tried so hard to protect. He never spoke to Sam again. The two brothers remained estranged until Lyndon's death in 1973. Sam died five years later.

WORKING FOR PEANUTS AND BEER

From the time Jimmy Carter entered politics, his brother Billy made headlines in his own right. The press loved his plainspoken, earthy manner and his often outrageous behavior. Jimmy Carter would say that people thought of Billy as a sort of southern folk philosopher. But people came to think of Billy as something much worse than that.

At first, Billy Carter would just hold court from his gas station across the street from the Carter family warehouse. The press ate up how he tossed off clever one-liners and bragged about smoking

pot in the White House, urinating in public, and drinking prodigious amounts of beer. As Billy's star began to rise, he capitalized on the growing national recognition of his name. He published a book, *Redneck Power: The Wit and Wisdom of Billy Carter.* He also introduced a new beer called Billy Beer, which he commended with the phrase, "It's the best beer I've ever tasted. And I've tasted a lot." After some initial public curiosity, the venture flopped. In the past few years, Billy Beer has become considered a collectible item. (If you still lust in your heart for a can of Billy Beer, it can be found on the Internet for as much as ten dollars.)

Later into the Carter administration though, Billy's antics became less laughable and more sinister. Along with other Georgia state officials and businesspeople, Billy involved himself in some dealings with the Libyan government. In July 1980, right before the presidential election, Billy registered himself as an agent of a foreign nation and acknowledged that he had accepted a $200,000 loan from Libya to facilitate oil sales. Accusations flew that he had peddled his influence with President Jimmy, who denied all these allegations. Jimmy also admitted that it was highly inappropriate for the brother of the president to be an agent of another country, but it was to no avail. The press had a field day, and the scandal became known as Billygate. The *Atlanta Constitution* remarked, "If [Billy's] not working for the Republican Party, he should be."

SINGING HIS OWN TUNE

Roger Clinton has been troubled for most of his life—a result, he has maintained, of growing up in a home dominated by an abusive, alcoholic father. In 1995 he cowrote a book titled *Growing Up Clinton*, wherein he recounted his struggles with cocaine and alcohol addictions. Ten years younger than his presidential half-brother Bill (whom he idolizes), Roger Clinton is an aspiring musician and actor of questionable talent.

Roger started causing headaches for his brother Bill back when he was governor of Arkansas. In 1984 Arkansas State Police approached Governor Clinton to tell him that brother Roger had been arrested for selling cocaine. In what Bill later described as an agonizing decision, Clinton chose not intercede on his brother's

The White House's first Web site debuted in 1994.

behalf. Roger Clinton was prosecuted and served a year in jail. Bill later said he felt it was the best thing that could have happened to his brother.

Years later during Bill's presidency, a few of Roger Clinton's alleged musical gigs caused more problems for his brother. It seems there were Asian businesses that were willing to pay very large sums of money to see Roger perform. Roger happily accepted the money, ostensibly for performing in their home countries; however, these payments were far larger than he had commanded for performances before or since. Was Roger peddling his influence, or did some Asian businessmen have a thing for his brand of music?

In the waning days of his presidency Bill Clinton did finally intercede for his brother and issued a full pardon for his brother's cocaine conviction way back in 1984. Roger's record was expunged. So how did he repay big brother? By getting involved in another scandal. This time Roger was accused of accepting money from people hoping to receive executive pardons. None of these "applicants" received anything—which begs the question of just how much (or how little) influence baby brother had. (We'll wager not very much.) Since his brother left the White House, Roger Clinton has been involved in various incidents, including drunk driving and disturbing the peace. So much for the clean record, Roger.

★　★　★　★　★

TO THE MOON, KENNEDY!

"Many years ago the great British explorer George Mallory, who was to die on Mount Everest, was asked why did he want to climb it. He said "Because it is there." Well, space is there, and we're going to climb it, and the moon and the planets are there, and new hopes for knowledge and peace are there."
—John F. Kennedy's address on the U.S. space program, September 12, 1962

NUMBER TWENTY-SIX: THEODORE ROOSEVELT

Served from 1901 to 1909

Vital Stats: Born on October 27, 1858, in New York City, New York. Died on January 6, 1919, in Oyster Bay, New York.
Age at Inauguration: 42
Vice President: None (first term); Charles Warren Fairbanks (second term)
Political Affiliation: Republican
First Wife: Alice Hathaway Lee (married 1880. died 1884)
Kids from First Marriage: Alice Lee (1884–1980)
Second Wife: Edith Kermit Carow (married 1886)
Kids from Second Marriage: Theodore (1887–1944); Kermit (1889–1943); Ethel Carow (1891–1977); Archibald Bulloch (1894–1979); Quentin (1897–1918)
Education: Harvard University. Attended Columbia University Law School
What he did before he was president: Writer; Historian; New York State Assemblyman; New York City Police Commissioner; Assistant Secretary of the Navy; Governor of New York; U.S. Vice President
Postpresidential Occupations: Writer; Politician

MEMORABLE QUOTES

"We are face to face with our destiny and we must meet it with a high and resolute courage. For us is the life of action, of strenuous performance of duty; let us live in the harness, striving mightily; let us rather run the risk of wearing out than rusting out."
—Theodore Roosevelt's address at the beginning of his New York gubernatorial campaign, October 5, 1898.

"A man who is good enough to shed his blood for his country is good enough to be given a square deal afterward. More than that no man is entitled to, and less than that no man shall have. "
—Theodore Roosevelt, July 4, 1903

... couldn't agree on a name. His father liked Isaac, and his mother, Warren.

NUMBER TWENTY-SEVEN: WILLIAM HOWARD TAFT

Served from 1909 to 1913

Vital Stats: Born on September 15, 1857, in Cincinnati, Ohio. Died on March 8, 1930, in Washington, DC.
Age at Inauguration: 51
Vice President: James S. Sherman
Political Affiliation: Republican
Wife: Helen "Nellie" Herron (married 1886)
Kids: Robert Alphonso (1889–1953); Helen (1891–1987); Charles Phelps II (1897–1983)
Education: Yale University. Cincinnati Law School
What he did before he was president: Lawyer; Assistant Prosecuting Attorney, Hamilton County, Ohio; Ohio Superior Court Judge; U.S. Solicitor General; Federal Circuit Court Judge; Civil Governor of Philippines; Secretary of War
Postpresidential Occupations: Kent Professor of Constitutional Law, Yale University Law School; Joint Chairman of the National War Labor Board; Chief Justice of the U.S. Supreme Court

MEMORABLE QUOTES

"We are all imperfect. We can not expect perfect government."
—William Howard Taft speaking at a banquet in his honor, May 8, 1909

"Lawyers are necessary in a community. Some of you . . . take a different view; but as I am a member of that legal profession, or was at one time . . . I still retain the pride of the profession. And I still insist that it is the law and the lawyer that make popular government under a written constitution and written statutes possible."
—William Howard Taft's thoughts on lawyers, November 4, 1909

At 18, Grover Cleveland worked on an uncle's cattle farm for room, board, and $10 a month.

WORDS TO CAMPAIGN BY

Candidates' catchphrase competition yields some superb slogans.

When U.S. presidential elections are held, half the fun is learning new campaign slogans. They're seen everywhere: on signs and buttons; pennants and posters; newsprint and knickknacks; and television commercials galore. These pithy little sayings often become what the public remembers first, last, and always about the elections. Uncle John has put together the most memorable mnemonic devices.

54-40 OR FIGHT
—James K. Polk, 1844
The "54-40" of the famed slogan was an area of the Oregon Territory under ownership dispute with Great Britain; Polk and his supporters wanted the U.S. to claim this area or go to war.

WHO IS JAMES K. POLK?
—Henry Clay, 1844
Some could be asking the same question today. Back in 1844, Henry Clay chose to capitalize on his fame by underscoring Polk's dearth of brand awareness. The slogan wins points for simplicity but not for efficacy. Polk, the Democratic dark horse nominee, not nominated until the ninth ballot, wound up winning the election.

FOR PRESIDENT OF THE PEOPLE
—Zachary Taylor, 1848
Born-and-bred Southerner Taylor meant it when he ran under this straightforward slogan. Old Rough and Ready's long and illustrious military career had made him a firm nationalist, and he refused to back either slavery or secessionism.

Ronald Reagan was the oldest inaugurated president at 69 years.

DON'T SWAP HORSES IN THE MIDDLE OF A STREAM
—Abraham Lincoln, 1864
Lincoln's second campaign had an ingeniously folksy slogan that belied the cunning tactics this incumbent employed while making a bid for reelection.

REJUVENATED REPUBLICANISM
—Benjamin Harrison, 1888
The grandson of former president William Henry Harrison, the 23rd president pursued American interests outside of our borders with zeal, establishing the Pan-American Union and annexing Hawaii for the first time (President Cleveland later repealed this action).

A FULL DINNER PAIL
—William McKinley, 1900
When McKinley ran for reelection, he wanted to remind voters of the prosperity America had experienced in the previous four years, referring to the tin buckets in which most blue-collar workers toted their midday meals.

HE KEPT US OUT OF WAR
—Woodrow Wilson, 1916
Wilson was a staunch isolationist—but his second administration didn't deliver the goods promised by his slogan. The winds of World War I blew too fiercely even for him to keep the U.S. out of conflict.

COX AND COCKTAILS
—Warren G. Harding, 1920
Hard to imagine this one being used today, but Harding's mnemonic device about his opponent James Cox's opposition to Prohibition must have struck a chord with the Temperance Ladies—he was reelected.

KEEP COOL WITH COOLIDGE
—Calvin Coolidge, 1924

The taciturn Coolidge chose an unexpectedly humorous slogan, considering that when he died, the sharp-tongued Dorothy Parker quipped, "How can they tell?"

A CHICKEN IN EVERY POT AND
A CAR IN EVERY GARAGE
—Herbert Hoover, 1928

In 1928 universal prosperity under Hoover seemed a bright possibility. Unfortunately the Great Depression was just around the corner and soon people were hard-pressed to find pots, let alone chickens.

I LIKE IKE
—Dwight D. Eisenhower, 1952

Even cleaner simplicity than "Who is James K. Polk?" The popular five-star general's nickname made an instantly recognizable slogan that most people who weren't even born during his administration know.

NOT JUST PEANUTS
—Jimmy Carter, 1976

Although Carter liked to play up his good-ole-boy, peanut farmer-from-Georgia persona, his campaign slogan was meant to remind voters that this U.S. Naval Academy graduate and keen businessman wasn't an empty shell.

★　★　★　★　★

FUN FACTS

- Both of Warren Harding's parents were doctors.
- John Tyler had fifteen children, more than any other president. His youngest child was born when Tyler was seventy and lived to see Harry Truman as president.
- When Teddy Roosevelt was running for president he didn't want cameras to record him playing tennis. He was afraid he'd look "too effeminate."

HIS LITTLE DOG FALA

*Surely no other dog in history witnessed more world-changing events
than Fala, Franklin Roosevelt's faithful black Scottie.*

F ranklin D. Roosevelt couldn't have known. He just couldn't
have known how much this gift of a little Scottie dog would
come to mean to him and his presidency. FDR's cousin
Margaret Suckley gave the dog, at the time called Big Boy, to
the president in 1940 hoping the terrier might lessen some of the
president's stress. FDR renamed the dog Murray the Outlaw of
Falahill after a Scottish ancestor, but he usually just called him
Fala for short.

CONSTANT COMPANIONS
The two became fast friends and Fala went almost everywhere
with the president. He played in the Oval Office, attended the
president's press conferences, slept on a blanket next to his bed,
and even rode in the president's limousine. He was very well
trained for the important meetings he attended with the president,
important officials, and foreign dignitaries; FDR taught him how
to shake hands and to stand at attention on his hind legs when
"The Star Spangled Banner" was played.

A worldly dog, Fala traveled often during the troubled times
of World War II. In 1941, Fala was with the president at the signing of the Atlantic Charter on the USS *Augusta* where he hung
out with British Prime Minister Winston Churchill's poodle Rufus.
In 1942 and 1943, Fala went on inspection trips of defense plants
and visited Monterey, Mexico, and President Camacho. In 1943
and 1944, he traveled to the Quebec Conferences.

A great supporter of the war effort at home, Fala was widely
photographed in the press to help boost wartime spirits at home
and abroad. 1n 1942, a film was made about Fala's life at Hyde
Park to show to the troops overseas. On board ships, sailors cut
locks of Fala's hair to send home. The Scottie even allowed his toy
bones to be melted down for scrap rubber.

CANINE CONTROVERSY

Famously on his travels, Fala had been mistakenly left behind in the Aleutian Islands. Roosevelt promptly sent a Navy destroyer to retrieve him. Republican opponents tried to turn the destroyer incident into a serious campaign issue in the 1944 presidential campaign saying that FDR spent $15,000 in taxpayer money on the dog. Roosevelt deftly responded and used Fala as a political tool:

> These Republican leaders have not been content with attacks—on me, or my wife, or on my sons. They now include my little dog, Fala. Well, of course, I don't resent attacks, and my family doesn't resent attacks, but Fala does resent them . . . He has not been the same dog since. I am accustomed to hearing malicious falsehoods about myself . . . But I think I have a right to resent, to object to libelous statements about my dog.

The Republicans had been swiftly reduced to being petty dog-haters. Quite the political victory for the FDR–Fala partnership!

REST IN PEACE

When the president died, it was natural that Fala ride beside the president's widow Eleanor Roosevelt as part of the president's funeral procession. When the dog later died in 1952, he returned to his master's side. Fala is buried next to Roosevelt at the president's Hyde Park estate. You can also see a bronze statue of the little Scottie dog at the FDR Memorial in Washington, DC, where Fala will always sit beside his master.

★　★　★　★　★

FDR FIRSTS

Franklin D. Roosevelt was the first president to visit Hawaii, the first president to go through the Panama Canal, and the first president to broadcast from a foreign country. In 1934, he gave a speech in Cartagena, Colombia, that was relayed to New York.

A STUDY IN OPPOSITES: THE LINCOLNS

The Lincolns' love story is a tale of two very different people with two very different spending habits.

Mary Todd was born in 1818 in Lexington, Kentucky, into a wealthy and influential family. Her mother had seven children and died at the age of thirty-one. Her father remarried within a year and had nine more children with his second wife (who Mary allegedly despised). Being a standout in that family was a tough business, so Mary took off for Springfield, Illinois to live with her sister.

COURTSHIP . . . INTERRUPTED

When Mary turned twenty, she was young, energetic, and wealthy. One of her suitors, a struggling lawyer named Abraham Lincoln, was just her opposite. Almost ten years her senior, Lincoln was quiet, sardonic, and still working on his fortune. They met at a dance and, like proverbial opposites, were immediately attracted to each other. "Miss Todd," he reportedly said to her, "I want to dance with you in the worst way." As the story goes, it sounds like Lincoln wasn't the best dancer, because Mary later reported to a friend, "He certainly did!"

Nevertheless, the two became an item and were first engaged in 1840. But they didn't make it to the altar the first time around. Mary's aristocratic family predictably disapproved of her marrying a "country" lawyer. Her sister even banned Lincoln from visiting the house—making it difficult for Mary and Abe to get together. Feeling the family's haughty attitude, Lincoln commented that though one *D* was good enough for God, it took two *D*s to spell Todd! Rumor has it that Lincoln broke off the engagement. Maybe he had some commitment issues? Another separation occurred after Lincoln was late picking Mary up for an 1841 New Year's Eve party. She became very frustrated and went by herself.

On the last day of his life, Calvin Coolidge worked on a jigsaw puzzle of George Washington.

By the time he arrived, she was busy flirting with others and told him to "never, never come back!"

Turns out it was more difficult than either one of them thought to stay away from each other. Springfield wasn't exactly a huge town. Since both Mary and Abe moved in the same social circles, they'd run into each other accidentally at parties and functions. Eventually, the two did reconcile and became secretly reengaged in 1842. So, despite everything, Abe and Mary got married in November 1842 at her sister's house, surrounded by thirty friends and relatives who had been invited just the day before.

THE ODD COUPLE
If you've ever seen pictures of the Lincolns, you know that they truly were opposites. Mary stood a mere 5 foot 2 inches tall while Lincoln towered at 6 foot 4 inches. Mary's body type was round and plump, and Abe was tall and lean. But their differences were more than skin deep—they went all the way down to their personalities. Quiet, introspective Abe was known to have a gentle, even-keeled personality coupled with sharp wit, able to cut to the quick with a sarcastic barb. Lively, spirited Mary was excitable and known to throw violent tantrums when criticized and upset. When Mary became so fitful, Lincoln would just leave the house for a bit. "It does her a lot of good," he wrote, "and it doesn't hurt me a bit."

IN THE NATION'S MONEY
Because Lincoln didn't earn a lot of money as a lawyer and then a politician, Mary had to adjust to a much more frugal life than what she was used to. During the first years of their marriage she learned to save money, but occasionally she'd slip back into her old habits and go on shopping binges.

Her problems became worse when the couple moved to Washington, DC, in 1860. Many folks said she was needlessly extravagant, especially in a time of war. In 1861 the press reported that she purchased more than 400 pairs of gloves in four months! During Lincoln's first term alone, she rang up debts of more than $25,000 from dresses and other expensive items she bought from shops. The press and the public were not pleased. We're willing to bet her husband wasn't either.

President Truman walked two miles every morning at a brisk clip of 128 steps per minute.

NUMBER
TWENTY-EIGHT:
WOODROW WILSON

Served from 1913 to 1921

Vital Stats: Born on December 28, 1856, in Staunton, Virginia.
Died on February 3, 1924, in Washington, DC.
Age at Inauguration: 56
Vice President: Thomas R. Marshall
Political Affiliation: Democrat
First Wife: Ellen Louise Axson (married 1885. died 1814)
Kids from First Marriage: Margaret Woodrow (1886–1933);
Jessie Woodrow (1887–1933); Eleanor Randolph (1889–1967)
Second Wife: Edith Bolling Galt (married 1915)
Kids from Second Marriage: None
Education: Princeton University. Attended University of Virginia
Law School. Received PhD from Johns Hopkins University.
What he did before he was president: Lawyer; College Professor;
President of Princeton University; Governor of New Jersey
Postpresidential Occupations: Retired

MEMORABLE QUOTES

"I would rather belong to a poor nation that was free than to a
rich nation that had ceased to be in love with liberty. But we shall
not be poor if we love liberty, because the nation that loves liberty
truly sets every man free to do his best and be his best, and that
means the release of all the splendid energies of a great people
who think for themselves."
—Woodrow Wilson's address on Latin American policy,
October 27, 1913

"In the last analysis, my fellow countrymen, as we in America
would be the first to claim, a people are responsible for the acts of
their government."
—Woodrow Wilson's address, given September 4, 1919

While Harding was still a candidate, his wife Flossie visited a clairvoyant . . .

NAME THAT OPERATION!

There have sure been some snappy names for military actions in recent years. Match wits with the military masterminds and match the code name to the correct operation.

1. Jimmy Carter's ill-fated attempt to rescue American hostages in Iran?

2. George H. W. Bush's punishing air war against Iraq in 1991?

3. Ronald Reagan's invasion of Grenada?

4. Franklin D. Roosevelt's invasion of Normandy in WWII?

5. George H. W. Bush's overthrow of Noriega in Panama?

6. John F. Kennedy's failed CIA-backed incursion into Cuba at The Bay of Pigs?

7. Bill Clinton's peacekeeping mission to Bosnia?

8. George H. W. Bush's deployment of troops to protect relief workers in Somalia?

9. Bill Clinton's invasion of Haiti?

10. George W. Bush's overthrow of the Taliban in Afghanistan?

A. Just Cause
B. Restore Hope
C. Eagle Claw
D. Urgent Fury
E. Joint Endeavor
F. Overlord
G. Enduring Freedom
H. Desert Storm
I. Zapata
J. Uphold Democracy

ANSWERS: 1. C, 2. H, 3. D, 4. F, 5. A, 6. I, 7. E, 8. B, 9. J, 10. G

She predicted that he was "a shoo-in," but that he would die in office. (He did.)

DEMAND A RECOUNT? THE ELECTION OF 1960

*Tricky Dick Nixon could have socked it to 'em
in a race that was too close to call.*

A fter a razor-thin presidential election, a sitting vice president has the right to decide whether to demand a recount
when allegations of voting fraud and irregularities arise.
Such was the case after the November 1960 presidential contest.
Richard Nixon of California, the Republican vice president under
outgoing President Dwight D. Eisenhower, faced off against John
F. Kennedy, the charismatic Democratic senator and war hero
from Massachusetts.

TV TIGHTENS THE RACE
In 1960 Kennedy at age forty-three and Nixon at forty-seven were
two of the youngest candidates ever to vie for the nation's highest
office. Despite the small difference in age, Nixon did not shy away
from presenting himself as the "experienced" candidate; Kennedy
came across as the more youthful candidate. In the fall, polls
showed that Nixon had a slight lead. But after the first-ever
nationally televised presidential debate, things changed. In that
evening debate Nixon appeared pale, sweaty, and scruffy with a
five-o'clock shadow, while a tanned Kennedy seemed relaxed and
well prepared. Kennedy began to gain on Nixon, tightening up
the race.

Kennedy's choice of Senate Majority Leader Lyndon B.
Johnson of Texas as his vice presidential running mate also helped
greatly in the pivotal state of Texas and in the South. Not to be
outdone, Nixon pledged to visit every state in the nation during
the campaign. And he kept his word when he finished up in
Alaska the Sunday before the election. He was exhausted to the
point of collapse, but his arduous nonstop campaigning had tightened up the race during the final weeks.

Warren G. Harding was the first U.S. president to visit Alaska. And the first to visit Canada.

UP ALL NIGHT

Election Day, November 8, 1960, brought a record turnout of nearly sixty-nine million voters. Early television news reports forecasted that Kennedy, with strong support in the East, would win. But as election night progressed Kennedy's lead began to shrink. Key remaining states of Illinois, Minnesota, Texas, and California remained undecided. Television forecasters hedged their predictions and relabeled the election a cliffhanger that was too close to call.

Kennedy, watching the returns from his house in Hyannis Port, Massachusetts, went to bed at 4:00 a.m., not knowing the outcome. When he woke up at 9:00 a.m., an aide congratulated him on his victory and informed him that Secret Service agents had surrounded the house as he was now the president-elect. Nixon, staying at the Ambassador Hotel in Los Angeles, also had gone to bed at 4:00 a.m. He awoke at 6:00 a.m. to discover that he had lost Illinois and Minnesota, and thus the election. He conceded soon afterward. Kennedy ended up with 303 electoral votes to Nixon's 219. A minor-party candidate, Harry F. Byrd won another 15 electoral votes in the South. But the popular vote totals were the closest in the twentieth century, with Kennedy winning with a plurality of only 119,000 votes.

DEMAND A RECOUNT?

Soon after the election, allegations of voting irregularities and illegal practices began to surface in Texas and Illinois, two states with long histories of voting fraud. Especially suspicious was the overwhelming turnout for Kennedy in Cook County, Illinois, home to Chicago mayor Richard Daley's powerful Democratic political machine. Kennedy had won Illinois by fewer than 9,000 votes. Texas was also tightly contested, where Kennedy's lead was only 46,000 votes. Republicans knew that if the electoral votes of the two states were reversed, Nixon would be the winner by a count of 270 to 252.

Nixon, after a much-needed vacation in Florida, returned to Washington in late November to consider what to do about the charges of election fraud. Outgoing President Dwight Eisenhower and other Republicans urged the vice president to demand a recount and start an investigation. Until that point, the United States never had a recount in its presidential history. Officials in Illinois estimated

Thomas Jefferson invented (among other items) the wooden coat hanger and the dumbwaiter.

that a recount could take more than a year. Texas did not even have mechanisms in place to conduct a recount—so no one knew just how long it would take the Lone Star State to recount its votes.

Although Nixon believed that strong legal grounds existed to request a recount, he responsibly and practically instructed Attorney General William P. Rogers not to launch a federal investigation. Nixon realized that a recount would mean that the country would be without a president for more than a year. He would later recall, "I could think of no worse example for nations abroad, who for the first time were trying to get free electoral procedures into effect, than that of the United States wrangling over the results of our presidential election, and even suggesting that the presidency itself could be stolen by thievery at the ballot box." Additionally, while there were irregularities with the Democratic turnout in Chicago, Nixon knew Kennedy could have challenged voting irregularities in rural Republican areas of Illinois. It was best for all to just move on.

Nixon's statesmanlike approach to the recount question revealed a little political savvy. Nixon realized that if he went through with a recount and lost, his political career would be over, and he wouldn't be around for kicking anymore. He had nearly won the presidency in 1960, and the closeness of the vote gave him hope that he could one day try again—and win.

★   ★   ★   ★   ★

NIXON GOES TO CHINA

"My hope is that in the future . . . that many, many Americans . . . will have an opportunity to come here . . . that they will be able to see this Wall, that they will think back to the history of this great people, and that they will have an opportunity . . . to know the Chinese people . . . What is most important is that we have an open world. As we look at this Wall, we do not want walls of any kind between peoples. I think one of the results of our trip, we hope, may be that walls that are erected, whether they are physical walls like this or whether they are other walls, ideology or philosophy, will not divide peoples in the world."
—Richard M. Nixon's remarks on the Great Wall of China, February 24, 1972

EXECUTIVE (BRANCH) EATS

The federal food files on chief execs, who have to eat too!

You can tell a lot about people by what they eat—their origins and personalities. American presidents bring their culinary tastes with them to the White House. Some of their favorite dishes become famous and others have remained well-kept secrets.

- George Washington had a number of favorite foods, including ice cream. His favorite dinner menu included cream of peanut soup, mashed sweet potatoes with coconut, string beans with mushrooms, and his wife's whiskey cake.

- Abraham Lincoln's slender physique wouldn't lead anyone to believe he was a foodie, but his favorite dish was his wife's scalloped oysters.

- Although each president has a personal chef, Dwight Eisenhower preferred to cook his own beef stew.

- Pity the poor Texan, Lyndon Johnson, who lived in our nation's capital with nary a Tex-Mex place (that he liked) in sight. He had to fly in caterers from Texas to get his mitts on some proper Texas barbecue and chili.

- President Nixon's culinary choices weren't exactly inspired—or inspiring! In keeping with the bland cooking of the late 1960s and early 1970s, Nixon often ate cottage cheese and ketchup, or cottage cheese and pineapple, for lunch. His dinner of choice was Salisbury steak with gravy.

- President Carter liked Southern classics like a breakfast of grits and buttermilk and a dinner of country ham with redeye gravy

or fried chicken. The former peanut farmer also brought peanuts to a new level of worldwide notoriety.

- George H. W. Bush's dislike of broccoli is famous, but what isn't as well known is that Poppy had a sweet tooth. Stewards on *Air Force One* kept Eskimo Pies ice cream treats, Baby Ruth candy bars, and Blue Belle brand ice cream on hand for him.

- Bill Clinton never met a Big Mac he didn't like, even though the press often chided him for his love of burgers. Like many of his appetites, burgers might not have been the best thing for him. His doctors worried that his increasing weight would adversely affect his health. Maybe he deserved a break that day, so he got up to get away to McDonald's. (They do it all for you!)

- Like LBJ, George W. Bush brought a bit of Texas with him to the White House, at least in his culinary choices. Dubya loves Tex-Mex and barbecue; the chefs on *Air Force One* serve barbecue when Bush flies to Washington from his Crawford, Texas, ranch. A rumored favorite DC eatery of the president and First Lady is the Cactus Cantina, famous for its fresh enchiladas and fajitas.

★　★　★　★　★

WHO'S THE YOUNGEST?

There's some argument over who the youngest president has been. Well, it all depends on which hairs you split. If you're interested in the youngest sitting president, then Teddy Roosevelt is your guy. He was just forty-two years and ten months old when he took office after President McKinley's death. But if you're talking the youngest elected president, then it's John F. Kennedy. When he took the oath of office in 1961, Jack was forty-three years and 236 days old.

VERY SUPERSTITIOUS

*Superstition is an American tradition in which even
the presidents have taken part. Sometimes, though,
their superstitions have been eerily justified.*

Athletes are notorious for their pregame rituals and good
luck charms. It turns out that American presidents are no
different, using superstition as one way to chart the course
of their administrations.

LINCOLN'S PREFIGURATION
The supernatural shaded Abraham Lincoln's White House, perhaps more than any other president. His wife Mary Todd had
visions of their children who had died young. She conducted
séances—some of which Abe attended, although he thought the
mediums were hucksters—to try to communicate with them. This
skepticism notwithstanding, Abe himself had dreams and visions
that he took very seriously. He announced once at a Cabinet
meeting when he was waiting for a report from General Sherman
that he knew good news was imminent, because he had just had a
recurring dream that always was a good omen for him.

Lincoln's most famous dream vision is described by his friend
Ward Lamon in a book of recollections. The dream began with
Lincoln hearing the sound of crying far away. He traveled through
a number of rooms in the White House searching for the source of
the sound, then arrived in the East Room to find a crowd surrounding a shrouded, dead body. The body's face was covered by
the shroud, making it unidentifiable. He asked one of the soldiers
guarding the body who was dead. The soldier replied, "The President! He was killed by an assassin!" The dream ended there.
Sadly, Lincoln was shot by John Wilkes Booth soon afterward,
and the story of premonition circulated far and wide.

MCKINLEY'S CARNATION
William McKinley made a habit of wearing a red carnation in his
lapel for luck. Occasionally, when he wanted to share the luck
with others, he would give it away. For example, if someone asked

him for a favor he couldn't grant, he would offer the carnation as a consolation prize. Once when two boys were visiting him in the White House, he gave one boy the carnation from his lapel, then he shrewdly took another out of a vase to put into his lapel for a while before giving that one to the other boy so his blossom would be lucky too.

When visiting the Pan-American Exposition in Buffalo, New York, in 1901, McKinley only had a short period scheduled for meeting, greeting, and shaking hands. At one point he gave his lucky red carnation to a young girl in the receiving line. Now without his good luck charm, McKinley was approached by a man with a bandage over his right hand. The man was Leon Czolgosz, and the bandage was hiding a gun. Czolgosz fired two shots at McKinley, and McKinley died eight days later.

ROOSEVELT'S NUMBERS GAME

Superstition also figured in the day-to-day life of Franklin D. Roosevelt. He strongly believed that it was bad luck to light three cigarettes with one match. Once a young man tutoring some of the Roosevelt children at their Hyde Park home received a warning from Roosevelt for doing this. When he did it again at lunch, Roosevelt laid into him, in what his lifelong secretary called, "one of the few occasions I know of when the President actually reprimanded someone brusquely in public."

Roosevelt had an acute case of triskaidekaphobia, or fear of the number 13. He would invite his secretary to come to dinner with him if there were otherwise going to be 13 guests present at the function. If his party was planning to travel on the 13th of the month, he would reschedule the departure for 11:50 p.m. on the 12th or 12:10 a.m. on the 14th. He avoided the date even in death, passing away in April 1945, on the afternoon of Thursday the 12th.

THE TRUTH IS OUT THERE, SAYS CARTER

UFOs are the kind of thing the government usually gets accused of covering up. Contrary to the stereotype, Jimmy Carter publicized his UFO sighting, which occurred when he was a fledgling politician in Georgia in 1969. Carter was standing outside with several other members of a Lions Club chapter in Leary, Georgia, before a meeting where he was scheduled to speak. Then, according to Carter's report,

the group saw an object in the sky that was as bright as the moon; changed color from blue to red; and moved toward and away from the observers twice. During his presidential campaign Carter promised, after having had a personal experience with UFOs, to open any existing government UFO files if he were elected.

Most of those who have researched Carter's sighting have figured that he probably saw the planet Venus, which was particularly bright in the early evening on the night in question (the date of which was definitively established by finding the record of his speech in the Lions Club archives). Some of the Lions who were there with him reported that it could have been Venus. Carter never did release any government UFO files, which sounds like the makings of a good episode of *The X-Files*.

THE REAGANS SEE STARS

In May 1988, former White House chief of staff Donald Regan published his book *For the Record*, in which he revealed that one of his tasks for President Ronald Reagan was to integrate his schedule with the advisements of an astrologer, whose reports came through First Lady Nancy Reagan. The astrologer, Joan Quigley, credited her work for President Reagan's surviving until the end of his second term and thwarting the 148-year curse by which the presidents elected in 1840, 1860, 1880, 1900, 1920, 1940, and 1960 had died in office. She also claimed to have almost total control over the timing of important public events. For example, after Congress nixed two of Reagan's appointments to the U.S. Supreme Court, Quigley advised that his third candidate, Anthony Kennedy, be nominated at precisely 11:32:25 a.m. on November 11, 1987. (Kennedy was confirmed 97–0.) Coincidence? You be the judge.

Quigley had been introduced to Nancy by talk show host Merv Griffin in 1973, and she stayed in sporadic contact with Mrs. Reagan for a number of years, with a spike during the 1980 presidential election. Then, after John Hinckley Jr.'s attempted assassination of Reagan, Nancy hired Quigley in May 1981 to be the Reagans' full-time astrologer after Quigley said she could have foreseen the assassination attempt had she been studying Ronald Reagan's charts. Nancy asked Quigley if she would waive her fee, but Quigley refused because, as she said, "People tend not to value advice they don't have to pay for."

... He played the helicon—a large tuba that coiled around his head, like a sousaphone.

NUMBER TWENTY-NINE: WARREN G. HARDING

Served from 1921 to 1923

Vital Stats: Born on November 2, 1865, in Corsica, Ohio. Died on August 2, 1923, in San Francisco, California.
Age at Inauguration: 55
Vice President: Calvin Coolidge
Political Affiliation: Republican
Wife: Florence "Flossie" Kling De Wolfe (married 1891)
Kids: None
Education: Attended Ohio Central College
What he did before he was president: Newspaper Editor; Member of Ohio Senate; Lieutenant Governor of Ohio; U.S. Senator
Postpresidential Occupations: None. Died in office.

MEMORABLE QUOTES

"With the nation-wide induction of womanhood into our political life, we may count upon her intuitions, her refinements, her intelligence, and her influence to exalt the social order. We count upon her exercise of the full privileges and the performance of the duties of citizenship to speed the attainment of the highest state."
—Warren Harding's thoughts on female suffrage, from his inaugural address, March 4, 1921

"My golf is miserably bad, and at other sports they kick me around with no more consideration than is given a prohibition enforcement officer in the down-town wards in the big cities . . . I have a challenge out to play under ninety at Chevy Chase before the year is done. I am going to win it or make a bonfire of all the golf sticks I possess."
—Warren G. Harding's lament on his golf game, from a letter dated April 29, 1922

NUMBER THIRTY: CALVIN COOLIDGE

Served from 1923 to 1929

Vital Stats: Born on July 4, 1872, in Plymouth Notch, Vermont. Died on January 5, 1933, in Northampton, Massachusetts.
Age at Inauguration: 51
Vice President: None
Political Affiliation: Republican
Wife: Grace Anna Goodhue (married 1905)
Kids: John (1906–2000); Calvin (1908–1924)
Education: Amherst College
What he did before he was president: Lawyer; Member of the Massachusetts House of Representatives; Mayor of Northampton, Massachusetts; Member and President of Massachusetts Senate; Lieutenant Governor of Massachusetts; Governor of Massachusetts; U.S. Vice President
Postpresidential Occupations: Writer

MEMORABLE QUOTES

"The government of the United States is a device for maintaining in perpetuity the rights of the people, with the ultimate extinction of all privileged classes."
—Calvin Coolidge in a speech, given September 25, 1924

"There is no dignity quite so impressive, and no independence quite so important, as living within your means."
—Calvin Coolidge in his *Autobiography*, 1931

"We draw our Presidents from the people. It is a wholesome thing for them to return to the people. I came from them. I wish to be one of them again."
—Calvin Coolidge in his *Autobiography*, 1931

George Washington is credited with introducing the mule to America.

PRIMARY INTENTIONS

Political primaries pick a pack of presidential possibilities.

E ver wonder how political parties go about picking possible
presidents? It might seem like they pick names out of hat or
flip a coin, but there really is a more complex and democratic
process behind Republican and Democratic choices of their presidential candidates. It's just a little ole process called the primary.

PREPRIMARY POLITICS

Relatively new to the political scene, presidential primaries have
only become influential during the past fifty years. This process
gives state voters a say in who will be chosen as the presidential
nominee of their party. Primary elections, which are held from
midwinter to late spring, are only composed of preliminary votes.
These elections are like the playoffs before the big game, which,
in this case is the party's national convention. There the candidate will be officially crowned prior to the even bigger game (the
general election) in November that elects the president.

When primary voters go to the polls they are voting to select
delegates to support their candidate choice at the parties' national
conventions, usually held in mid- to late summer. Since 1831,
these conventions have been the place where a presidential candidate has been chosen and officially presented to the American
public. In much of the nineteenth century, powerful party bosses
and leaders often hand picked their convention delegates, who
then selected candidates after a lot of wheeling and dealing in
the much-disparaged "smoke-filled rooms" of the conventions.
Average citizens in the states had little say at all.

Progressives fought back against this backroom dealing and
used the primary as a strong method in making the selection
process more democratic and open to public view. In the early
1900s, Progressive reformer Robert La Follette of Wisconsin
pushed hard for the direct election of convention delegates, and
by 1912 twelve states had presidential primaries. However it
would take decades before primaries really flexed any political

---

Draft dodger? Grover Cleveland hired someone to enter the military in his place . . .

muscle. In 1912, for example, former president Theodore Roosevelt's wide popular support gave him eight victories out of the twelve primaries that year, but that didn't secure his nomination, and his political comeback ended. Defying the primaries' results, the Republican convention gave the nomination to his rival and incumbent president Howard Taft.

Despite these early setbacks primaries grew and grew in importance for the next sixty years. By 1976, twenty-seven states held primaries, and that year's winners, Jimmy Carter for Democrats and Gerald R. Ford for the Republicans, would go on to capture their parties' nominations. From 1976 on, the Republican and Democratic Parties have not nominated a presidential candidate who did not first win the majority vote in the primaries. Primaries have become so efficient at selecting a party's nominee that they've stolen a little of the national conventions' thunder. There's just not much suspense anymore at the parties' pep rallies, where nominees are crowned in front of a national television audience.

PRIMARY ETIQUETTE

So how does it all work? Well, primary rules and regulations vary from state to state. As there is no federal law on how to run a primary, the parties themselves decide state by state what sort of primary to have. An "open" primary allows any voter to participate in either the Democratic or Republican primary. These primaries often cause the most anxiety among party leaders over the possibility that voters of the opposing party will "cross over" to vote for a weak candidate. So most presidential primaries are "closed," allowing only party members to participate.

Some states, like Iowa for instance, don't have primaries. They generally have caucuses, whose rules and regulations also vary from state to state. A caucus consists of a series of meetings that can stretch out over days or even weeks. The first meeting is usually held at the precinct level, where voters participate in public discussion of the candidates and then choose a delegate to attend the next level meeting. The same process occurs, rising through each level of government until eventually the meetings select delegates to attend a state party convention, which then picks the delegates to the national party convention. Although

the caucus, like the primary, opens the candidate selection process up to many voters, it demands a lot of time (some precinct gatherings can take up a whole evening) and generally only attracts the most active of the party faithful.

THE CAUCUS (AND PRIMARY) RACE

Every year brings a different array of primaries and caucuses. In 2004, thirty-nine states and the District of Columbia held presidential primaries, with most of the remaining states holding caucuses. One recent change in the primary calendar has been the fact that more and more states have moved their primaries earlier and earlier in the presidential election year. In 1960 there were sixteen primaries, with the first one (New Hampshire) taking place on March 8; the next one (Wisconsin) not until April 5; and the rest spaced out until California and South Dakota voted on June 7. As state political leaders began to realize that the earlier primaries received the most national attention and allowed states to exert a stronger influence on the selection process, states began to move up their primaries. By 1996, two thirds of the primary contests were held by the end of March. Now presidential nominees are determined earlier and earlier in the campaign season. In 2000, George W. Bush and Al Gore had secured their unofficial party's nomination by early March; Bush and John Kerry accomplished this again in 2004.

Some people wonder if this "front-loading" of the primaries is a good thing. Having so many primaries grouped together at the beginning of year does not allow for a lot of time for candidates to campaign in all parts of the country before a nominee is chosen. Some proposed changes include having a national primary, where everyone votes on the same day, or having four regional primaries, where the states from one region, for example, the West, could all vote at once. Most likely the parties will only tinker a little with the current process every election season. Whatever happens, the primary is here to stay.

WHITE HOUSE CONFIDENTIAL

More stuff you might not know about the presidents—some serious, some silly—presented in pop quiz form.

1. How many children did George Washington, the Father of His Country, have?
   A. None
   B. One
   C. Seven

2. Abraham Lincoln carried one particular book around with him so much that it got to be frayed and falling apart. What was it?
   A. The Bible
   B. *Joe Miller's Joke Book*
   C. *Uncle Tom's Cabin*

3. Who was the only twentieth-century president who didn't attend college?
   A. Calvin Coolidge
   B. Harry S. Truman
   C. Gerald Ford

4. Theodore Roosevelt's daughter Alice said, "[He] was not a bad man. He was just a slob." Years later, in 1991, 500 historians decided to agree. Who did they elect as the worst American president in history?
   A. Millard Fillmore
   B. Woodrow Wilson
   C. Warren G. Harding

5. While in office Thomas Jefferson ran up a bill of more than $10,000 for one comestible. What was it?
   A. Wine
   B. Candles
   C. Paper

Washington wrote that in a note to his gardener in 1794.

6. When Ronald Reagan announced his intention to run for governor of California in 1966, studio head Jack Warner said, "No, no! [It should be] Jimmy Stewart for governor, Ronald Reagan for . . ."—what?
   A. lieutenant governor
   B. best friend
   C. dogcatcher

7. When Jimmy Carter was elected, country singer Loretta Lynn commented, "It sure is nice to have a president who . . ."
   A. "is from the South, has a PhD, and is just as nice as country folks."
   B. "lusts after women, but only in his heart."
   C. "don't speak with an accent."

8. What president warned the nation to beware of the influence of the "military-industrial complex"?
   A. Franklin Roosevelt
   B. Dwight Eisenhower
   C. John Kennedy

9. Which president called Richard Nixon "a no-good lying bastard?"
   A. Harry S. Truman
   B. Gerald Ford
   C. John Kennedy

10. Andrew Johnson was superbly accomplished at what one particular thing?
    A. Making his own clothes
    B. Spitting tobacco
    C. Dancing

ANSWERS: 1. A, 2. B, 3. B, 4. C, 5. A, 6. B, 7. C, 8. B, 9. A, 10. A

Truman, on the U.S. Constitution, "It's a plan, but not a straitjacket, flexible and short . . ."

CLOSE CALLS IV

September 1975 was definitely not your month, Gerry.

I f there's a prize for the president with the most assassination attempts, Gerald Ford definitely gets it. In the same month, in the same state, Ford was threatened by two completely unconnected women, the only two women to ever shoot at a president. After the two California attacks, Ford continued his schedule as usual, but he seemed hesitant to accept more invitations to the Golden State. Can you blame him?

LYNETTE "SQUEAKY" FROMME: GERALD FORD
Terrified and alone, Lynnette Fromme sat on Venice Beach after her father threw her out of their suburban home. An elfish man approached her and said, "So, your father kicked you out." Amazed that he knew her story, Fromme ran after the man, Charles Manson, and so became one of the Manson "family."

When Manson was arrested for the vicious Tate–LaBianca murders, Fromme, called Squeaky because of her voice, carved a cross into her forehead and sat outside the courthouse in protest. After the conviction Fromme dedicated her life to freeing Manson, whom she viewed as the Son of God.

Fromme and her roommates, all Manson followers, founded the International People's Court of Retribution to strike against leaders of polluting corporations. Fromme ordered others to kill, but no one listened. She wrote to the judge on the Manson trial and asked that Charlie be freed, but the judge didn't quite understand that she was threatening him. She wore red robes to symbolize her cause, but the press didn't care. She tried to get Manson's prison writings published, but the press refused. People saw her as a slight, childish woman and didn't feel threatened by anything she did.

Attention Grab
Feeling desperate for the attention she thought necessary to free Manson, Fromme noticed in the papers that President Ford was

coming to Sacramento, California, right in her own backyard. She borrowed a .45-caliber gun from an unwitting friend and waited in a crowd outside the state Capitol building. With Ford less than two feet away, Fromme leveled the gun at his nether regions. Although the gun was loaded, there was no bullet in the chamber, so Ford escaped with both his life and his manhood intact. Fromme was tackled by the Secret Service as she shouted, "It didn't go off!"

Squeaky Fromme was the first woman to attempt an assassination and the first person arraigned under the new assassination law. This law, passed after the JFK assassination, allowed a sentence of life in prison for anyone who attempted to assassinate the president of the United States. Prior to this, there was no federal law against attempting to assassinate the president and criminals were subject to state laws.

Fromme assumed that she would represent herself in her trial, and could call Charles Manson as a witness. This was her plan: get Manson on the stand and he would save the world. Not only did the judge refuse to let Manson be called as a witness, but he also ordered that Fromme be given court-appointed counsel. She became enraged and her outbursts in court became so disruptive that she was removed. Fromme barely participated in her own defense. Her lawyers argued that she had never intended to kill the president, just threaten him—hence, no bullet in the chamber. The jury sided with the prosecution, which argued that she had pulled the trigger, but just didn't know how to load a gun. Fromme was sentenced to life in prison.

On December 23, 1987, Fromme escaped from prison. She was caught walking along a road not two miles away on Christmas Day, and she has remained in prison ever since.

SARA JANE MOORE: GERALD FORD
At forty-five, Sara Jane Moore, called Sally by her friends, didn't quite know what to do with herself. She had been married five times (twice to the same man), and had four children, three of whom she left to her parents to raise. Sally had tried being a nurse, being a certified public accountant, and joining the Woman's Army Corps, but nothing seemed to stick.

When her last marriage was annulled because she failed to get

Martin Van Buren was the first president not born a British subject.

a divorce from her fourth husband before jumping into her fifth marriage, Sally turned to the street scene of hippie San Francisco. This was shortly after heiress Patty Hearst was kidnapped by the Symbionese Liberation Army, whose only ransom demand was that Patty's rich Daddy Dearest distribute millions of dollars worth of food to the poor. People in Need, the distribution program Randolph Hearst set up to meet this demand, needed workers, and Sally Moore, CPA, fit right in. Moore was only tangentially involved, but she was heady with her entrance into the radical left. She approached the FBI in April 1974 and offered her skills as an informant.

The middle-aged housewife was now thrust into a cloak-and-dagger netherworld, and for a few months she thrilled in her new role. But soon she found herself drawn to the very people she was spying on. Among these antiestablishment zealots, Moore felt accepted for the first time. After only three months, she was so torn by her betrayal of her new friends that she told them she was a narc. They threw her out. Moore went to the FBI, but they fired her because she had blown her cover.

Trying to Fit In
For a while, Moore bounced back and forth between the FBI and the radical Left, unable to choose a side. Desperate to find acceptance again, Moore taped a confession of her dealings with the FBI and gave it to her former companions on the fringe. Shortly afterward, a friend Moore had implicated was murdered outside her apartment, and she began receiving threatening phone calls.

Afraid for her life, Moore asked the FBI to place her in protective custody, but they referred her to the San Francisco Police. At this time, she heard of Fromme's attack on President Ford and decided what she must do to work her way back into the Left's good graces. Hearing that Ford would be in San Francisco on September 21 and 22, Moore bought a gun and took trips to the shooting range for practice. After this stunt, she reasoned, no one would be able to doubt her true loyalties.

On September 20, Moore called the San Francisco Police Department and asked the officer there to arrest her. She said she

---

Victoria Clafin Woodhull, the first female candidate for president, ran in 1872.

was planning to "test" the presidential security system when Ford appeared at Stanford University the next day. The officer immediately notified the FBI and the Secret Service. The next morning the officer interviewed Moore and arrested her for carrying a concealed weapon. The police confiscated her gun and ammunition, then handed her over to the Secret Service. Two agents met with her that night and determined that she was incapable of assassination and no security risk. They released her.

The next morning, September 22, Moore dropped her nine-year-old son off at school and purchased another gun, a .38. On her way back toward the St. Francis Hotel she drove recklessly, hoping to be pulled over and arrested again. No such luck this time. She made it into the crowd waiting for the president, thinking to herself, "Oh this is ludicrous. What am I doing standing here?" At one point she tried to leave, but there were too many people packed in for her to get out of the crowd.

Gerald Ford at last emerged from the hotel with his beefed up security force. Moore drew her gun and fired once from across the street, some 40 feet away, but missed. An ex-marine in the crowd saw her draw the gun and knocked her hand up before she pulled the trigger. Moore said at her trial that she was glad she missed.

Moore pleaded guilty and was sentenced to life. She was sent to the same prison as Squeaky Fromme. Moore had another thing in common with her fellow assassin: while a youngster, Moore went to the same grocery store as Charles Manson.

★ ★ ★ ★ ★

TRUMAN TRIES HIS DAMNDEST

"You know, the greatest epitaph in the country is here in Arizona. It's in Tombstone, Ariz., and this epitaph says, 'Here lies Jack Williams. He done his damndest.' I think that is the greatest epitaph a man could have. Whenever a man does the best he can, then that is all he can do; and that is what your President has been trying to do for the last three years for this country."
—Harry S. Truman on his presidential efforts, June 15, 1948

NUMBER THIRTY-ONE: <u>HERBERT HOOVER</u>

Served from 1929 to 1933

Vital Stats: Born on August 10, 1874, in West Branch, Iowa.
Died on October 20, 1964, in New York City, New York
Age at Inauguration: 54
Vice President: Charles Curtis
Political Affiliation: Republican
Wife: Lou Henry (married 1899)
Kids: Hebert Clark (1903–1969); Allan Henry (1907–1993)
Education: Stanford University
What he did before he was president: Miner; Engineer;
Chairman of Commission Relief for Belgium; U.S. Food
Administrator; Chairman of Supreme Economic Council;
Secretary of Commerce
Postpresidential Occupations: Chairman of the Commission for
Polish Relief; Chairman of Finnish Relief Fund; Coordinator of
European Food Program; Chairman of the Hoover Commission;
Writer

MEMORABLE QUOTES

"I am convinced that . . . we have reestablished confidence.
Wages should remain stable. A very large degree of industrial
unemployment and suffering which would otherwise have
occurred has been prevented."
—Herbert Hoover's thoughts on economic recovery,
December 3, 1929

"No greater nor more affectionate honor can be conferred on an
American than to have a public school named after him."
—Herbert Hoover, at the dedication of Herbert Hoover Junior
High School, San Francisco, California, June 5, 1956

A TELL-ALL
DOG-OGRAPHY

Presidents best beware of a dog with a literary streak.
She just might write a best seller!

When George H. W. Bush moved into the White House in 1989, he knew the ins and outs since he had served as vice president for eight years under Ronald Reagan. Luckily for him, his English Springer Spaniel Millie was equally familiar with the demands of the highest office in the nation. After all, she had eight years of training too and was more than ready for the step up to the White House. She quickly became a favorite of staff, press, and public alike due to her generally gracious behavior. But who knew that Millie had a literary streak as well?

A BEST SELLING AUTHOR

Millie became the first First Pet to write a book entitled *Millie's Book*. First Lady Barbara Bush took long hours of scrupulous dictation to capture every one of Millie's words on paper. A resounding success, first-time author Millie gave an insider's view to a day in the life of the First Family—from morning briefings, meetings in the Oval Office, and apologies for digging up tulips on the White House grounds. In her book, she recalls chasing four squirrels, three rats, and a pigeon on the White House lawn. (Even a presidential pooch has to blow off some steam.) The book earned $900,000 in royalties, which the Bush family donated to literacy charities. Millie's tales of life inside the White House eventually outsold her master's presidential memoirs.

MOMMA MILLIE!

In 1989, Millie became a mommy and gave birth to six puppies (five girls and one boy) in the White House. One of the females was given to the president's son George W. Bush, who named her Spot. Spot would eventually return to the White House when her master became president, the first dog to serve nonconsecutive terms as a first pet!

Truman believed in prayer but blamed much of the world's troubles on religious differences . . .

A GOOD COLLEGE EDUCATION

*Get out your civics books! It's time to go back to school
to learn about college, the electoral college that is.*

One of the oddities of American democracy—which is the oldest and, arguably, most celebrated of democracies in the world—is the fact that the average citizen does not vote directly for president. It's true. Instead, when U.S. voters go to the polls to cast a ballot for president, they are actually voting for a slate of electors from their state, who in turn elect the president. The electors make up the electoral college—which is not a type of school, despite its name.

Because the outcome of the presidential race is determined by the vote of this electoral college, it is possible that the candidate who becomes president is not the candidate who takes in the most votes. In fact, this unusual outcome has occurred four times in U.S. history: in 1824, 1876, 1888, and, most recently, 2000, when Democrat Al Gore received in excess of 500,000 popular votes more than the eventual winner, Republican George W. Bush. How could it be that the most popular guy was not elected president? Go figure.

ELECTORAL PREP SCHOOL

When the Founding Fathers drew up the U.S. Constitution in 1787, they were wary of letting the public directly choose the president. They were afraid the uneducated masses might select local favorites or untested popular heroes. They were also afraid that smaller states could be overshadowed by larger ones if the president were directly elected. So the founders created the new electoral college system as a buffer between the people and the presidency, and as a balance between the influence of larger and smaller states.

The way the electoral system works is as follows: each state is given a number of electors equal to the number of U.S. representa-

tives and senators it has in Congress. The small states agreed to this calculation at the time of the Constitution because it guaranteed that no matter what the size of a state, it still received at least three electoral votes. In addition, the Twenty-third Amendment in 1961 gave the District of Columbia its own three electoral votes. As there are currently 435 members of the House, 100 senators, and 3 District electors, this adds up to 538 members of the electoral college. Today a candidate must have the majority of electoral votes or at least 51 percent (that's 270 of them if you're counting) to win the election. So technically, individual citizens do not elect president, entire states do. This winner-take-all nature of the electoral college allows a candidate to secure the most electoral votes even if he or she does not capture the popular vote.

If there is ever a case where an election is split between more than two candidates, and no candidate receives the required 270 majority, the election is "thrown" to the U.S. House of Representatives, which selects the president from among the top three contenders. This has occurred only twice in history (the elections of 1800 and 1824).

VOTE, VOTE, WHO'S GOT THE VOTE
So just how do electors get picked then? Since 1836 states have been using the popular vote to select their electors. Over the years, the tradition set in that the electors would simply confirm the popular vote of their states. Maine and Nebraska are the exception: they allocate their electors to the winner of their congressional districts, so the electoral vote could be split in those two states.

Nearly all states stipulate that the candidate who wins a plurality (the most votes) in a state wins all of that state's electoral votes. But, according to the Constitution, electors still can vote as they please. Only tradition has made them vote as their state has done. A few times in United States history a "faithless elector" has switched and voted contrary to his or her state's wishes, but it has never directly affected the outcome of an election, yet. The most recent example occurred in 2000, when an elector from the District of Columbia, who although pledged to Democrat Al Gore, abstained from voting to protest the District's lack of voting

representation in Congress. Thus Gore received one fewer electoral vote than he should have.

COLLEGE TRANSFER?

Right from the get go, the electoral college was one aspect of the Constitution that was criticized. Thomas Jefferson called the indirect election system "the most dangerous blot on our Constitution," and the arrangement has been hotly debated ever since. One suggestion has been to make the electoral vote proportional to the popular vote in a state—which would make it better represent all of a state's voters. For example, if a candidate receives 60 percent of a state's vote, that candidate would only receive a corresponding fraction of the electoral votes rather than a winner-take-all situation. Others have argued that in a democracy a president should be elected by nothing other than direct popular vote. These folks want the electoral college done away with entirely.

One difficulty of making any change to the current system is that such a change requires an amendment to the Constitution, which is not an easy thing to accomplish. Others say that the electoral college has worked relatively well over the past 220 years, so why make a change? However, a popular movement for change may arise if there are any more elections where the popular vote winner is denied the White House.

★　★　★　★　★

PRESIDENT, FISHERMAN, PHILOSOPHER

"Fishing is much more than fish . . . It is the great occasion when we may return to the fine simplicity of our forefathers."
—Herbert Hoover

"There are only two occasions when Americans respect privacy, especially in Presidents. Those are prayer and fishing."
—Herbert Hoover

TAKE THE HIGH ROAD, <u>CLEVELAND</u>

It's been almost a century since his death in 1908,
but Grover Cleveland still fails to capture the imagination.
It's too bad because this hard-drinking, womanizing guy
had a moral streak a mile wide.

He is mostly remembered as a dull president with the same name as a Muppet. But if you take a deeper look, there was more to President Grover Cleveland than first meets the eye. A regular party guy, he had a deep and gorgeous thirst for cold beer and easy women alike. He certainly wasn't shy about showing it. Despite Grover's taste for a good time, his fierce moral integrity set him apart from your typical party-hearty types. His honesty helped launch this sheriff from New York to the White House as a man who strove to do the right thing during an era fraught with corruption.

GROVER "BIG STEVE" CLEVELAND

Stephen Grover Cleveland (he later dropped the Stephen) began his political career as the sheriff of Erie County. With his rotund waistline, a walrus mustache, and a penchant for drinking, gambling, and frequenting saloons, he didn't exactly fit the type for a future candidate for president. Nicknamed Big Steve for the size of both his body and his personality, this son of a Presbyterian minister defended his rather impious pastimes by remarking, "My father used to say it was wicked to go fishing on Sunday, but he never said anything about draw poker."

While serving as the sheriff Cleveland gained a reputation as a tough, hard-working, honest man. Although he spent a lot of time off duty drinking at the local tavern and fraternizing with the rougher element of society, he never allowed this familiarity to cloud his judgment. He didn't hesitate to prosecute his own friends if they broke the law. His dedication to his professional duties was such that he would even step beyond the boundaries of

---

Theodore Roosevelt was the first American recipient of a Nobel Prize in 1906.

the office when necessary to perform society's most unpleasant tasks—such as executing criminals. That's right. On more than one occasion Cleveland personally acted as the executioner of convicted murderers when the agent who usually carried out such sentences was not available. Enemies used this unenviable duty against him by nicknaming Cleveland The Hangman of Buffalo. Among the general public, however, these actions garnered Cleveland a reputation for unusual integrity.

LOVE CHILD!

Cleveland liked to party with a group of fellows called the Jolly Reefers, bachelors who would meet on Niagara Island where they "gave parties to which no ladies were invited but accommodating women were always welcome." One of these "accommodating women" was Mrs. Maria Crofts Halpin, a pretty widow and regular party gal. She dallied with both Cleveland and his married friend Oscar Folsom, the Democratic district leader. When Mrs. Halpin became pregnant and in due course gave birth to a son, she named him Oscar Folsom Cleveland. Despite the paternal uncertainty inherent in this name, she insisted that the child was Cleveland's and demanded that he marry her.

Cleveland refused. In an honorable move, he did agree to support the child. Cleveland eventually became very concerned for the boy's welfare and urged Halpin to give him up for adoption. She refused at first, but then Cleveland offered her $500—a small fortune at the time—if she would agree to let the boy go to a loving home. She took the money and shortly afterward disappeared from Buffalo. Cleveland then arranged for the boy to be adopted by a good family.

This episode would come back to haunt Cleveland during his first run for the White House in 1884. It was a time of rampant political corruption that historian Henry Adams described as "poor in purpose and barren in results." Public officials were known for taking bribes, selling favors, setting up protection rackets, and writing legislation to cover their respective posteriors. Cleveland used his reputation for integrity to set him apart from the opposition. It worked. Joseph Pulitzer's newspaper, the *New York World*, listed four good reasons for endorsing Grover of

---

Eisenhower gave the first televised presidential news conference in 1955.

Buffalo: "1. He is an honest man; 2. He is an honest man; 3. He is an honest man; 4. He is an honest man." So honest in fact, that he publicly acknowledged, during a tight presidential election, the incident with Mrs. Halpin.

BLAINE FROM MAINE IS A PAIN

Cleveland's opponent, Senator James Blaine from Maine, was not above getting down and dirty in a campaign. Blaine blatantly dug up the "Halpin Love Child" to undermine Cleveland's reputation and distract attention from the two candidates' political records. They even came up with a derogatory chant to immortalize Cleveland's indiscretion: "Ma, Ma, where's my pa?" Cleveland's supporters tried to reply in kind, chanting back, "Gone to the White House, ha, ha, ha!"

Cleveland's campaign managers—certain that the story would ruin him—advised him to either deny the rumor as completely false or to tell the people that the love child actually belonged to Oscar Folsom. Cleveland refused both suggestions. Folsom had since died, and Cleveland had taken in both Folsom's widow and daughter; to sully a dead man's name would be painful to his family and to Cleveland, who treasured their friendship while Folsom lived. He unflinchingly admitted to his own relations with Maria Halpin and angrily rebuked his advisers for proposing such escape tactics.

Even more impressive was Cleveland's restraint when presented with the chance to wreak his revenge on James Blaine. Cleveland's supporters presented him with documents proving that Blaine had a surprisingly similar personal skeleton in his closet. Apparently Blaine had been forced to marry his own wife in a literal shotgun wedding, after he too had fathered a child out of wedlock. Cleveland tore up and burned the incriminating documents, refusing to settle the score with Blaine by stooping to his opponent's shameless tactics.

THE VETO PRESIDENT

Once in office Cleveland did his best to demonstrate the concept that a leader could be honest and should serve his people and not betray their trust. He worked tirelessly at vetoing unscrupulous

bills and corrupt legislation that crossed his desk, so much so that people began to call him the Veto President. His advisors often warned him that his stances could cost him his reelection, to which he replied: "What is the use of being elected or reelected unless you stand for something?" His honesty may have cost him consecutive terms, but it did secure his place in history as both the twenty-second and the twenty-fourth presidents.

FAMOUS LAST WORDS
After his second term Cleveland retired to Princeton, New Jersey. Sadly, an economic depression had soiled both his reputation and his legacy; he vanished from the public radar as one of the most unpopular men in the country. On his deathbed in June 1908, Cleveland left the world with the parting words, "I have tried so hard to do right."

★　★　★　★　★

A HOUSE OF A DIFFERENT COLOR
History happens in presidential homes other than the White House

Theodore Roosevelt's estate in Oyster Bay, New York, was named Sagamore Hill ("Sagamore" is Algonquin for chief). After he became president, it became known as the Summer White House. There, Roosevelt mediated a settlement of the Russo-Japanese War, an action that won him the Nobel Peace Prize. (The settlement, known as "The Treaty of Portsmouth," was actually signed in New Hampshire, but all the dirty work was done in Oyster Bay.)

Ronald Reagan's Rancho del Cielo ("ranch of the sky" in Spanish) was his home away from DC. Located near Santa Barbara, California, Reagan's private residence had a nickname too—the Western White House. There, the Reagans hosted many important visitors including Margaret Thatcher, Queen Elizabeth II, and Mikhail Gorbachev who wore a cowboy hat, a gift from Reagan, while he toured the grounds.

Florence Harding was the first First Lady to fly in an airplane.

NUMBER THIRTY-TWO: FRANKLIN DELANO <u>ROOSEVELT</u>

Served from 1933 to 1945

Vital Stats: Born on January 30, 1882, in Hyde Park, New York. Died on April 12, 1945, in Warm Springs, Georgia.
Age at Inauguration: 51
Vice President: John Nance Garner (first and second terms); Henry A. Wallace (third term); Harry S. Truman (fourth term)
Political Affiliation: Democrat
Wife: Anna Eleanor Roosevelt (married 1905)
Kids: Anna Eleanor (1906–1975); James (1907–1991); Elliott (1910–1990); Franklin Delano (1914–1988); John Aspinwall (1916–1981)
Education: Harvard University. Attended Columbia Law School
What he did before he was president: Lawyer; Member of the New York State Senate; Assistant Secretary of the Navy; Governor of New York
Postpresidential Occupations: None. Died in Office.

MEMORABLE QUOTES

"If the fires of freedom and civil liberties burn low in other lands, they must be made brighter in our own. If in other lands the press and books and literature of all kinds are censored, we must redouble our efforts here to keep them free."
—Franklin D. Roosevelt's address to the National Education Association, June 30, 1938

"We are a nation of many nationalities, many races, many religions—bound together by a single unity, the unity of freedom and equality."
—Franklin D. Roosevelt in a campaign address, November 1, 1940

Martha Washington's image was used on a silver certificate in 1886.

NUMBER THIRTY-THREE: <u>HARRY S. TRUMAN</u>

Served from 1945 to 1953

Vital Stats: Born on May 8, 1884, in Lamar, Missouri. Died on December 26, 1972, in Independence, Missouri.
Age at Inauguration: 60
Vice President: Alben W. Barkley
Political Affiliation: Democrat
Wife: Elizabeth "Bess" Virginia Wallace (married 1919)
Kids: Margaret Truman (b. 1924)
Education: Public High School. Attended Kansas City School of Law
What he did before he was president: Timekeeper for a Railroad Construction Company; Bank Clerk; Farmer; Haberdasher; Missouri National Guard; Captain in the 129th Field Artillery; Judge, Jackson County, Missouri; U.S. Senator; U.S. Vice President
Postpresidential Occupations: Writer

MEMORABLE QUOTES

"Sixteen hours ago an American airplane dropped one bomb on Hiroshima and destroyed its usefulness to the enemy . . . It is an atomic bomb. It is a harnessing of the basic power of the universe. The force from which the sun draws its power has been loosed against those who brought war to the Far East."
—Harry S. Truman's announcement on the bombing of Hiroshima, Japan, August 6, 1945

"The atom bomb was no 'great decision' . . . It was merely another powerful weapon in the arsenal of righteousness."
—Harry S. Truman on the decision to employ atomic bombs, April 28, 1959

She is the only First Lady to have her image used on U.S. currency.

FIGHT FOR YOUR RIGHT TO PARTY

Think we only have two parties to choose from?
America has a long history of third-party choices.

T he United States has a long history of a two-party political system. But three is not always a crowd when the presidency is on the line. Here's a quick sample of some of the most important third parties to populate the political field.

KNOW-NOTHINGS
At the beginning of the 1850s, many people were feeling economically and socially uneasy due to the large and steady influx of immigrants into the United States. Anti-Catholic sentiment was also very high, and secret Protestant societies with arcane rituals sprung up around the country. The Know-Nothings were one such group, called so because of their elusive response to any questioning. Their message caught on very quickly, and soon the Know-Nothings controlled state legislatures throughout the Northeast. However the party factionalized over the slavery issue, and soon these rival groups were absorbed by other political parties.

BULL MOOSE PARTY
Republican Teddy Roosevelt felt confident that his hand-picked successor William Howard Taft would continue his progressive policies. But Roosevelt was quickly disappointed and began to actively oppose Taft within the party during the 1912 campaign. Things became so heated that at one point during the Michigan convention two separate factions were trying to nominate their own candidate from the same podium, at the same time. Taft finally won the nomination, and Roosevelt decided to split from the Republicans to form his own party. Originally called the Progressive Party, it quickly took on the nickname of its flamboyant nominee Roosevelt. After being shot in the chest during a public appearance while president, TR had bravely continued on

with his speech instead of going to the hospital; as blood soaked his vest, he had simply said to a shocked audience, "It takes more than that to kill a Bull Moose." In the end, Roosevelt did beat Taft in the national election. The only problem being that there was a bigger progressive in the race, Woodrow Wilson, who beat them both.

DIXIECRATS

Infuriated by President Truman's pro-civil rights platform at the 1948 Democratic Convention, several Southern delegations walked out in protest, refusing to renominate him for president. Instead they picked Strom Thurmond, who managed to get himself on the ballot in four Southern states as the Democratic candidate. He won all four, but Thurmond failed to make a dent outside of the South, getting just 2.4 percent of the vote nation-wide. However his run did make a political impact: Truman put integration on the back burner, to keep the party together.

AMERICAN INDEPENDENT PARTY

The year was 1968, and civil rights protests and unrest were igniting the South, making the Southern, white establishment very anxious. The time was ripe for a politician to champion the status quo, and George C. Wallace seized the moment. The Democratic governor of Alabama left his party to form the American Independent Party and announced his candidacy for president. His right-wing platform of segregation, staunch anticommunism, and general distrust of the federal government resonated with voters. He won nearly 14 percent of the vote, including five Southern states. Wallace did return to the Democratic Party, but the AIP anemically carries on to this day.

LIBERTARIAN PARTY

Founded in 1971, the Libertarian Party believes in absolute personal and economic freedom, leading members to support a variety of political causes, such as being pro-choice and being anti-gun control, that are traditionally not found under the same roof. They had their strongest showing in the 1980 presidential election, garnering 921,000 votes, or 1.1 percent. While party support

has decreased somewhat over the years—nominee Harry Browne came in fifth place overall in 2000 by receiving only 386,000 votes—they boast hundreds of Libertarians in office, mostly in state legislatures and city councils.

GREEN PARTY
Originally an import from Europe, the liberal and ecology-friendly Green Party began to take root in the United States in the early 1980s. It was organized on a local level, but that all changed when Ralph Nader decided to run for president in 1996. He came in fourth place, receiving more than 700,000 votes, and gave himself and the Green Party a national presence. When Nader tried again for the presidency in 2000, many blamed him for siphoning off enough votes from Gore to let Bush win.

THE REFORM PARTY
After an amazing showing in the 1992 presidential election, where he garnered 19 million votes, billionaire Ross Perot founded the Reform Party to launch his next White House bid. His mixture of economic isolationism and plain-spoken irreverence for Washington, DC, appealed to voters. Yet, in 1996, he didn't fare as well, getting fewer than half the votes he did the first time. In-fighting has since fractured the party, which is hurting without Perot's deep pockets.

INDEPENDENCE PARTY
Although former professional wrestling superstar Jesse "The Body" Ventura was elected governor of Minnesota on the Reform Party ticket, he quickly bolted and formed a party all on his own. The Independence Party was similar to the Reform Party except skewed socially more to the left, supportive of gay rights and pro-choice. When Ventura retired in 2002, IP candidate Tim Penny threw his hat in the ring for the Minnesota gubernatorial race. He lost quite badly. An IP politician has served in the Senate, however: while governor, Ventura tapped IP cofounder Dean Barkley as the man to fill a Senate seat made vacant by the death of an incumbent.

ALWAYS A BRIDESMAID, NEVER A BRIDE

"The President has only 190 million bosses.
The Vice President has 190 million and one."
Hubert H. Humphrey

Everybody dreams of being president, but do people aspire to be the nation's second banana? "Look at all the vice presidents in history. Where are they? They were about as useful as a cow's fifth teat," President Harry S. Truman, himself once a vice president, said of the job. He had first-hand experience with the vice presidency, but is it really all that useless? In total, forty-six men have held the position of vice president of the United States from the first veep John Adams to the current VP Dick Cheney. Would they all agree with Truman?

JOB DESCRIPTION
The vice president officially has only two roles—to preside over the Senate, breaking tie votes, and to replace the president should he be unable to fulfill his duties. The Twenty-fifth Amendment solidified this presidential succession. So it seems that the position could be pretty dull, unless you make it into something better.

Only in recent years have vice presidents done more than look nice, keep quiet, and go to funerals of foreign leaders. Al Gore, Bill Clinton's vice president, and Dick Cheney have started a new trend by taking active roles in governing the nation and foreign relations. The vice president now is seen as a crucial member of the president's staff, at times a trusted adviser and valuable asset on the campaign trail.

HOW TO GET THE JOB
So what does it take to reach the office of vice president of the United States? Being from New York might help. More vice presi-

dents (11 of 'em) have been residents of the Empire State than any other. Having the last name Johnson could help too; there have been three with that name (Richard Mentor Johnson, Andrew Johnson, Lyndon Johnson).

Otherwise, serving in Congress is a good stepping-stone to the job. Since 1928, just two Democratic vice presidential nominees did not serve in Congress at any point in his or her career. Since 1940, only three Republican VP nominees did not serve in Congress. Having a birthday in October can help too—seven VPs were born during that month.

WHAT ABOUT A PROMOTION?

After a number of years in the shadow of the president, many vice presidents decide to run for the top job, but on the whole, they don't fare as well as one might think. Unless the chief executive dies or is removed from office, VPs tend not to do too well as presidential candidates. In fact George H. W. Bush was the only vice president in the twentieth century directly elected to the presidency immediately following completion his vice presidential term. All the other VPs first became president because the head honcho died or resigned.

A BUCKET OF WARM SPIT?

John Nance Garner thought the office was as useful as "a bucket of warm spit." (Some sources say the Texan VP used a more colorful word that rhymes with "spit," but we've decided to keep it clean.) It turns out though that some important strides have been made through the vice presidential path. In 1984, Democrat Geraldine Ferraro became the first woman to run as vice president (with Walter Mondale) on a major party ticket. In 2000, Senator Joseph Lieberman became the first Jewish American to be nominated for the vice presidency when he ran with Al Gore on the Democratic ticket. Many political pundits believe that our first female president may very well come up through the ranks, serving as vice president first.

Rutherford and Lucy Hayes celebrated their silver wedding anniversary in 1877.

PRESIDENTIAL GEMS

They've sat in the Oval Office. They've met the press.
They've done the job. Now hear what they've got say.

ON THE JOB

"All the president is, is a glorified public relations man who spends his time flattering, kissing, and kicking people to get them to do what they are supposed to do anyway."
—Harry S. Truman

"I'm proud to be a politician. A politician is a man who understands government, and it takes a politician to run government. A statesman is a politician who's been dead 10 or 15 years."
—Harry S. Truman

"The pay is good and I can walk to work."
—John F. Kennedy

"Being president is like being a jackass in a hailstorm. There's nothing to do but stand there and take it."
—Lyndon Johnson

"Why would *anyone* want to be president today? The answer is not one of glory, or fame; today the burdens of the office outweigh its privileges. It's not because the Presidency offers a chance to *be* somebody, but because it offers a chance to *do* something."
—Richard Nixon

NUMBER TWO

"My country has, in its wisdom, contrived for me the most insignificant office [the vice president] that ever the invention of man contrived or his imagination conceived."
—John Adams

The White House is the only private residence of a head of state that is open, free, to the public.

"The second office of this government is honorable and easy, the first is but a splendid misery."
—Thomas Jefferson

"The office of the Vice-President is a greater honor than I ever dreamed of attaining."
—Chester A. Arthur

CONGRESSIONAL COMMENTARY

"Congress has scarcely any thing to employ them, and complain that the place [Washington, DC] is remarkably dull."
—Thomas Jefferson

"Thank God she doesn't have to be confirmed by the Senate."
—Herbert Hoover, on hearing of the birth of his granddaughter

"When they call the roll in the Senate, the Senators do not know whether to answer 'present' or 'not guilty.'"
—Theodore Roosevelt

"There were two unpleasant surprises [about Washington]. One was the inertia of Congress, the length of time it takes to get a complicated piece of legislation through . . . and the other was the irresponsibility of the press."
—Jimmy Carter

"Congress in session is Congress on public exhibition, whilst Congress in its committee-rooms is Congress at work."
—Woodrow Wilson

"It is the duty of the President to propose and it is the privilege of the Congress to dispose."
—Franklin D. Roosevelt

MEET THE PRESS

"If one morning I walked on top of the water across the Potomac River, the headline that afternoon would read: 'President Can't Swim.'"
—Lyndon Johnson

"The great curse of public life is that you are not allowed to say all the things that you think. Some of my opinions about some men are extremely picturesque, and if you could only take a motion picture of them, you would think it was Vesuvius in eruption."
—Woodrow Wilson

"I understand that the press sometimes has to put politicians under a microscope. But when they use a proctoscope, that's going too far."
—Richard Nixon

ON NAPPING

"Is the country still here?"
—Calvin Coolidge, waking from a nap

"I have orders to be awakened at any time in the case of a national emergency, even if I'm in a cabinet meeting."
—Ronald Reagan

HE'S LEAVING OFFICE, BYE-BYE

"Private life would be a paradise compared to the best situation here; and if once more there, it would take a writ of habeas corpus to remove me into public life again."
—Andrew Jackson

"There's nothing left . . . but to get drunk."
—Franklin Pierce, on what a president should do when out of office

"If I'd known how much packing I'd have to do, I'd have run again."
—Harry Truman, on leaving office

It was formerly the home of the superintendent of the U.S. Naval Observatory.

NUMBER THIRTY-FOUR: DWIGHT D. EISENHOWER

Served from 1953 to 1961

Vital Stats: Born on October 14, 1890, in Denison, Texas.
Died on March 28, 1969, in Washington, DC.
Age at Inauguration: 62
Vice President: Richard M. Nixon
Political Affiliation: Republican
Wife: Marie "Mamie" Geneva Doud (married 1916)
Kids: Doud Dwight "Icky" (1917–1921); John Sheldon (b. 1922)
Education: U.S. Military Academy, West Point, New York;
Command and General Staff School
What he did before he was president: Soldier; Commander of
European Theater of Operations; Supreme Commander of Allied
Forces in Western Europe; General of the Army; Army Chief of
Staff; President of Columbia University; Supreme Commander of
the Allied Powers in Europe
Postpresidential Occupations: Writer; Political Adviser

MEMORABLE QUOTE

"The United States pledges . . . its determination to help solve the
fearful atomic dilemma—to devote its entire heart and mind to
finding the way by which the miraculous inventiveness of man
shall not be dedicated to his death but consecrated to his life."
—Dwight D. Eisenhower's address to the United Nations,
December 8, 1953

"Some day there is going to be a man sitting in my present chair
who has not been raised in the military services and who will have
little understanding of where slashes in their estimates can be
made with little or no damage. If that should happen. . . I shud-
der to think of what could happen in this country."
—Dwight D. Eisenhower in a letter dated August 20, 1956

Cleveland's second daughter, Esther, was the first and only child of a president . . .

THE PRESIDENT'S DREAM HOUSE

Barbie can keep her dream house. We want to move our toys on into this miniature replica of the White House with working TVs, bubbling fountains, and a whole library of books.

Did you ever wish you could go behind the scenes at the White House to see where and how the president and his family really live? What kinds of books do they shelve in the presidential library? What kinds of photos are on the desk in the Oval Office? Just where is that mythical bowling alley in the White House basement? Thanks to one man with an amazing gift for creating miniature replicas (some call them "dollhouses"), more than 43 million curious folks have been able to see into the private White House, on a much smaller scale, all thanks to John Zweifel.

ZWEIFEL WANTS AN EYEFUL

In 1956 John Zweifel took his first public tour of the White House. Like other visitors he saw the usual sites: the East Room, the Blue Room, the Green Room, the Red Room, and the State Dining Room. As lovely as these spaces were, Zweifel felt unsatisfied. He was more intrigued by the tantalizing thought of just what lay beyond the velvet ropes where the public was not permitted. What about all those other rooms like the Oval Office and the Lincoln Bedroom? Just how big are the president's private bathroom and the First Lady's closet?

Zweifel's curiosity proved an inspiration to him. A professional miniature maker who had been dubbed the King of the Miniatures by Walt Disney, Zweifel decided to create a miniature replica of the White House so everyone could venture behind those closed doors to see those off-limits rooms for themselves. Zweifel didn't know it then, but his life and that of his family would be dominated by this project for the next forty years. It would be their gift to the American people.

MAKING A MODEL HOME

From the time of his first White House visit, Zweifel worked on his proposal for the miniature. He presented it to the Kennedy administration, which approved the idea and gave Zweifel their cooperation. But after President Kennedy's assassination, security tightened, and the White House became off-limits to Zweifel for the Johnson and Nixon administrations. During this time Zweifel contented himself with taking hundreds of public tours, observing all he could from behind the ropes, and committing everything to memory (he was forbidden to take notes or photos). He extensively researched and studied all the public information he could get his hands on to create his replica. But he knew he needed to get back on the inside.

It wasn't until after Nixon's resignation and the Watergate scandal that a sense of openness returned to the presidency. President Ford allowed the Zweifel family and their team of volunteers to measure and photograph all of 1600 Pennsylvania Avenue. Nineteen years after Zweifel's first White House tour—more than one million dollars spent and more than one hundred of thousand hours of labor later—a completed mini-White House went on tour.

GETTING THOSE TINY DETAILS

Even though it is technically one of the world's greatest miniatures, Zweifel's White House replica isn't exactly small. Built on a scale of 1 inch to 1 foot, it measures nearly 70 feet long and 30 feet wide and weighs 10 tons. Not only does the beauty of the presidents' home amaze viewers, but also the miniature's richness and incredible accuracy. The mini-chandeliers light up, the phones ring, the fountain in the Jacqueline Kennedy Garden bubbles continually, and the tiny televisions work.

More than twenty-two thousand craftspeople volunteered their time and talent to create each item in the miniature. The wooden tables and chairs are hand carved from the same kind of wood as the originals. The carpets are stitch-for-stitch replicas. The walls sport exquisite, hand-painted mini masterpieces. One volunteer, Robert C. Robinson, spent five years donating time to make 2,250 miniature books that actually can be read with the help of a magnifying glass.

Thomas Jefferson held the first inaugural open house at the White House in 1805.

The Zweifels found the White House china among the most difficult items to create in miniature, but they crafted 120 tiny reproductions of the White House place settings with 40 pieces to each place setting.

Like most homes the miniature White House undergoes seasonal changes. In winter smoke curls up from the chimney. During the December holidays, there's a decorated Christmas tree in the Blue Room. But just as the real White House has new tenants at least once every eight years, the miniature version gets an update too. The president's personal photos on the Oval Office desk change with each administration. In 1976, Zweifel reproduced tiny roller-skate marks on the white house wood floors, just like those left behind by President Jimmy Carter's daughter. When the real White House floor was refinished its mini twin's floors were refinished too.

ON THE ROAD AGAIN

The mini-White House is a true mobile home. It has traveled to all fifty states, as well as to Europe and Japan. It's even visited in the Grand Ole Opry! During its stay at the Smithsonian in Washington, DC, it was one of the most popular attractions there. Zweifel has had offers to create miniatures of other capitals, but still thinks the White House is the most special. "It's because no other country has a house like the White House." Zweifel says, "The White House is the people's house."

★   ★   ★   ★   ★

SOBER AND SLOSHED SIDEBOARD

When Chester Arthur moved into the White House, he relished redecorating the place. One of the first things to go was Lucy Hayes's sideboard, given to her by the Women's Christian Temperance Union (Lucy didn't allow alcohol in the White House). The sideboard was sold off to a DC tavern owner, who subsequently filled it with liquors and displayed it in his bar on Pennsylvania Avenue.

The bodies of 7 presidents, including Lincoln and Kennedy, have lain in state in the East Room.

THE PRESIDENT SEZ II

More of the most memorable words from our commanders in chief.

"It is hard to fail, but it is worse never to have tried to succeed."
—Theodore Roosevelt

"The only thing we have to fear is fear itself—nameless, unreasoning, unjustified terror which paralyzes needed efforts to convert retreat into advance."
—Franklin D. Roosevelt

"More than an end to war, we want an end to the beginning of all wars—yes, an end to this brutal, inhuman and thoroughly impractical method of settling the differences between governments."
—Franklin D. Roosevelt

(Motto kept on a plaque on his desk during his administration):
"The buck stops here."
—Harry S. Truman

"I like to believe that people, in the long run, are going to do more to promote peace than our governments. Indeed, I think that people want peace so much that one of these days governments had better get out of the way and let them have it."
—Dwight D. Eisenhower

"Let the word go forth from this time and place, to friend and foe alike, that the torch has been passed to a new generation of Americans."
—John F. Kennedy

"Ask not what your country can do for you—ask what you can do for your country. My fellow citizens of the world: ask not what America will do for you, but what together we can do for the freedom of man."
—John F. Kennedy

Looking for a hand-carved, hand-painted mahogany model of the Boeing 747 Air Force One?

"If government is to serve any purpose it is to do for others what they are unable to do for themselves."
—Lyndon B. Johnson

"I will not seek, and I will not accept the nomination of my party for another term as your president."
—Lyndon B. Johnson

"You won't have Nixon to kick around anymore, because gentlemen, this is my last press conference."
—Richard Nixon

"I am not a crook."
—Richard Nixon

"My fellow Americans, our long national nightmare is over. Our Constitution works; our great Republic is a government of laws and not of men. Here the people rule. But there is a higher Power, by whatever name we honor Him, who ordains not only righteousness but love, not only justice but mercy."
—Gerald R. Ford

"War may sometimes be a necessary evil. But no matter how necessary, it is always an evil, never a good. We will not learn how to live together in peace by killing each other's children."
—Jimmy Carter

"The measure of a society is found in how they treat their weakest and most helpless citizens."
—Jimmy Carter

"There is no question that we have failed to live up to the dreams of the founding fathers many times and in many places. Sometimes we do better than others. But all in all, the one thing we must be on guard against is thinking that because of this, the system has failed. The system has not failed. Some human beings have failed the system."
—Ronald Reagan

It's yours for a mere $110 from the George Bush Library and Museum Store.

"General Secretary Gorbachev, if you seek peace, if you seek prosperity for the Soviet Union and Eastern Europe, if you seek liberalization: Come here to this gate! Mr. Gorbachev, open this gate! Mr. Gorbachev, tear down this wall!"
—Ronald Reagan

"The crew of the space shuttle Challenger honored us by the manner in which they lived their lives. We will never forget them, nor the last time we saw them, this morning, as they prepared for their journey and waved good-bye and slipped the surly bounds of Earth to touch the face of God."
—Ronald Reagan

"There is nothing wrong with America that cannot be cured by what is right with America."
—Bill Clinton

"I ask you to join in a re-United States. We need to empower our people so they can take more responsibility for their own lives in a world that is ever smaller, where everyone counts . . . We need a new spirit of community, a sense that we are all in this together, or the American Dream will continue to wither. Our destiny is bound up with the destiny of every other American."
—Bill Clinton

"A great people has been moved to defend a great nation. Terrorist attacks can shake the foundations of our biggest buildings, but they cannot touch the foundation of America. These acts shattered steel, but they cannot dent the steel of American resolve. America was targeted for attack because we're the brightest beacon for freedom and opportunity in the world. And no one will keep that light from shining."
—George W. Bush

Decked out in a blue power suit, Barbie bobbed her hair and ran for president in 2000.

GOING TO THE LIBRARIES

*Each presidential library contains something
just a little bit unexpected!*

E very president since Herbert Hoover has had a presidential
library established in his name. The National Archives and
Records Administration (NARA), an independent federal
agency that calls itself, "America's national record keeper," admin-
isters all the libraries (except Nixon's, which is privately funded)
According to NARA, "These are not traditional libraries, but
rather repositories for preserving and making available the papers,
records, and other historical material." Yawn, right?

Although a trip to the library can sound like a trip to dulls-
ville, each presidential library holds a little something unexpected.
In addition to papers and archives, every presidential library and
museum also has on display some of the gifts received by its hon-
oree during his term of office—from exorbitant presents from foreign dignitaries to homespun gifts from average Joes. Come with
us as we take you on a virtual road trip of presidential libraries and
point out the small gems in each.

THE HERBERT HOOVER
PRESIDENTIAL LIBRARY AND MUSEUM
WEST BRANCH, IOWA

In addition to the Hoover collections, this library also houses a
research collection devoted to the work of Rose Wilder Lane—the
daughter of Laura Ingalls Wilder, author of the *Little House on the
Prairie* series of books.

Lane led a fascinating life as a journalist, editor, and philosopher,
and her collection includes a wealth of diaries, correspondence,
drafts, and other writing. The collection reveals the important role
that Rose Wilder Lane played in the development of her mother's
much-loved series of children's books. She helped her mother find a
publisher, Harper Brothers, who encouraged Ingalls Wilder to turn

---

Mattel also issued a presidential Barbie in 1991, complete with a red, white, and blue gown.

her memories into the multivolume memoirs about pioneer life. Lane even became her mother's editor.

But what is it doing, you might ask, in Hoover's presidential library? In 1919, Lane wrote *The Making of Herbert Hoover*, the president's first biography. In the process the two became close friends, a friendship which lasted over forty years.

THE HARRY S. TRUMAN LIBRARY AND MUSEUM
KANSAS CITY, MISSOURI

In addition to a collection of endearing love letters the president wrote to his wife Bess (he was better known for the acerbic letters he wrote, such as the one excoriating a music critic for his trashing of daughter Margaret's musical talent), the Truman Library could serve as a garage. It houses two vintage Chryslers, meticulously restored by the Chrysler Corporation to appear just as they did when Harry and Bess purchased them in 1940. The Royal Club Coupe and the four-door Windsor set them back a grand total of $2,703.00. They even sprung for a radio!

THE LYNDON BAINES JOHNSON
LIBRARY AND MUSEUM
AUSTIN, TEXAS

The Johnson Library contains over 4,000 original editorial cartoons dealing with LBJ's political career. It also has on display a 1910 Model T Ford, donated by Henry Ford II. The car is similar to the Model T that served as the Johnson family car during the president's childhood. There is also a 1968 Lincoln stretch limousine. But best of all is a life-size animatronic figure of LBJ himself. It moves, it talks, and it tells five of LBJ's funniest stories.

THE JIMMY CARTER LIBRARY AND MUSEUM
ATLANTA, GEORGIA

The Carter Library proudly displays Carter's Nobel Peace Prize and an exact replica of the Oval Office. But Carter also holds the crown too, the Crown of St. Stephen. Just how did the former peanut farmer get his hands on a saint's crown?

Known as "The Holy Crown of Hungary" (Magyar Szent Korona), the crown has long been a powerful symbol for the

---

George Washington divided his estate into 5 farms, covering more than 3,000 acres, • • •

Hungarian people. At the end of World War II, with the Soviet army approaching, the crown was entrusted to the U.S. army for safekeeping. Cold War tensions precluded returning it to the communist-controlled nation, so it was safeguarded in the U.S. Gold Depository at Fort Knox, Kentucky. In 1977 President Jimmy Carter decided to return the Crown to Hungary, where it is now on permanent display at the Hungarian National Museum in Budapest.

On March 18, 1998, the grateful Hungarians awarded Carter an exact replica of their beloved crown. Accepting the gift, Jimmy Carter said, "The people of Hungary trusted us to keep one of their greatest treasures. We returned it when conditions permitted. This replica of the magnificent Crown is a generous and gracious gesture of the abiding faith and trust that exists between our two countries."

THE RONALD REAGAN
PRESIDENTIAL LIBRARY AND MUSEUM
SIMI VALLEY, CALIFORNIA

The Reagan Library is the largest of all the presidential libraries. It contains over 55 million pages of government documents, 1.5 million photographs, and nearly 770,000 feet of film. You'll find an entire wall covered with 400 magazine covers that feature Ron and Nancy from their acting careers well into their political ones.

In addition, all 200,000 of the gifts kept by the Reagans are housed there and are often on exhibit. From a custom made silver belt buckle with the words "President Ronald Reagan" spelled out in inlay to a Russian army surplus cap, there are a ton of interesting objects that people showered on the first family. There is also a section of the Berlin Wall, presented to Reagan at the library in 1990 by Germany.

While you're there, grab a bite to eat at the Reagan Country Café. Soups, salads, sandwiches, and pizza are all on the menu, but you'll have to check the gift shop for the jellybeans!

NUMBER THIRTY-FIVE: JOHN FITZGERALD KENNEDY

Served from 1961 to 1963

Vital Stats: Born on May 29, 1917, in Brookline, Massachusetts. Died on November 22, 1963, in Dallas, Texas.
Age at Inauguration: 43
Vice President: Lyndon Baines Johnson
Political Affiliation: Democrat
Wife: Jacqueline Lee Bouvier (married 1953)
Kids: Caroline Bouvier (b. 1957); John Fitzgerald (1960–1999); Patrick Bouvier (b. and d. 1963)
Education: Harvard University
What he did before he was president: Writer; Lieutenant in the U.S. Navy; U.S. Congressman; U.S. Senator
Postpresidential Occupations: None. Died in office.

MEMORABLE QUOTE

"I hope that no American . . . ill waste his franchise and throw away his vote by voting either for me or against me solely on account of my religious affiliation. It is not relevant."
—John F. Kennedy on why people should vote for him, July 25, 1960

"With a good conscience our only sure reward, with history the final judge of our deeds, let us go forth to lead the land we love, asking His blessing and His help, but knowing that here on earth God's work must truly be our own."
—John F. Kennedy in his inaugural address, January 21, 1961

NUMBER THIRTY-SIX: LYNDON BAINES JOHNSON

Served from 1963 to 1969

Vital Stats: Born on August 27, 1908, near Stonewall, Texas. Died on January 22, 1973, in Stonewall, Texas.
Age at Inauguration: 55
Vice President: Hubert Humphrey
Political Affiliation: Democrat
Wife: Claudia Alta "Lady Bird" Taylor
Kids: Lynda Byrd (b. 1944); Luci Baines (b. 1947)
Education: Southwest Texas State Teachers College. Attended Georgetown University Law School
What he did before he was president: Teacher; National Youth Administration Director, Texas; U.S. Congressman; U.S. Senator; Vice President
Postpresidential Occupations: Retired.

MEMORABLE QUOTES

"The Great Society is a place where every child can find knowledge to enrich his mind and to enlarge his talents . . . It is a place where men are more concerned with the quality of their goals than the quantity of their goods."
—Lyndon Baines Johnson in his "Great Society" speech, May 22, 1964

"I don't believe in labels. I want to do the best I can, all the time. I want to be progressive without getting both feet off the ground at the same time. I want to be prudent without having my mind closed to anything that is new or different."
—Lyndon Baines Johnson, March 15, 1964

THE PRESIDENT
<u>WAS A CROOK</u>

*Turns out that troublemakers do abound in the Oval Office,
but some offenses are worse than others.*

We are only too familiar with the exploits of President
Richard Nixon during the Watergate scandal and the
perjury charges against Bill Clinton. But they aren't the
only ones to engage in a little criminal mischief. Here are some
lesser-known examples of presidents living above the law.

THOMAS JEFFERSON, SMUGGLER
While touring the south of France, Jefferson noticed that the
locals were turning up their noses to American rice imports, pre-
ferring to gobble up their own native strain. Sensing an opportunity to diversify the Southern economy, this decidedly agrarian
president literally took matter into his own hands, illegally filling
his pockets with rice seeds that he could then smuggle out of the
country. Undeterred that this was a capital offense punishable by
death, he bribed a mule driver to keep quiet and made it back
to the United States with his contraband. And while it didn't
exactly break the South of its cotton habit, his risky venture was-
n't a complete failure: the rice is still grown in the U.S. today.

ANDREW JACKSON, ARSONIST
He was famous for his brash demeanor and hot temper while in
the White House. Yet the seventh president's misbehavior began
long before his elevation to the highest office in the land. While
a law student in North Carolina, a seriously sloshed Jackson
and friends ironically decided to break the law and completely
destroyed a neighborhood tavern. After breaking dishes and
smashing furniture, this future president and his cohorts then
burned the place down. But not all of his youthful exploits were
so violent—he was a great fan of the practical joke. He just loved

essing with people, whether it was scandalously inviting prosti-
tutes to classy Christmas Balls or causing a stink by hiding people's
outhouses.

FRANKLIN PIERCE, HIT AND RUN
Often overlooked (as outgoing president, he missed Buchanan's
inaugural parade because they had simply forgotten to come get
him), Pierce's brush with the law was ironically a failure to notice
someone. While on his way home from a friend's house, the president ran over an old woman with his carriage. Yet there are defi-
nite perks to the Oval Office, which Pierce soon learned: although
at first arrested, he was quickly released after the cops realized who
he was.

RICHARD NIXON, BREAKING AND ENTERING
The nation shouldn't have been surprised by the Watergate scandal:
Nixon's adolescence was filled with break-ins that foreshadowed
things to come. He was arrested while in college for sneaking into
a movie theater, although he got away with it by calling a judge
who was an alumnus of his school. When he was impatient to find
out his grades for a class in law school, he got a couple of friends
together and broke into the dean's office.

★ ★ ★ ★ ★

REMEMBERING RONNIE

"President Reagan had spoken to Parliament, handled complex
files with skill and good humor, strongly impressing his Canadian
hosts. And here we were waiting for our wives. When their car
drove in a moment later, out stepped Nancy and Mila looking like
a million bucks. And as they headed towards us, President Reagan
beamed. He threw his arm around my shoulder. And he said with
a grin, 'You know, Brian, for two Irishmen, we sure married up.'"
—Former Canadian Prime Minister Brian Mulroney eulogizes
Ronald Reagan

. . . became the first president to have a gallstone surgically removed.

MEASURING UP

As David Letterman could tell you, making lists has always been a part of American culture. So it's only natural that ranking the presidents would fascinate Americans.

T he U.S. presidents, taken together, are a pretty extraordinary group. Thomas Jefferson and James Madison were among the greatest intellects of their day, George Washington was the most respected soldier of his, and Teddy Roosevelt, when he wasn't storming San Juan Hill or on an African safari, won the Nobel Peace Prize. It's obvious that they're pretty exceptional in comparison to schmoes like you and me. But how do they compare to each other?

POLL POSITION
Historian Arthur M. Schlesinger wanted to know the answer to that question too. So he did the first in-depth exploration of this question in 1948. Schlesinger polled fifty-five historians, asking them to categorize the presidents as Great, Near Great, Average, Below Average, or Failure. There were no requirements given about giving out as many Greats as Failures to fit everyone into a neat bell curve. The historians also only considered the presidents' terms of office rather than all their lives' achievements. Schlesinger then averaged the individual rankings for each president and used the averages to create an overall rank to place each president in a category. The poll included all the presidents from Washington through Franklin Roosevelt (excluding William Henry Harrison and James A. Garfield because they died so shortly into their terms of office). Schlesinger also chose to exclude Harry S. Truman, who was the sitting president when the survey was taken and published. Then results were published in *LIFE* magazine for all to see.

In Schlesinger's survey, six presidents were Great. These were, in order, Lincoln (who was unanimously judged Great by the historians), Washington, Franklin D. Roosevelt, Wilson, Jefferson, and Jackson. The top ten was rounded out by the four ranked Near great: Theodore Roosevelt, Grover Cleveland, John Adams,

and James K. Polk. Ulysses S. Grant and Warren G. Harding were the only two presidents to rank as Failures.

The list ran in order on the first page of the article; then Schlesinger spent the rest of his piece musing on what it takes to attain presidential greatness, based on the similarities of the administrations of the Great presidents. He concluded that they always serve at a turning point in U.S. history, advocated progressivism and reform, are idealistic but not to a fault, are moral leaders, expand the power of the executive branch, and are opposed by the popular press, among other things.

UPDATE: NO CHANGE

Fourteen years later in 1962, Schlesinger took a new survey of seventy-five experts, in which he was able to add Truman and Eisenhower to the list. (In keeping with the precedent set in 1948, the sitting president, Kennedy, was excluded from consideration.) The results were mostly the same. The top seven presidents were all in the same order, although Jackson was demoted from Great to Near Great. Eisenhower debuted in the bottom of the Average guys in twenty-second place. One thing remained the same; Grant and Harding were still the Failures. In the text of the article, Schlesinger reiterated his earlier points about progressivism and expanding the power of the executive branch. He also downplayed any of the changes in ranking, noting that while a few presidents moved up or down a few slots in the overall hierarchy, the only president who actually changed categories was Jackson.

RANKINGS RUN RAMPANT

Since then, presidential rankings surveys have proliferated like bunny rabbits. Among them were historians Robert K. Murray and Tim H. Blessing, who conducted a very thorough poll over a number of years in the early 1980s, and Arthur Schlesinger, Jr., who took up his father's mantle for the *New York Times Magazine* in 1996. The year 2000 saw even more lists put out by C-SPAN and the conservative Federalist Society (with the participation of the *Wall Street Journal*).

Some of these surveys grew directly out of critiques of the Schlesinger surveys. Murray and Blessing investigated possible

Chester Arthur taught penmanship to earn tuition.

biases of the historians who were polled; they tested for correlations with birthplace, place of residence, and area of expertise and found few surprising connections. Scholars of African-American history had a lower opinion of Confederacy apologist Andrew Johnson. Military historians were harshest with Carter. Another not-so-surprising finding was that lesser-known presidents tend to be ranked more highly by historians who specialize in that president's historical period. Regionalism played a part too; Northerners tended to go easier on Hayes, the Southerners on Fillmore. In perhaps the easiest bias to spot, the Midwesterners liked Truman.

The Federalist Society detected a whiff of liberal bias (which Murray and Blessing didn't consider) in Schlesinger Sr.'s work, so they attempted to control for political affiliation. Their results were also unsurprising, with conservatives Reagan and Coolidge getting big boosts in their ratings and liberals Kennedy and Lyndon Johnson falling from loftier perches. In a slight change, Washington came out on top instead of the usual winner, Lincoln. Grant escaped being a Failure, but Andrew Johnson, Pierce, and Buchanan were sucked into it to join perennial bottom-dweller Harding. (At least everybody can agree on something.)

TELLING TRENDS

A few overall trends are clear from these surveys, even among the torrent of data. The top three presidents are almost always Lincoln, Washington, and Franklin Roosevelt, in that order. Grover Cleveland's stock has continued to fall in every poll. Eisenhower, on the other hand, is on his way up. Little redemption is in sight, however, for poor Warren G. Harding even though he did snatch second-to-last in the Federalist Society's poll, leaving James Buchanan in the mush pot.

If all these rankings tell us anything, it's that Americans love rankings. (To Uncle John's knowledge, no one has yet attempted a ranking of the rankings.) And given the speed with which rankings have accumulated, there are sure to be plenty of studies ranking the presidents in the future. With opinions so mercurial and politics so volatile, though, it's fairly certain that none of them will ever settle the hierarchy of greatness once and for all.

NUMBER THIRTY-SEVEN: RICHARD MILHOUS NIXON

Served from 1969 to 1974

Vital Stats: Born on January 9, 1913, in Yorba Linda, California. Died on April 22, 1994, in New York City, New York.
Age at Inauguration: 56
Vice President: Spiro T. Agnew; Gerald R. Ford (from December 6, 1973)
Political Affiliation: Republican
Wife: Thelma Catherine "Pat" Ryan (married 1940)
Kids: Patricia (b. 1946); Julie (b. 1948)
Education: Whittier College. Duke University Law School
What he did before he was president: Lawyer; Lieutenant Commander in the U.S. Navy; U.S. Congressman; U.S. Senator; U.S. Vice President
Postpresidential Occupations: Writer

MEMORABLE QUOTES

"I should say this, that Pat doesn't have a mink coat. But she does have a respectable Republican cloth coat, and I always tell her she'd look good in anything."
—Richard M. Nixon on Pat Nixon's outerwear in his "Checkers" speech, September 23, 1952

"Life isn't meant to be easy. It's hard to take being on the top—or on the bottom. I guess I'm something of a fatalist. You have to have a sense of history, I think, to survive some of these things . . . Life is one crisis after another."
—Richard Nixon's fatalism, September 1980

NUMBER THIRTY-EIGHT: GERALD R. FORD

Served from 1974 to 1977

Vital Stats: Born on July 14, 1913, in Omaha, Nebraska.
Age at Inauguration: 61
Vice President: Nelson A. Rockefeller
Political Affiliation: Republican
Wife: Elizabeth "Betty" Ann Bloomer Warren (married 1948)
Kids: Michael Gerald (b. 1950); John Gardner (b. 1952); Steven
Meigs (b. 1956); Susan Elizabeth (b. 1957)
Education: University of Michigan; Yale University Law School
What he did before he was president: Lawyer; Lieutenant
Commander in the U.S. Navy; U.S. Congressman; U.S. Vice
President
Postpresidential Occupations: Speaker; Businessman

MEMORABLE QUOTES

"I have not campaigned either for the Presidency or the Vice
Presidency. I have not subscribed to any partisan platform. I am
indebted to no man, and only to one woman—my dear wife—as
I begin this very difficult job."
—Gerald Ford's remarks upon taking office, August 9, 1974

"Now, therefore, I, Gerald R. Ford, President of the United States
. . . have granted and by these presents do grant a full, free, and
absolute pardon unto Richard Nixon for all offenses against the
United States which he, Richard Nixon, has committed or may
have committed or taken part in during the period from January
20, 1969 through August 9, 1974."
—Gerald Ford pardons former President Nixon,
September 8, 1974

TEE TIME
WITH THE PRESIDENT

*Horse racing may be the sport of kings, but golf is the leading
contender for the sport of presidents.*

A president needs a way to defuse the stress of leading the
free world. Some presidents have blown off steam using
the tranquil yet supremely addictive sport of golf. "While
you are playing, you cannot be worried and be preoccupied with
affairs. Each stroke requires your whole attention and seems the
most important thing in life," said Woodrow Wilson, who played
an average of six times a week.

ON THE LINKS
William Howard Taft, Warren Harding, Theodore Roosevelt,
Dwight D. Eisenhower, John F. Kennedy, Gerald R. Ford, Ronald
Reagan, George H. W. Bush, and Bill Clinton are among those
who played while in office. In fact, fourteen of the last seventeen
presidents have been golfers.

Taft was the first president to take up the sport. He began
playing while in office and became such an avid golfer that he
missed the ceremonial signing of the General Arbitration Treaty
with Great Britain because he snuck out for a round of golf.

Dwight Eisenhower, who often carried a golf club while walking around the White House, may have been the most famous
presidential golfer. He spent about 150 days out of the year hitting
the greens and played 800 rounds of golf during the span of his
two terms in office. Along with Arnold Palmer, Ike is credited
with increasing the popularity of the sport during the 1950s and
1960s. Citizens liked to poke fun at Ike's game. Bumper stickers
began to appear that said, "Ben Hogan for President. If We're
Going to Have a Golfer, Let's Have A Good One."

George H. W. Bush got into hot water for saying that the first
Gulf War would not keep him hostage in the White House and
that he would keep playing golf. Arnold Palmer is a friend of the

. . . because it was commonly believed then that flowers gave off unhealthy vapors.

former president and says, "What you've heard about George Bush the golfer is true: he plays fast and takes no prisoners."

Bill Clinton was frequently photographed on the links, often taking a leisurely five hours to play a round of eighteen holes. (Pity the poor golfers playing behind him.) He had a reputation for playing fast and loose with the rules, taking a mulligan (that's a do-over to the nongolfers out there) whenever he was unhappy with a shot. He freely admitted that the mulligans certainly didn't help his scores all that much anyway.

Before taking office, George W. Bush had to adjust to having the press and public watch his every swing. "I went out to play golf, and it just didn't dawn on me that when I came to the hole on the road, there would be 300 people there. It affected my swing, I want you to know," he said. He still often plays golf with his father. The two of them play what they call polo golf, or what others have termed aerobic golf. Basically, it's golf at a breakneck pace. No dawdling between shots. It's a fast and furious game when the Bushes take the links.

★　★　★　★　★

GOOD THINGS COME IN SMALL PACKAGES

The only thing diminutive about these guys is there size. Here are the smallest sized presidents.

1. **5 foot 4 inches:** James Madison
2. **5 foot 6 inches:** Martin Van Buren, Benjamin Harrison,
3. **5 foot 7 inches:** John Adams, John Quincy Adams, William McKinley,
4. **5 foot 8 inches:** William Henry Harrison, James Polk, Zachary Taylor
5. **5 foot 8 1/2 inches:** Ulysses S. Grant, Rutherford B. Hayes

The 6 floors of the White House have a total floor area of about 55,000 square feet.

PRESIDENTIAL Q&A

It's another presidential pop quiz. Test your knowledge or just guess your way through. You might be surprised to see who was a cheerleader and who is in the family of the chief executives.

1. During the Depression, homeless settlements were called "Hoovervilles," old newspapers were called "Hoover blankets." What were "Hoover wagons"?
   A. Railroad cars that hoboes rode in
   B. Roller skates
   C. Broken-down cars pulled by mules

2. Andrew Jackson ran for president as the "Man of the People," so thousands of "the People" swarmed into the White House at his 1829 inauguration. What did Jackson do?
   A. He signed thousands of autographs
   B. He hid upstairs and called out the militia
   C. He escaped out a window

3. At over 300 pounds, President William Howard Taft was by far the heaviest president, a fact that caused which very embarrassing moment?
   A. He got stuck in the White House bathtub
   B. He broke the carriage that was bringing him to his inauguration
   C. He split his trousers when he bowed to Queen Victoria

4. John Quincy Adams and Jimmy Carter are the only two presidents who were:
   A. pastors of their local churches
   B. published poets
   C. peanut farmers

5. The two Bush presidents are distantly related to Benedict Arnold, Abraham Lincoln, Winston Churchill, the Roosevelts, Gerald Ford, and who among the following?

The Easter Egg Roll, held on Easter Monday, has been a White House tradition since 1878.

A. Mister Rogers
B. Marilyn Monroe
C. Britney Spears

6. Charles Guiteau, the man who shot and killed James Garfield, used a .44-caliber British Bulldog because:
   A. It was the most accurate pistol of the day
   B. It was easy to conceal
   C. He thought it would look good in a museum

7. In 1835, when future president Zachary Taylor was a colonel in the army, his daughter Sarah ran away to marry the man who would later become president of:
   A. Wells Fargo
   B. The New York Stock Exchange
   C. The Confederacy

8. What president said, "Religious faith has permitted me to believe in my continuing possibility that I can become a better person every day."
   A. Jimmy Carter
   B. Bill Clinton
   C. George W. Bush

9. Ulysses Grant once said, "I have never altogether forgiven myself for . . . that." To what was he referring?
   A. Taking part in the war against Mexico
   B. Marrying a woman whose parents were slaveholders
   C. Being drunk throughout most of the Civil War

10. What president was a cheerleader for his college's basketball team?
    A. Gerald Ford
    B. Ronald Reagan
    C. Richard Nixon

ANSWERS: 1. C, 2. C, 3. A, 4. B, 5. B, 6. C, 7. C, 8. B, 9. A, 10. B

The movements of the president, First Lady, and others are tracked within . . .

NUMBER THIRTY-NINE: "JIMMY" JAMES EARL CARTER

Served from 1977 to 1981

Vital Stats: Born on October 1, 1924, in Plains, Georgia.
Age at Inauguration: 52
Vice President: Walter F. Mondale
Political Affiliation: Democrat
Wife: Rosalynn Smith (married 1946)
Kids: John William (b. 1947); James Earl (b. 1950); Donnell
Jeffrey (b. 1952); Amy Lynn (b. 1967)
Education: Attended Georgia Southwestern College and Georgia
Institute of Technology; U.S. Naval Academy, Annapolis,
Maryland
What he did before he was president: Lieutenant Commander in
the U.S. Navy; Farmer; Businessman; Georgia State Senator;
Governor of Georgia
Postpresidential Occupations: Writer; Humanitarian

MEMORABLE QUOTES

"Our decision about energy will test the character of the American
people and the ability of the President and the Congress to govern
this Nation. This difficult effort will be the 'moral equivalent of
war,' except that we will be uniting our efforts to build and not to
destroy."
—Jimmy Carter addresses the nation during the energy crisis,
April 18, 1977

"America did not invent human rights. In a very real sense . . .
human rights invented America."
—Jimmy Carter's words from his farewell address,
January 14, 1981

THE VERY MODEL OF A MODERN FIRST LADY

*When the twentieth century kicked off, Modernism
was all the rage in art, in literature. It's no surprise that
the movement spread to First Ladies, too.*

Maria Kennedy Shriver, whose husband Arnold Schwarzenneger recently became governor of California, told a journalist she doesn't like the term First Lady; she prefers First Woman—although she didn't explain why. Maybe the term "lady" sounded a bit old-fashioned to her and she wanted to give the title a modern spin. It's no wonder, with all the very modern women who filled the role in the twentieth century. Here are just a few.

EDITH BOLLING GALT WILSON, TAKING THE REINS
Aristocratic Washington widow Edith Bolling Galt met and married widower President Woodrow Wilson in 1915 just as World War I began to affect the United States. After a 1919 stroke left him partially paralyzed, Edith Wilson took over many routine duties of the presidency and controlled people's access to her husband. Some say she was running the country, but historians debate the full scale of her influence. In her memoirs she emphasized that the president's doctors had urged her "stewardship" of the Executive Branch. Woodrow Wilson died in 1924, and Edith Bolling Galt Wilson on her husband's birthday, December 28, in 1961. The two of them are buried in the National Cathedral in Washington, DC.

ELEANOR ROOSEVELT, A UNIQUE PRESENCE
Anna Eleanor Roosevelt married distant cousin Franklin Delano Roosevelt just after her 1903 debut and was at first a "conventional, quiet young society matron," in her words. Through his years as Assistant Secretary of the Navy and after his polio diagnosis, Eleanor remained his helpmate—but developed political

President Hoover held the last New Year's Day Reception at the White House in 1932.

interests of her own, and transformed the role of First Lady with her active speaking and writing on many cause, most notably civil rights. Even though after her husband's 1945 death she said, "The story is over," her story was still unfolding. President Truman appointed her a delegate to the United Nations, where she served as chairman of the Commission on Human Rights and played an important part in drafting the "Universal Declaration of Human Rights." She died in November 1962 and is buried beside her husband at their Hyde Park estate.

JACKIE KENNEDY, YOUTHFUL AND CHIC
Recent Vassar grad Jacqueline Lee Bouvier worked as an inquiring photographer in the nation's capital when she met its most eligible bachelor, Senator John Fitzgerald Kennedy. Their 1953 wedding was a publicity fest, and never again would the stylish, reserved Jackie have the privacy she craved. After her husband was elected president in 1960, they and their young children Caroline and John, Jr., brought liveliness to the White House. An educated woman, Jackie charmed diplomats and public officials alike. Her famous husband noted her immense popularity during a 1961 tour of France by referring to himself as "the man who accompanied Jacqueline Kennedy to Paris." Her courage during the tragedy of her husband's assassination won her admiration. After a seven-year marriage to Greek millionaire Aristotle Onassis, she lived in New York City and worked as a book editor until her 1994 death.

BETTY FORD, OPEN AND HONEST
A former dancer under the tutelage of Martha Graham, Elizabeth Anne "Betty" Bloomer Ford wasn't expecting to be First Lady, but in 1974, Richard Nixon's resignation changed all that. She and her husband Gerald moved on in to the White House. Only a few weeks later, Betty underwent a mastectomy to remove her cancerous right breast. At that time, women were not open about the illness, but Betty publicly disclosed her condition, a decision that moved women all over the country to visit their doctors for examinations. Betty also struggled with drug dependency and alcoholism, another aspect of her life she chose to reveal, which

The First Lady has trimmed the White House Christmas tree since 1929.

resulted in her establishing the Betty Ford Center in Rancho Mirage, CA.

NANCY REAGAN, JUST SAY NO

"My life really began when I married my husband," says Nancy Reagan, who majored in theater at Smith College and performed in films while meeting actor Ronald Reagan, whom she married in 1952. During her husband's long political career and two terms in the White House, she drew criticism for everything from her son Ron and daughter Patti's lifestyles to the expensive fashions she wore. Far from flighty, Nancy crusaded for the fight against drug and alcohol abuse among young people. Calling on her acting chops, she guest-starred on the sitcom *Diff'rent Strokes* to promote the "Just Say No!" message. Since her husband's long struggle with and recent death from Alzheimer's disease, she has become a crusader again, speaking out for stem cell research and new methods of treating the illness.

HILLARY RODHAM CLINTON, MADAME SENATOR

Valedictorian of her Wellesley class and graduate of Yale Law School alongside her husband, Bill Clinton, Hillary Rodham Clinton came to the White House determined not to be "some little woman," to quote her famous *60 Minutes* interview. But the fiercely independent and intellectual Rodham Clinton turned some people off when she tried to launch her health-care initiative; then she gained the pity of others during her husband's extramarital dalliances. Despite endless carping about her hairstyle, her political influence, and her role in the Whitewater scandal, Hillary Clinton managed to carve her own successful niche in politics, and in 2001 was elected to the Senate from New York state. She is the first First Lady to be elected to office.

BEWARE OF PRESIDENTS ACCEPTING GIFTS?

A centuries-old tradition, American presidents continue the exchange of gifts between heads of state, dignitaries, and even the common man.

The exchange of gifts among kings and chiefs and presidents and premiers and even the common man is an ancient tradition and perhaps the oldest form of diplomacy. In 1787 a young America chose to ban acceptance of foreign gifts by government officials so that the new democracy might not be subject to bribes; however, the strong tradition could not be entirely done away with; every U.S. president, including George Washington, has accepted foreign gifts on behalf of the United States of America.

The phenomenon grows with each administration. Today a president may receive 15,000 gifts a year, coming from every state in the nation and every country in the world. Gifts from foreign leaders continue a rich diplomatic tradition of exchange between heads of state; those from citizens, both Americans and others, symbolize an inherently democratic exercise—ordinary people freely addressing, in every manner and form, the leader of the world's largest democracy.

BLESSED ARE THE CHEESEMAKERS?

One of the oddest gifts ever received by a president has to be Thomas Jefferson's Mammoth Cheese. On New Year's Day, 1802, President Thomas Jefferson received a gigantic wheel of cheese, delivered to the White House by Baptist preacher John Leland. It measured more than 4 feet in diameter, 13 feet in circumference, and 17 inches in height; once cured, it weighed 1,235 pounds. Made by citizens of Cheshire, Massachusetts, in gratitude for Jefferson's devotion to religious freedom, the cheese was transported by sailing ship and sleigh and arrived highly ripened to be received by the president himself.

The most ironic thing about Leland's outsized gift was that Thomas Jefferson (along with John Tyler and Andrew Johnson)

had instructed his family not to take any gifts, in order to avoid the inevitable conflicts arising from accepting domestic gifts. Surprisingly, presidents have few restrictions on what they can and cannot accept—the one hard-and-fast rule is that they cannot take a gift intended for the White House itself. Although the criticism over President Bill and Hillary Clinton's 2001 White House boodle is the most recent, their "take" was within legal limits.

Other U.S. presidents have come under fire for their use of gifts. The first uproar occurred when President James Monroe sold his personal furniture to the White House (ostensibly to finance his travels as president), then "reacquired" the furniture when he left office in 1825.

Other questionable gift recipients have included Ulysses S. Grant, who considered all presidential gifts to be rewards for his battlefield achievements; Jacqueline Kennedy, who moved out with several tables that had been intended for the White House restoration; and Nancy Reagan, who was criticized for "borrowing" $20,000 couture dresses from designers (she claimed that by wearing the gowns she supported the fashion industry).

Less-controversial domestic gifts come in droves for all presidents. President Lincoln received clothing and food, President Wilson took home a White House limousine, President Reagan accepted a $2.5 million house in Bel Air, and President George H. W. Bush accepted thirty-nine fishing rods.

HEY, THAT FISH BAIT WAS FRESH!
Today gift giving between heads of state still forms a part of modern diplomacy and retains its significance as symbols of cooperation and friendship. They take many forms, from native arts, to treasured antiques, to natural resources from a country. The latter can cause controversy, as it recently did when in 2003 Canadian Prime Minister Jean Chretien gave all the leaders at a G8 Summit, including President George W. Bush, a pen holder carved from 70-million-year-old Alberta fossils, inlaid with Canadian maple, and topped with a 24-karat-gold fountain pen.

The U.S. State Department, responsible for receiving and dispatching such gifts, valued the "marble base with wooden pen rest" at $20 and sent it to the archives. The Canadian public was

An avid gardener, President John Quincy Adams expanded the White House garden to 2 acres.

not pleased to learn that its Prime Minister's valuable offering had been listed just above a $15 commemorative coin from the Czech Republic and a $3 jar of fish bait from Morocco.

AND THE GIFTS JUST KEEP ON COMIN'

From foreign leaders President George W. Bush has received, among other items, a million-dollar painting from Saudi Arabia and $18,000 pen from the United Arab Emirates. While he cannot personally accept gifts of state, the president and his family are allowed to accept domestic gifts—anything worth more than $260 must be made public. In 2003, the Bushes declared seventeen gifts valued at $22,355 that included a boat dock for their Crawford home, $1,000 gold cufflinks from the pianist Van Cliburn, an outdoor barbecue/smoker from the White House staff, and an autographed copy of the book *Forrest Gump*.

Only a few presidential gifts will ever be displayed; there are simply too many to rotate. Now, White House aides log the foreign gifts given to the Bush family and send them to the National Archives where the gifts are stored for Bush's future presidential library, while a few are kept on display in the White House or in the Crawford, Texas "White House."

★　★　★　★　★

FDR'S FOUR FREEDOMS

"We look forward to a world founded upon four essential human freedoms. The first is freedom of speech and expression—everywhere in the world. The second is freedom of every person to worship God in his own way—everywhere in the world. The third is freedom from want—which, translated into world terms, means economic understandings which will secure to every nation a healthy peacetime life for its inhabitants—everywhere in the world. The fourth is freedom from fear—which, translated into world terms, means a world-wide reduction of armaments to such a point and in such a thorough fashion that no nation will be in a position to commit an act of physical aggression against any neighbor—anywhere in the world."
—Franklin D. Roosevelt's State of the Union address, January 6, 1941

Hal Holbrook played President Lincoln in the 1985 epic miniseries *North and South*.

FILL MORE OF JACKSON'S BATHTUBS

*Rumor has it that the spiffy President Fillmore installed
the first White House bathtub. Turns out that's false!
Here's the real poop on the matter.*

E arly twentieth-century newspaper columnist and political
pundit H. L. Mencken was known for having a sly sense of
humor. But when he wrote a tongue-in-cheek story entitled
"A Neglected Anniversary" in 1917, somehow his reading public
didn't realize he was joshing. The column, which appeared in the
New York Evening Mail on December 28, lambasted Americans for
not celebrating an important anniversary, the installation of the
first American bathtub on December 20, 1842.

According to Mencken it was Adam Thompson, a Cincin-
natian who frequented England on sales trips and there acquired a
habit of bathing. Thompson devised a system of pipes and pumps
to ferry running water to his bathroom, installing a tub that was
(as Mencken puts it) "the grandfather of all the bathtubs of
today." Many in Cincinnati were opposed to the new invention,
Mencken wrote, in fact the *Western Medical Repository* had
claimed that bathing brought on "phthisic, rheumatic fevers,
inflammation of the lungs and the whole category of zymotic dis-
eases." But the tub still caught on, particularly when President
Millard Fillmore took a bath in the tub in 1850 and liked it so
much he had one installed in the White House.

THE TUB GROWS LEGS
Truth be told, Mencken's column isn't really that funny, which is
perhaps why readers didn't get the joke. Despite his inventing
publications, people, and statistics, the story grew legs and ran.
The false tale began appearing in articles about the bathtub and
Fillmore, as well as in encyclopedias and other books. Mencken
was amused, as well as disturbed by the public's acceptance of an
utterly fake new "fact," and wrote another column debunking

Grover Cleveland was the first president born in New Jersey.

the rumor in 1926 called "The American Public Will Swallow Anything."

Clearly he was right. Even though the second column appeared in thirty newspapers across America, the bathtub legend still didn't die. Most media sources, including to Mencken's annoyance some of the newspapers that printed his exposé, still thought the Fillmore piece was true. Three weeks after running the second column, *The Boston Herald* re-ran the original fake story as news!

JACKSON COMES CLEAN

Andrew Jackson was the real White House bathroom innovator. Jackson first installed running water in 1833, building iron pipes that reached into a nearby reservoir and brought water to the White House's first floor. That running water made it possible to install the bathtub erroneously attributed to Fillmore. But Jackson did the fake Fillmore story one better—he installed two tubs, one for hot baths and one for cold, and even a shower! To commemorate the hoax today, each year Moravia, New York, has bathtub races in its street as part of its Fillmore Days celebration.

★　★　★　★　★

IT'S A BIRD, IT'S A PLANE, IT'S SUPER PRESIDENT!

Saturday morning's crime fighter in chief didn't live in the Hall of Justice, the Fortress of Solitude, or the Bat Cave!

Believe it or not, the greatest American hero on Saturday morning was *Super President*, a cartoon that ran on NBC for one season (1967–1968). When President James Norcross wasn't balancing the budget, he donned a red-and-white, form-fitting costume to go fight crime. Super President's powers came from a mysterious "cosmic storm" that gave him the ability to alter his molecular composition. When evildoers encroached, Norcross also used his secret exit from the Oval Office to access a secret cave under the Presidential Mansion. One wonders though if his high-powered Omnicar and flying suit came at the taxpayers' expense?

Harding installed the White House's first radio set in his second-floor study in 1922.

NUMBER FORTY: RONALD WILSON <u>REAGAN</u>

Served from 1981 to 1989

Vital Stats: Born on February 6, 1911, in Tampico, Illinois.
Died on June 5, 2004, in Bel Air, California.
Age at Inauguration: 69
Vice President: George H. W. Bush
Political Affiliation: Republican
First Wife: Jane Wyman (married 1940. divorced 1948)
Kids from first marriage: Maureen Elizabeth (1941–2001);
Michael (adopted) (b. 1945)
Second Wife: Nancy Davis (married 1952)
Kids from second marriage: Patricia "Patti" Ann (b. 1952);
Ronald Prescott (b. 1958)
Education: Eureka College
What he did before he was president: Broadcaster; Film Actor;
Captain in the U.S. Army; Governor of California
Postpresidential Occupations: Public Speaker

MEMORABLE QUOTES

"Thomas Jefferson once said, 'We should never judge a president
by his age, only by his works.' And ever since he told me that I
stopped worrying."
—Ronald Reagan's words on running for president at age 73,
February 8, 1984

"Everywhere we go, Nancy makes the world a little better."
—Ronald Reagan's words for his wife Nancy, August 22, 1984

President Eisenhower was the first to use helicopters to travel to and from the White House.

NUMBER FORTY-ONE: GEORGE HERBERT WALKER BUSH

Served from 1989 to 1993

Vital Stats: Born on June 12, 1924.
Age at Inauguration: 64
Vice President: J. Danforth "Dan" Quayle
Political Affiliation: Republican
Wife: Barbara Pierce
Kids: George Walker (b. 1946); Robin (1949–1953); John Ellis "Jeb" (b. 1953); Neil Mallon (b. 1955); Marvin Pierce (b. 1956); Dorothy Pierce (b. 1959)
Education: Yale Univeristy
What he did before he was president: Lieutenant, j.g. and Pilot in the U.S. Navy; Co-founder of Zapata Petroleum and Zapata Off-Shore; U.S. Congressman; U.S. Ambassador to the United Nations; Chairman of the Republican National Committee; U.S. Liaison to China; Director of the CIA; U.S. Vice President
Postpresidential Occupations: Writer; Public Speaker

MEMORABLE QUOTES

"I will keep America moving forward, always forward—for a better America, for an endless enduring dream and a thousand points of light."
—George H. W. Bush accepts the Republican nomination, August 18, 1988

"As his vice president for eight years, I learned more from Ronald Reagan than from anyone I encountered in all my years of public life. I learned kindness; we all did. I also learned courage; the nation did."
—George H. W. Bush eulogizes Ronald Reagan, June 11, 2004

Musical instruments were among the earliest items purchased for the President's House.

PARDON ME?

The government may be full of checks and balances. But the academy president seems to have a monopoly on the power to pardon.

I f you're ever unjustly imprisoned for a crime, don't worry. The president can get you out with a little thing called a pardon. The presidential power to pardon is derived directly from Article II of the United States Constitution: *"The President . . . shall have power to grant reprieves and pardons for offenses against the United States."* These words entrust the presidency with the ability to reduce a sentence, to stay a sentence, to rescind a fine, as well as to unconditionally absolve a person of guilt, before or after conviction. The power is a broad one that demands discretion. Whether presidents have exercised such discretion is a matter of debate.

There have been as many controversial pardons as there have been presidents. Pardons have gone to everyone from Jimmy Hoffa (jury tampering and fraud) to George Steinbrenner (campaign finance-related crimes). Not to mention some less notable names like Private William Scott. He was standing before the firing squad when he received a pardon from Lincoln. His offense? Falling asleep on guard duty. And Oscar Collazo—his death sentence was commuted by Truman, for his attempted assassination of Truman.

I AM NOT A CROOK

Few presidential pardons have been as controversial, however, as the one granted to Richard Nixon by Gerald Ford in 1974. Not only was the pardon preemptive—for any past crimes Nixon might later be convicted of—but President Ford, the pardon-grantor, had become president because of Nixon, the pardon-grantee. When Nixon's popularly elected running mate Spiro Agnew resigned (following charges of tax evasion) in 1973, Nixon nominated affable Ford, the sitting House minority leader, for the post of vice president. Barely nine months after becoming vice president, Ford took over for Nixon when he was forced to resign because of the Watergate scandal. One month after that, Ford pardoned his former boss as his first act in office.

During the 1790s, the White House lavatory consisted of an outdoor wooden privy.

GET OUT OF JAIL FREE CARD

Questionable? Maybe, but the presidential power to pardon is absolute. Despite their desire to create a government constrained by checks and balances, the nation's founders decided that the pardon power would be best exercised by a single individual. They reasoned that one man would have a greater sense of responsibility in its use than a collective legislative body. One person is a lot easier to target than a whole body of legislators.

So, like we said, the presidential power to pardon is absolute . . . with one exception. The president has the power to grant pardons for any crime, except for those people who are impeached from office. (That Nixon resigned before the House had voted to impeach him was probably not coincidental.) So while even high treason may be pardoned, a crime of impeachment means you're out of luck and must face the music. It may sound a little out of whack, but you can get your head around it once you know about a scandal that took place in seventeenth-century England.

DO NOT COLLECT YOUR £200

In 1678, the English Parliament voted to impeach the Lord High Treasurer of England, a man named Thomas Osborne, Earl of Danby. Danby's crime had been to broker a secret deal with Louis XIV of France, the arrangement promised England's support to France in return for generous payments to the British king, Charles II. Unfortunately, Danby had negotiated the deal with France unbeknownst to Parliament, who, at that time, was raising money for a war against France. One of Danby's enemies exposed the whole deal. Parliament was furious with King Charlie, but knew he was beyond its grasp to punish.

Luckily Danby was easily in reach. Parliament promptly set out to impeach him. Danby was officially charged with taking over powers reserved for the king by negotiating matters of war and peace without the approval of Parliament. In addition, Parliament charged Danby with obstructing its actions through corruption and embezzlement in the office of the treasury. It looked like Danby was in serious trouble.

In seventeenth-century England, impeachment did not just result in the offender's removal from office. Conviction could

---

In 1801 Thomas Jefferson had two water closets installed, one at each end of the house.

mean exile, imprisonment, or even death. Fortunately for Danby, his 1679 impeachment only resulted in imprisonment in the Tower of London. Luckily, King Charles II intervened and pardoned Danby. Parliament and Charles wrestled back and forth over Danby's fate for five years while he sat locked in the Tower. The pardon came through and Danby went free in 1684.

GO DIRECTLY TO JAIL

So why the wrestling match? Couldn't Charles II pardon anyone he wanted? Technically, yes he could and Parliament was legally powerless to stop him. The legislative body needed to create new policies that would make their impeachments stick and help keep their power intact. If the King could pardon all their "impeachees," then Parliament was totally toothless. After the Danby affair had ended and a new king was on the throne, legislators went to new lengths to restrict the king's power to pardon, something finally accomplished in 1701.

The framers of the U.S. Constitution were apparently well versed enough in English history to remember that little fracas. When designing their government, they wanted to be sure that Congress and the president didn't get into a wrestling match every time someone was impeached. They were smart enough to nip the problem right in the bud and worked it right into the Constitution.

★　★　★　★　★

THANKFUL TURKEYS

Since Lincoln's time, presidents have received Thanksiving turkeys to celebrate the holiday. The event became annual in 1947 when Truman was presented with the first National Thanksgiving Turkey. Since then, the week before the presentation, the National Turkey Federation selects the very best turkey from a wide field of competitors to present to the president. (They also pick an alternate, in case the National Turkey cannot fulfill its duties.)

In a recent tradition started by George H. W. Bush, presidents now grant presidential pardons to the National Turkey and the alternate, so that they spend the rest of their days at a petting zoo in Virginia. Thanks, Mr. President!

NUMBER FORTY-TWO: WILLIAM JEFFERSON CLINTON

Served from 1993 to 2001

Vital Stats: Born on August 19, 1946, in Hope, Arkansas.
Age at Inauguration: 46
Vice President: Albert "Al" Gore, Jr.
Political Affiliation: Democrat
Wife: Hillary Diane Rodham (married 1975)
Kids: Chelsea Victoria (b. 1980)
Education: Georgetown University; Attended Oxford Univeristy; Yale University Law School
What he did before he was president: Law Professor; Attorney General of Arkansas; Governor of Arkansas
Postpresidential Occupations: Writer; Public Speaker

MEMORABLE QUOTES

"In 1996, like 1896, we really do stand at the dawn of a profoundly new era. I have called it the Age of Possibility because of the revolution in information and technology and market capitalism sweeping the globe—a world no longer divided by the Cold War. Just consider this: there's more computer power in a Ford Taurus . . . than there was in Apollo 11 when Neil Armstrong took it to the moon. Nobody who wasn't a high-energy physicist had even heard of the World Wide Web when I became president. And now even my cat, Socks, has his own page."
—Bill Clinton's remarks to the Princeton class of 1996, June 4, 1996

.. the role of Richard Nixon on film.

PET NAMES

You've probably heard of Dubya's dog Spot and Bill Clinton's Socks, the cat. But you'd have to be a true devotee to know the name of the last cow at the White House or the moniker of Alice Roosevelt's pet snake! They will magically appear as you fill in this puzzle's grid—of course, you can look 'em up elsewhere in the book. Is that "cheating"? Certainly not—it's your puzzle, and you can do it any way you like!

ACROSS
1. Ask for ID
5. Sills trills
10. Tiny jumper
14. What Bo Derek was in 1979
15. Fast Eddie shot, perhaps
16. On a ___ (enjoying a winning streak)
17. Country's McEntire
18. Demean
19. Bacon partner
20. Last cow at the White House
23. Kett and James
24. Star center from Shanghai
28. Lowest adult male singing voice
32. Pave over
33. Holliday or Severinsen
36. Irish setter of the Nixon White House
39. Love god

41. "The Age of Anxiety" poet
42. Tibetan holy man
43. Coolidge bull-dog
46. Morse click
47. Scuttlebutt
48. Japanese-American
50. Penitent ones
53. Windows fore-runner
57. Alice Roose-velt's pet snake
61. Fizzy drink
64. Two-door
65. Grammy winner Puente
66. Move heavily
67. "___ Thro' the Rye"
68. Norwegian king
69. Irritated
70. Classic tooth-paste
71. MacLachlan of film

DOWN
1. Seize, to Caesar
2. Bothered
3. Argue, in a debate
4. CSI venue
5. To ___ (unani-mously)
6. "Hurlyburly" playwright
7. What "vidi" means
8. Test for precious metal
9. Ciao!: Colloq.
10. Restaurant comp
11. Ship's record
12. Finnish actress Taina
13. Capp and Capone
21. Author Dinesen
22. Hefty regular at Cheers
25. "___ to Be You" (2 words)
26. Actress Watts
27. "Excellent!"

What's the main attraction at the Presidents Park in Lead, South Dakota?

29. Actress Phillips
30. Slight
31. Poet Nash
33. Winger of film
34. "Are you in
___?" (two words)
35. "That ___ Girl"
37. "___ drink with
jam and bread..."
("Do Re Mi" line)
38. Roadhouses
40. Alley Oop's time

44. City near Provo
45. Eighteen-
wheeler
49. Doesn't work
51. Christina of
"Casper"
52. John B
54. Kind of news-
paper
55. Of base eight
56. Elbow
58. "3:10 to ___"

(1957 film of an
Elmore Leonard
story)
59. Carville or
Matalin specialty
60. Pitcher
Alejandro
61. Radical '60s
campus org.
62. Guadalajara
gold
63. ___ es Salaam

Turn to page 315 for Answers.

There you can gawk at 15 feet tall heads of all the U.S. presidents.

NUMBER FORTY-THREE: GEORGE W. BUSH

Serving from 2001 to 2005

Vital Stats: Born on July 6, 1946, in New Haven, Connecticut.
Age at Inauguration: 54
Vice President: Richard "Dick" Bruce Cheney
Political Affiliation: Republican
Wife: Laura Welch (married 1977)
Kids: Barbara Welch and Jenna Pierce (b. 1981)
Education: Yale University; Harvard Business School
What he did before he was president: Lieutenant in the Texas Air National Guard; Founder of Arbusto Energy, Inc.; CEO of Spectrum 7; Board Member of Harken Oil and Gas; Managing General Partner of the Texas Rangers; Governor of Texas

MEMORABLE QUOTES

"The enemies of liberty and our country should make no mistake: America remains engaged in the world by history and by choice, shaping a balance of power that favors freedom. We will defend our allies and our interests. We will show purpose without arrogance. We will meet aggression and bad faith with resolve and strength."
—George W. Bush in his inaugural address, January 20, 2001

"In an age when space flight has come to seem almost routine, it is easy to overlook the dangers of travel by rocket, and the difficulties of navigating the fierce outer atmosphere of the Earth. These astronauts knew the dangers, and they faced them willingly, knowing they had a high and noble purpose in life. Because of their courage and daring and idealism, we will miss them all the more."
—George W. Bush's words on the Space Shuttle *Columbia* tragedy, February 1, 2003

Harry S. Truman was the name of the sheriff on *Twin Peaks*, David Lynch's oddball TV series.

WHERE ARE THEY NOW?

The last known addresses of some of our commanders in chief.

The chief executives' final resting places are as varied as the men who occupy them. Some are ornate, others plain. But they all have one thing in common; they attract a lot of curious tourists all anxious to see how the commanders in chief have be laid to rest. Is it tough to rest in peace with so many visitors?

JOHN ADAMS & JOHN QUINCY ADAMS
United First Parish Church; Quincy, Massachusetts. There are only four graves in the crypt of this church, and they are all occupied by the illustrious Adams family. The second President Adams is there with his wife Abigail, as well as their son, the sixth president, and his wife Lucretia.

JAMES MONROE
Hollywood Cemetery; Richmond, Virginia. Although a staunchly Virginian politician his whole life, Monroe was forced to sell his estate there to settle his debts and then move to New York to be with his daughter after the death of his wife, Elizabeth. He died a year later and was buried in New York. Yet this separation from his wife would not last: twenty-seven years later he was moved back home to Virginia. He now rests inside a Gothic, wrought iron tomb next to her.

ANDREW JACKSON
The Hermitage; Nashville, Tennessee. Although known as a rugged frontiersman and soldier, Jackson now rests within a tomb resembling a Greek temple. He had built it for his wife, who died shortly before he took office. Their graves are now together, in the garden of his mansion.

Lyndon Johnson was the first president to confer in the U.S. with a Pope in 1965.

JOHN TYLER

Hollywood Cemetery; Richmond, Virginia. Tyler, a loyal Virginian who joined the Confederate cause, now rests in the same cemetery as Jefferson Davis, former president of the Confederacy. He is joined by many of his sixteen children, as well as his second wife, Julia, the vivacious, controversial woman he married while in office. Tyler's grave is ornate, with an obelisk and two bronze eagles clutching a Greek urn at the top.

ZACHARY TAYLOR

Zachary Taylor National Cemetery; Louisville, Kentucky. Although he died in 1850, Taylor's remains were not moved into this ornate, limestone mausoleum until 1926. A massive, marble statue of the president atop, a granite pillar is nearby, as well as the graves of sixty-six other Taylor family members.

ABRAHAM LINCOLN

Oakridge Cemetery; Springfield, Illinois. Known for his humble origins, Lincoln now resides in a huge, domed tomb. In addition are a 117-foot obelisk; a 10-foot-high, bronze statue of Lincoln himself; and ornate depictions in bronze of key moments in his storied life. Plunked down in the middle of it all is his sarcophagus. Yet he's not even in it. To frustrate grave robbers, Lincoln was buried 10 feet below his tomb.

ULYSSES S. GRANT

Grant's Tomb; New York City, New York. And what about the most famous tomb of all? Roughly 90,000 people donated over $600,000 for its construction, the largest fund-raising campaign in history at the time. One million people attended the opening, and it remains to this day the largest mausoleum in North America.

JAMES GARFIELD

Lake View Cemetery; Cleveland, Ohio. Assassinated while in office, Garfield now resides with his wife, Lucretia, in matching bronze caskets below Memorial Hall, a museum dedicated to the president's life.

Originally named Hiram Ulysses, Grant flip-flopped his names because he didn't like his . . .

GROVER CLEVELAND
Princeton Cemetery; Princeton, New Jersey. Although Cleveland's political life blossomed in New York, this president was born in Caldwell, New Jersey. Buried nearby is Aaron Burr, infamous vice-president to Jefferson and duelist who killed Alexander Hamilton.

BENJAMIN HARRISON
Crown Hill Cemetery; Indianapolis, Indiana. Harrison, the 23rd President, was often described as dull, frosty, and boring. He has a monument to match: a boxy, granite tomb inscribed with the words "Lawyer and Publicist" below his name.

THEODORE ROOSEVELT
Youngs' Memorial Cemetery; Oyster Bay, New York. William Jones Youngs was Roosevelt's personal secretary when Teddy was governor of New York. Now, the former President, his second wife Edith, and many others from the Roosevelt clan reside within this peaceful bird sanctuary. The president, known for his swift rise to political power, can be found in a gated area at the top of the cemetery's hill.

WOODROW WILSON
Washington National Cathedral; Washington, DC. Wilson is the only president to rest inside the National Cathedral. His Gothic, marble tomb is just one of the 150 people buried there. His wife Edith is buried in a vault below him.

CALVIN COOLIDGE
Plymouth Cemetery; Plymouth, Vermont. Unlike many of his fellow presidents, Coolidge has an unassuming headstone situated within a modest cemetery. Every July 4, his birthday, a wreath is laid upon his grave.

HERBERT HOOVER
Herbert Hoover Historic Site; West Branch, Iowa. Buried on the property where he was born, Hoover is kept company by his wife, Lou.

FRANKLIN ROOSEVELT

Franklin D. Roosevelt National Historic Site; Hyde Park, New York.
FDR and Eleanor are buried in the rose garden of their family
home. Yet this was not Eleanor's only option: she had maintained
another house for herself several miles away, so that she could
escape her domineering mother-in-law.

HARRY S. TRUMAN

Harry S. Truman Library and Museum; Independence, Missouri.
Often chided for marrying above himself, especially by his mother-
in-law, Harry now rests alongside his devoted wife, Bess. President
Truman is lucky enough to also have an eternal flame in his
honor. The "Eternal Flame of Freedom," dedicated by the
Independence, Missouri American Legion, has been burning at
the library since 1991.

DWIGHT D. EISENHOWER

Eisenhower Center; Abilene, Kansas. Our 34th president rests comfortably, with his wife and four-year-old son, Doud, inside a small
chapel on the grounds of his childhood home.

JOHN F. KENNEDY

Arlington National Cemetery; Arlington, Virginia. An eternal flame
flickers above the flat, granite slab marking his grave, the path to it
paved with stone from his beloved Cape Cod. His brother Robert's
grave is nearby, unadorned except for a white wooden cross.

LYNDON BAINES JOHNSON

Lyndon Baines Johnson Ranch; Johnson City, Texas. His rough-
hewn, granite tombstone dwarfs those of his relatives, all lined up
under the shade of oak trees.

RONALD WILSON REAGAN

The Ronald Reagan Presidential Library; Simi Valley, California.
Before his death, Reagan chose one of his quotations as his epitaph: "I know in my heart that man is good. That what is right
will always eventually triumph. And there's purpose and worth to
each and every life."

George Washington is the only president with a state named for him.

ANSWERS

Solution to "Leading Ladies" from page 34.

G	R	A	B		E	B	B	S		A	M	A	S	S
R	O	N	A		U	R	A	L		C	A	S	I	O
I	L	A	Y		P	A	R	A		T	N	U	T	S
E	L	L	E	N	H	E	R	N	D	O	N			
V	O	O	D	O	O		G	E	N	E	S	E	E	
E	N	G		T	R	O	Y		N	E	R	U	D	A
		S	O	I	R	E	E		I	M	A	N		
	F	R	A	N	C	E	S	F	O	L	S	O	M	
L	A	I	T		G	E	T	H	I	M				
E	U	N	I	C	E		S	S	G	T		I	N	T
I	N	K	N	O	T	S		R	H	A	M	E	S	
	G	R	A	C	E	G	O	O	D	H	U	E		
G	O	T	O	N		A	V	O	W		M	O	R	T
I	N	A	W	E		M	E	N	U		A	M	O	S
A	L	I	N	A		P	R	E	P		N	E	N	E

Solution to "Pet Names" from page 308.

C	A	R	D		A	R	I	A	S		F	L	E	A
A	T	E	N		M	A	S	S	E		R	O	L	L
R	E	B	A		A	B	A	S	E		E	G	G	S
P	A	U	L	I	N	E	W	A	Y	N	E			
E	T	T	A	S		Y	A	O	M	I	N	G		
		B	A	S	S	O		R	E	T	A	R		
D	O	C		K	I	N	G	T	I	M	A	H	O	E
E	R	O	S		A	U	D	E	N		L	A	M	A
B	O	S	T	O	N	B	E	A	N	S		D	I	T
R	U	M	O	R		N	I	S	E	I				
A	T	O	N	E	R	S			M	S	D	O	S	
		E	M	I	L	Y	S	P	I	N	A	C	H	
S	O	D	A		C	O	U	P	E		T	I	T	O
D	R	A	G		C	O	M	I	N		O	L	A	V
S	O	R	E		I	P	A	N	A		K	Y	L	E

THE LAST PAGE

Uncle John's new Readers are already in the works! Keep your eyes out for:

- **Uncle John's Slightly Irregular Bathroom Reader**—the biggest and best! (Nov. 04)
- **Uncle John's Plunges into History Again!** (Oct. 04)
- **Uncle John's Colossal Collection of Quotable Quotes** (Oct. 04)
- **Uncle John's Presents Book of the Dumb 2** (Nov. 04)
- **Uncle John's Plunges into Michigan** (Dec. 04)

For more information on what's new with Uncle John and to keep abreast of any new developments, why not become a member of the Bathroom Readers' Institute! Just send a self-addressed, stamped envelope to:

Bathroom Readers' Institute
P.O. Box 1117
Ashland, Oregon 97520

You can also sign up at our website: **www.bathroomreader.com.**

Members receive an attractive membership card, a permanent spot on the BRI honor role, *and* issues of the BRI email newsletter, filled with special offers on our books and other Uncle John's merchandise. As always, we thank you for your support and look forward to your thoughts and comments.

Enjoy!